Inside Leeds United
THE STORY OF THE MILLENNIUM SEASON

BY DON WARTERS

LEEDS UNITED
PUBLISHING

KEVIN SPEIGHT AND CHRISTOPHER LOFTUS

Leeds United's Millennium campaign was as exciting as they come. It was a season in which David O'Leary's emerging young team took another giant step forward to finish third in the Premiership and qualify for the Champions' League for the first time in the club's 80 year history.

The team treated us to many memorable moments as that objective was achieved and there were also some great European nights at Elland Road to savour as United's UEFA Cup campaign extended as far as the semi-final stage.

But there was also the tragedy in Turkey when supporters Kevin Speight and Christopher Loftus, in Istanbul to cheer United on against Galatasaray, were knifed to death on the eve of the game.

This sickening act overshadowed the UEFA Cup run and saddened right-minded supporters every-where. It is something we should never forget and pray never happens again.

AUTHOR'S THANKS

It has been a privilege and a pleasure to be closely associated with Leeds United at a time when the future of the club has not looked as exciting and so full of promise since the early years of the Don Revie era.

I owe a debt of gratitude to club chairman Peter Ridsdale, who had the idea for this book and commissioned me to pen it.

Doing so was a very memorable experience and I would like to take this opportunity to place on record my grateful thanks to all – management, players, officials, coaches, administration staff and the like - who helped me in my task.

My hope now is that you will have as much enjoyment reading the book as I had writing it.

Don Warters

Published by: **Leeds United Publishing Limited.**
Sub edited by: **Paul Green.**
Designed & Printed by: **Polar Group, Leicester.**
Photographs by **Andrew Varley Picture Agency, Leeds.**
Additional photography: **Don Warters and John M. Wainwright.**

First Published 2000 by Leeds United Publishing Limited, Elland Road, Leeds LS11 0ES

No part of this publication may be reproduced or used in any form by means of graphic, electronic or mechanical, including recording, taping or information storage or retrieval systems - without prior permission in writing from Leeds United Publishing Limited.

ISBN 1-903415-05-5

A catalogue record is available for this book from the British Library

Inside Leeds United

PREFACE

David O'Leary and **Eddie Gray** herald the dawn of a new and exciting era

DAVID O'LEARY has fondly labelled Leeds United's talented and fast emerging team as his young musketeers. There isn't a better description.

"All for one and one for all" - nowhere can that famous battle cry of the musketeers have been more appropriately applied than at Elland Road during this history-making rollercoaster of a season which culminated in United reaching the Champions' League.

Strong in defence, fearless and exciting in attack and with an almost cavalier-like approach at times in which they finished off opponents with rapier-like precision - true musketeer style.

"I work on the theory that we are all in it together, we win together, we lose together and we take our rollickings together," the United manager said.

The fans have loved virtually every minute of it. Attendances hit a record high and burst through the one million barrier for the first time as fans flocked to Elland Road in tens of thousands.

United's games have been featured on television more than in any other season and their enterprising brand of football has never been more popular with the public than it is now.

Of course it has not all been plain sailing. United have had to endure and overcome circumstances that were unprecedented. And though they created a new winning sequence of ten games they also equalled the club's record for losing when they were beaten six times in a row. A seventh reverse would have set an unwanted new record.

I cannot bring to mind any manager who has had to face such a traumatic, action-packed tragedy-tinged season as O'Leary experienced in his first full campaign as team boss at Leeds United. It cannot have been easy – and it wasn't - though the genial Irishman has taken it all in his elegant stride.

With the experienced and ever-dependable Eddie Gray at his side, and a fine backroom team as well, O'Leary has taken the club to the threshold of what promises to be another golden era. Not since the days of Don Revie's regime has the future at Elland Road looked so full of rich promise.

CONTENTS

FOREWORD

By David O'Leary

PLAYING OUR WAY into Europe again and into the highly prized Champions' League has made my first full season in management one of immense satisfaction. The club is where we want to see it – at the forefront of football.

Sadly, the season was also tinged with tragedy and we cannot ever forget that two of our supporters lost their lives in following the club they loved and supported. The killings of Kevin Speight and Christopher Loftus had a big effect on the team and I think the incident in Leeds that led to Lee Bowyer and Jonathan Woodgate being charged had a terrible effect on both players.

Having had to take these on board makes our achievement of going into the premier European club competition all the greater and more commendable. Now we can relive the season that got us there through this book written by Don Warters.

I have known Don since I first came to Elland Road as a player seven years ago though I have worked more closely with him since I became manager. He is a writer who has been associated with Leeds United for most of his life and is one who understands the club. He also understands and appreciates the season we have just had.

What you will read in this book reflects, I think, just how great his understanding of the club really is. It has been a pleasure to work with him on this project. I would also like to thank the chairman for giving me the job as manager and, of course, our supporters, who have been behind me from day one in the job. Your backing has been such a great help, not only to me but to the players as well. Thank you.

■ Harte and Hopkin sweat it out during pre-season training

CHAPTER ONE

TOIL AND SWEAT

A HOT summer's day in early July 1999 is where it all began. The sun was shining out of a clear blue sky on Soldiers' Field in Roundhay Park and the temperatures were heading for the high seventies.

Great news if you happened to be on holiday and were there to relax and enjoy yourself. But Leeds United's first team squad players weren't.

Pre-season training was under way and it was not long before assistant manager Eddie Gray was dripping with sweat. "I always say to people they should book their holidays when pre-season training is due to start because it's always hot and sunny," said Gray.

"The players hate it, of course, but it's just the sort of weather you hope for when you go on holiday."

There were some notable absentees. Skipper Lucas Radebe, whose summer was dotted with

and Tony Hackworth had also suffered long term injuries.

Manager David O'Leary was enjoying a belated family holiday in Portugal, leaving his trusted right hand man to front the necessary leg work in the first few days of pre-season training. But the rest were there, pounding away in energy-sapping conditions morning and afternoon on the hard surface of Soldiers' Field with not a football in sight.

"It was hot – very hot – but the lads worked hard all the same. It is important to do some running first and we didn't look at a football for the first few days," added Gray.

Two players in particular who lapped up the laps were Republic of Ireland defender Gary Kelly and Austrian international Martin Hiden. Heat or no heat, they were delighted to be in at the start,

> "Some players will put on a pound or maybe two in weight, but years ago you could have players returning as much as a stone or a stone-and-a-half overweight."
>
> Eddie Gray

international matches for South Africa as well as a trip to Australia to play for the World XI against the Socceroos to mark the opening of Australia's new national stadium, had been given an extra week off to rest.

Central defender Robert Molenaar was still battling to recover from a cruciate knee ligament injury. And promising young strikers Lee Matthews

having battled back from serious injuries that had wrecked the previous season for both.

Kelly didn't kick a ball in first team football because of shin problems, while Hiden's cruciate knee ligament injury, suffered in the 3-2 defeat at Manchester United, took him out of action in mid-season.

All that was in the past. Thoughts were now very much on trying to prove their fitness – and then catch the manager's eye in the hope of forcing their way back into the team. No easy feat that, considering how well the team had performed without them and with four new summer signings to compete with as well.

Kelly, who had twice attempted what proved to be unsuccessful comeback bids in the reserves during the previous season, was keeping a low profile this time, politely refusing an invitation from Bryn Law to talk about his hopes in front of the Sky TV cameras.

Hiden spoke of his determination to get back into the swing of first team football, while accepting it wouldn't be easy. "What I am hoping for is to have a few pre-season games and see how it goes," he said. "I was fit enough to do some running before the end of last season and then worked hard during the summer. I feel really fit and my hope is to get in a few pre-season games and take it from there."

Obviously, the importance of pre-season work was not lost on the former Rapid Vienna defender, though even United's assistant manager was forced to admit that virtually all the players had reported back in good shape following the summer break.

"It is a bit different now to what it was when I was a player," said Gray. "In my day players used to get ten, 11 or even 12 weeks off at times. Now it's down to just a few weeks so they tend to come back for pre-season training in quite reasonable shape. But these days when the rewards for players are so high it is in their best interests to keep themselves fit. They would be fools to themselves if they didn't.

"You look at players when they come back and you can tell right away if any of them have been slacking during the summer. But it doesn't happen now. Some players will put on a pound or maybe two in weight, but years ago you could have players returning as much as a stone or a stone-and-a-half overweight.

"When we began pre-season work, one or two of the lads struggled a bit more than the others. You always get that. In general, though, they looked well. But it was necessary that we did some running first and once that was out of the way, we could get down to working with the ball, which, of course, is what players enjoy doing most."

Some people may have regarded David O'Leary as still being a little wet behind the ears compared with experienced managers like Alex Ferguson. But the amiable Irishman can be tough when he needs to and he is no one's fool. He proved himself a quick learner in his first season as a manager and quickly fostered a tremendous team spirit among his young side.

I cannot recall a better team spirit at the club since the days, more than 25 years ago, when Don Revie's United side were at the height of their power. More mature followers of the club will recall only too well how successful that time was.

Hard work and dripping sweat failed to dampen the spirits of the United squad. And once the players became aware that the further development of the training complex at Thorp Arch included the construction of a large lake, it was only a matter of time before someone was given an involuntary soaking.

Not surprisingly, some would say, the honour of being first soon fell to chief security officer Jack Williamson, closely followed by Lee Bowyer. Jack, as any visitor, whether authorised or not, will confirm, presented a formidable barrier as one tried to gain access to the complex.

The archetypal security man, was nicknamed by Gordon Strachan during the little Scot's days at Elland Road as 'The Rotweiller' and handed a T-shirt on which were printed the words: "Jack 'You can't park that car here' Williamson."

He was the prime candidate for a ducking and following one training session a group of first team players seized upon the opportunity, grabbed him and threw him fully clothed into the lake. When the laughter died down Lee Bowyer offered him a helping hand – and was promptly pulled into the water!

Light-hearted pranks and leg pulling are very much part and parcel of football and United's players are certainly no exception. Had he still been at the club Jimmy Floyd Hasselbaink could have confirmed that.

Some time before his £12million departure to Atletico Madrid, the Dutch international fell victim to a carefully laid trap and very nearly got himself arrested by the long arm of the law - much to the amusement of his team-mates.

Senior physiotherapist David Swift and Jack Williamson hatched the plan. The original target was said to have been young central defender Jonathan Woodgate, but a late change of mind led to Hasselbaink becoming the victim.

Local police were in on the act, the idea of which was to have Jimmy charged with poaching. One pheasant, a wood pigeon and a rabbit were brought to the training ground and unknown to the Dutchman, placed in the boot of his car.

After training, police officers arrived at the ground and, armed with a bogus warrant for Jimmy's arrest, asked to speak to him about a serious matter. They informed him there had been reports of poaching in the area and they had reason to believe he was one of the culprits. "Do you own a seven series BMW with the registration JYM?" he was asked. He replied that he did and was then told they had a warrant to search his car.

"There's nothing in my car," he protested, but was then marched out to his vehicle and ordered to open it. A search of the glove compartment and the interior of the car revealed nothing and by the time he was asked to open the boot Jimmy was beginning to get angry.

"I'm telling you, the boot is empty – I've nothing in it," he protested strongly. "Mr Hasselbaink, we have a warrant and if you don't open the boot we will have to take you and the car to the police station," replied an officer.

When he did finally open the boot, his face fell at the sight of a black plastic bin liner containing one dead pheasant, a wood pigeon and a rabbit.

The police van was ready and out came the handcuffs as Jimmy mouthed: "What the f---- are these?" The police informed him he would have to accompany them to the station for further questioning.

It was only then that he noticed people in the background trying hard not to laugh out loud and the game was up. He had been well and truly stitched up.

Pranks such as those help to promote team spirit. "We are a dedicated bunch and we are serious about wanting to improve all the time and

"Mr Hasselbaink, we have a warrant and if you don't open the boot we will have to take you and the car to the police station"

A Police Officer

■ Could we have a look in your car sir! Former Leeds United striker Jimmy Floyd Hasselbaink was 'set up' by his team mates as a 'poacher' in a practical joke.

bring success to the club. But we like a laugh or two along the way," said goalkeeper Nigel Martyn

Improvements costing in the region of £5million were undertaken at Thorp Arch last summer and involved the club in purchasing 20 more acres of agricultural land for the siting of a further half dozen full-sized grass pitches in addition to a number of smaller workout areas. United now have eight full-sized grass pitches and one all-weather pitch at the complex.

In addition, the purchase of the majority of the Thorp Arch Grange building has given United a development valued in total at some £8million and which can now house up to 38 Academy trainees and provide the classrooms, library and recreational facilities necessary for clubs to be granted Academy status.

While the lake, which measures some 45 metres in length and is 30 metres wide, fits nicely into the landscaping of the complex, it is not just there for

appearance. Nor was it constructed to satisfy Lee Bowyer's love of fishing!

Filled with water that drains off the pitches, the lake incorporates an irrigation system allowing the water to be filtered and then used again to water the pitches when necessary.

DAVID BATTY is regarded as the club's Number One prankster, though Press Officer Dick Wright says that Gary Kelly is not far behind, while young defender Jonathan Woodgate claims to be Number One apprentice.

While most practical jokers like eventually to own up to their pranks and bask in the glory of them, midfielder Batty rarely admits to being the instigator. It's a sure-fire bet that he was at the forefront when Jack was given his "baptism" in the lake, though he was evasive when questioned about it, simply claiming that most of the first team squad had been in on it.

It was David O'Leary who labelled Batty the

■ Phew! Harry Kewell puffs and Lee Bowyer grimaces as Leeds United go though a gruelling pre-season run on Soldiers' Field, Roundhay Park.

club's Number One joker. "When he told Batts, Woody piped up – and I'm his apprentice," said Wright.

Tricks with mobile phones are commonplace on the team bus. Batteries can be removed without the owner realising and it is not uncommon for a player to ring another who is sat just in front of him to ask him to fetch a cup of tea from the back of the bus!

Jokers are not, of course, confined to the first team. Portuguese Under-21 international Bruno Ribeiro and experienced Scottish left-back David Robertson, both out of first team favour and in the reserves, were suspected of trashing the Press Officer's office not long after they had returned from the rigours of a week of army training at Catterick Garrison in North Yorkshire.

"I left my office unlocked and when I returned the chairs were all on the table and desk, the rubbish bin was on the door and my spectacles and mobile phone had both disappeared," Wright recalled.

Ribeiro was the chief suspect but he answered the accusation by claiming Derek Lilley was the culprit. "I could not think of anyone less likely to do it than Derek," said Wright. "It was Bruno. I didn't mind the upset but I really needed my glasses and phone."

The phone was found by dialling the number and tracing the ring to a drawer in the corner of the room, but the glasses were more of a problem. Eventually they were found taped to the ceiling in a corner of the office.

The five days the reserves spent at the army camp proved to be a humbling experience. "Stepping off the luxury first team coach, which has white leather upholstery and all mod cons, straight into the corporals' barracks at Catterick was a rude awakening," said Wright.

"Having to get up at 6am and live by military discipline, four to a room and having to make their own beds and all the rest of it amounted to a major shock at first. But they soon realised when they saw the young squaddies, and what they were having to do, that they weren't so badly off."

Six-mile runs with backpacks were the order of

the day, but those who prided themselves on their fitness were in for a shock when paratroopers carrying logs on their backs overtook them.

Malicious talk at Thorp Arch centred on which player might be the first back home with an injury,

> # "Some of the lads suggested I should get the referee to agree to play 15 minutes each way or whoever scores the first goal wins the game."
>
> **Dick Wright**

genuine or otherwise, with Ribeiro's name cropping up. But everyone lasted the pace and returned claiming to feel much fitter and better for it.

The reserves went straight from Catterick to play a friendly game against Goole Town. "Some of the lads suggested I should get the referee to agree to play 15 minutes each way or whoever scores the first goal wins the game," said Wright.

Meanwhile the first team squad were going through their paces – and how – on a trip to Sweden and Finland where, against lesser opposition, they knocked in a bucketful of goals – 20 in all without one conceded in their three games.

"This tour was low key in relation to the teams we played," said assistant manager Eddie Gray, who was in charge of the party. "It was really about getting the boys fit and providing the new lads with a chance to bed into the team and the pattern of our play. So it was particularly successful from that point of view.

"Danny Mills, Michael Duberry and Eirik Bakke fitted in great. They are intelligent footballers and they seemed to know just how we wanted them to play and what was required of them."

Four goals from Alan Smith, three for Jimmy Floyd Hasselbaink, a couple of penalties from Gary

Kelly and goals also from Alfie Haaland, David Hopkin, Lee Bowyer, Stephen McPhail, Matthew Jones and Harry Kewell gave United a 15-0 victory over Byske IF in the opening game of the tour.

A journey into Finland provided tougher opposition for United, who beat Tervarit RY 1-0 with a goal from Hasselbaink, though both Harry Kewell and Gary Kelly missed penalties. United had rung the changes in both games in a bid to give all players match practice but in the third game of the tour, back in Sweden against Bodens BK, club skipper Lucas Radebe had his first run out.

He had been given an extra week to recover from his hectic schedule with South Africa and he helped United to keep their third clean sheet of the tour. Goals from Hopkin, Hasselbaink and Ian Harte, who scored twice, gave United a 4-0 success.

The goals flowed again when United returned home and made the short trip to Huddersfield Town, where Hasselbaink and Kewell helped themselves to two goals each after Smith had opened the scoring.

United followed their 5-0 mauling of the Terriers with a 1-0 win at Birmingham City, courtesy of another goal from Smith, and completed their pre-season matches with a visit to Parkhead, where they beat Celtic a lot more comfortably than a 2-1 scoreline suggested.

Smith and an own-goal from Oliver Tebily, who turned a cross from Smith into his own net, brought United their goals and when Bobby Petta scored for Celtic it was the first goal United had conceded in their six pre-season matches.

Satisfactory preparations in anyone's language, so when David O'Leary dug into his own pocket to treat his players to a night out at a local restaurant three days before the big kick-off, spirits were high.

It was rumoured afterwards that one player had suffered a slight disappointment when he was served a lobster with only one claw. "Excuse me," he asked the waiter. "Don't lobsters have two claws?"

"Yes sir, but this one has had a fight with another lobster," the waiter replied. "Well take this one back and bring me t'winner," the player replied.

Whether this was a true story or not, there was no denying that team spirit was sky high and even the controversial departure of Hasselbaink, whose departure to Real Madrid dominated the week leading up to the big-kick off, didn't dent it.

Hasselbaink's £12½million move provided United with a whacking £10million profit on a player George Graham had signed from Portuguese club Boavista for £2million a couple of seasons earlier. No one, of course, can argue with Hasselbaink's contribution to United's cause in his two years at the club.

Forty-two goals in two campaigns represented powerful enough testimony. With two more years remaining on his contract, however, his determination to break that and go elsewhere for mega-money left a sour taste in the mouths of many supporters.

Contracts are seemingly not worth the paper they are written on these days and despite United being prepared to make him the club's highest paid player, he remained adamant that he wanted to move to Spain where Atletico Madrid were reported to be ready to pay him £45,000 a week.

> "I think, once and for all, we buried the myth that this club does not back its managers in the transfer market."
>
> Peter Ridsdale

Faced with that scenario, United had no alternative but to get as much as possible for the player and an extra £2million was squeezed out of Atletico, to take the fee to £12million.

The transfer went through rapidly, but there was the little matter of an unpaid Council Tax bill to settle in Leeds and Hasselbaink returned to Thorp Arch two days after his transfer to ask for directions to the tax office. "He said it was only a few hundred pounds, which I suppose would not have meant much to him at all, but I had to tell him

that we all have to pay it – and off he went," said Dick Wright.

United knew all along that the biggest problem they were likely to have in negotiating new contracts with several of their present players would centre on Hasselbaink.

"That was why we left his until last," explained chairman Peter Ridsdale, who was successful in negotiating new deals last summer for Alan Smith, Jonathan Woodgate, Stephen McPhail, Matthew Jones, Harry Kewell, David Hopkin and Lee Bowyer.

There was also total success for United in their summer transfer quests. The players at the top of David O'Leary's summer shopping list – Danny Mills, Eirik Bakke, Michael Duberry, Michael Bridges and Darren Huckerby - were all signed for a total of £20million.

"All in all I think you have to say we had a very good summer," said the United chairman. "I think, once and for all, we buried the myth that this club does not back its managers in the transfer market.

"While I always said in George Graham's time here that we would support him – and we did – regrettably the public did not seem to believe me because the manager was never consistent in saying what the board were saying."

Graham spent close on £15million bringing 12 players in during the two years he was manager at Elland Road and with the signing of David Batty in December 1998, United spent a total approaching £25m between the time that O'Leary succeeded Graham and a new season began.

"We backed George and I don't think anyone could justifiably criticise the way we supported David O'Leary 100 per cent last summer in his task of getting together the squad he wanted to challenge for honours," added Ridsdale.

SETTLING in at a new club can be a difficult experience, but Michael Bridges had no problems at all – once he had managed to talk his way past security at Thorp Arch.

"Getting past Jack (Williamson) was an experience to savour," he recalled. "He did let me in, though he took a bit of persuading!"

Bridges celebrated his 21st birthday shortly after his protracted transfer to United from Sunderland went through. At £5million he became United's record signing, his price topping the £4.5million fees paid first for Swedish international Tomas Brolin and then Lee Sharpe.

Bridges enabled United to put one over on former manager George Graham by turning down

■ How much more is there to come? The tree trunk provides welcome support for Eirik Bakke who was having his first taste of pre-season training with Leeds United.

Tottenham and delighted David O'Leary with his desire to play for the Elland Road club.

"He's a very exciting player and he's joined a squad already very high on talent. I believe he will become a very polished performer for us over the years," said the United boss.

Bridges himself said: "Settling in at Leeds was easy for me. They're a great bunch of lads here and I knew half of the younger lads before I came, from being in the England Under-21 squads.

"The set-up here is quite fantastic and once I knew Leeds wanted me I could not get hold of the pen fast enough to sign. Obviously you have to hear what a club has to say, but I did not really have to think twice about coming here. Everything went through very quickly in the end."

Bridges fitted neatly into O'Leary's quiet revolution. He is a promising young player with a hunger for success and just the type the United boss was looking for.

"There are a lot of things to achieve here," he said. "I have joined what is basically a very young side. When you have 'Young' v 'Old' practice games and you see 22-year-olds in the 'old' team you realise just how young the squad at Leeds really is."

"It's possible that we could be together for the next six or seven years and if that's the case then I don't see why we can't do something similar to what Manchester United did when they had a lot of talented youngsters coming through together."

Premier League football was available to him had he stayed at Sunderland, but Bridges wanted a fresh challenge and United offered just that.

"In some respects I was a little upset at leaving the Sunderland fans because the support the fans give up there is outstanding and I actually had a lot of letters from Sunderland supporters wishing me all the best at Leeds which I thought was tremendous of them," he said.

"But it was time for me to move on and face new challenges and I regard having come to Leeds a great challenge."

The offer of a big money move to Tottenham never really appealed to him. That was something

that took me totally by surprise. I had to go and see what they had to say but the move, I felt, was not right for me," he said.

"It had nothing to do with the money. There was just something that did not feel quite right to me and if you think you will not be happy you would be unwise to go ahead with a move."

Danny Mills also found it easy to settle into new surroundings following his £4million move from Charlton Athletic. "It's great to be here and I'm looking forward to a successful season," said the right back who also has experience at Under-21 squad level.

Michael Duberry hoped to inherit the good points of central defensive play from David O'Leary who, of course, knows all there is to know about that particular art, having played for the best part of 20 years in that role with Arsenal, before ending his playing career at Elland Road

"I am very keen to learn from him. He knows the position inside out. I've joined a club that's buzzing so I reckon there could hardly be a better time to move here," he added.

Eirik Bakke, the Norwegian Under-21 international skipper and midfield player was delighted to have secured a move to the Premiership with United. The youngster from Sogndal had impressed United manager David O'Leary when on trial for a few days at Thorp Arch towards the end of the previous season.

Described by his new manager as "one for the future" the Norwegian knew he had a fight on his hands to get into United's starting line up. "I liked what I saw from Eirik when he was here on trial and I am pretty sure he will turn out to be a very strong midfield player for us," was the United manager's view.

More immediately, however, the countdown to the new season was well and truly under way.

An ankle injury suffered by Alan Smith in a private practice match against York City three days before the opening game of the Premier League campaign at home to Derby County was an unwanted team selection problem for O'Leary.

Having sold Clyde Wijnhard to Huddersfield Town and then lost Jimmy Hasselbaink to Atletico so close to the season's start, Smith's injury was more of a worry than it otherwise might have been.

Despite intense treatment the teenager was still limping on the eve of the Derby game so it was a surprise when he was included in the starting line-up against the Rams.

Understandably perhaps, he did not have the most effective of games and his manager admitted afterwards that Smith was not fit and would not have played had the circumstances been different.

United paraded two of their new signings, English players Mills and Bridges both gaining a place in the starting line-up against the Rams, with another, central defender Michael Duberry, having a place on the substitute's bench.

With players like Smith and Jonathan Woodgate also in the side it was no wonder that England coach Kevin Keegan was among the interested spectators in a 40,000-plus crowd at Elland Road.

United, and O'Leary, (even though he's an Irishman!) can safely be described as doing more than their bit to help further the cause of English football. In times when many top English clubs were going foreign, O'Leary's "British is best"

■ Danny Mills soon settled into new surroundings!

policy must have been a real boost for the England coach.

Expectations were sky high among United fans, so high in fact that the manager was prompted to issue a note of caution. "The biggest problem at this club right now is that some people will be thinking we can win the League," the United boss told me the day before the Derby game.

"I think they will be wrong and if people become too impatient that could spoil the overall picture at the club in the next few years. I think that

So what were the targets in this Millennium season? "Breaking into the top three and securing one of the Champions' League places would be a major step up and I would also like a good run in at least one of the cup competitions," the United boss replied.

The search for another striker had begun before the start of the season. An inquiry for the £10million rated Emile Heskey was quickly rebuffed by Leicester, though the young England striker was to sign for Liverpool in March.

> ## "The biggest problem at this club right now is that some people will be thinking we can win the League."
>
> David O'Leary

eventually we are going to have a very, very good side. We have a good team now but they are still quite young. They need to mature, to get older together and gel.

"We all talk about Manchester United and what they have become but Alex Ferguson needed time – and a little bit of luck as well - to sort things out at Old Trafford and for his side to gel together. Eventually they got there, but supporters had to have patience.

"To be honest, though, I don't really look at that too much. My job here is to try to do the best I can for Leeds United and that is what I am concentrating my efforts on. If people think there is a faster way to do things, then that is up to them," he added.

Taking a leaf out of the Frank Sinatra songbook, O'Leary will do things his own way. "Lots of managers have said privately to me how impressed they were with our team last season," he said.

"Some people have also told me that with the success we enjoyed last season I have made a rod for my own back. That's the sort of thing you have to expect but I don't let it concern me.

"I love the job I'm doing and my plan has been - and is - to try to build a team that will keep me here at Leeds for a long time and keep the club challenging for top honours for a long time," he explained.

United drew a blank against a Derby side who were quick to get men behind the ball. After amassing 28 goals in their last six pre-season matches, United had to be content with a 0-0 scoreline in their opening Premier League game.

Harry Kewell had the best chance to end the deadlock when an ill-judged back pass put him clean through but he fluffed the opportunity to beat goalkeeper Mart Poom.

It was inevitable that after having watched United's forwards fire blanks some would point to the absence of Hasselbaink as a key factor. The United manager, fully aware that his squad was thin on the ground so far as strikers were concerned, stressed he would not be rushed into a signing.

With £12million nestling in the bank, the urge must have been to spend it quickly but the United boss insisted: "I'll spend it only when I can get the player I want. This club of ours deserves only the best and I intend to get the best," he added.

DAVID HOPKIN reached a high point in his career – literally – when he put pen to paper on a new deal with Leeds United designed to keep him at the club until the year 2003.

The Scottish international was 25,000ft in the air aboard the chartered jet that was carrying the United squad back home from their midweek game at Southampton when he signed his new and improved contract.

Maybe United felt it the ideal time to secure his signature on the document. After all, they were in high spirits after a resounding 3-0 hammering of Southampton at the Dell on the night of August 10.

Club secretary Ian Silvester approached with the contract as the clock ticked towards midnight and duly got the signature United wanted. I have to admit it was a bit unusual," Hopkin said. "I can't think there will have been many players who have signed their contracts in mid-air like that.

"I think the club were keen for it to be signed and I was just happy that everything had been sorted out and that my new contract was giving me the security I wanted."

His new deal was for four years. "You are always going to have some differences when negotiating a new contract but it didn't take too long for things to be agreed," he said.

■ David Hopkin put to pen paper in mid-air!

The Greenock-born midfielder, who was brought to Elland Road by former manager George Graham in the summer of 1997 in a £3.4million move from Chelsea, is one of the more mature players in United's side and had sought greater security from his contract talks.

"I am happy at Leeds and was keen to stay but I was almost 29 years old and at the stage where I was looking for security," he explained.

Hopkin still had another 18 months of his old contract to go when he opened talks over a new one. "These days, once you are in that situation you begin to think about being offered a new one but you think a little differently than when you were younger," he explained.

"Maybe when you are 22 or 23 you think more about money but when you get older you are looking for a bit of security. In my case a four-year deal will take me to the age of 33 and that suits me fine," the Scottish international added.

Getting back into the Scotland side was another of Hopkin's aims though he admitted this was not at the forefront of his mind. Staying in the United side and playing well for the club was.

Injuries and illness had combined to interrupt his attempts to establish a place in the Scotland side and there is no doubt Hopkin would like to force his way back into the national side – but preferably in his favoured central midfield role.

Before the season began he spoke with Scotland boss Craig Brown about the situation. "When he's played me it has been in a wide right position but I prefer to play in a more central role – as I do for my club most times," he said.

"I do want to play for Scotland but if you play most of your games in centre midfield in such a league as the Premiership – and do well – then I think you should warrant your place on merit.

"I don't like going to play for Scotland in a wide right position. It's strange to me and I don't think you do yourself justice playing at international level out of position. I prefer to play in a more attacking role – I've played there once and scored twice so that's not a bad return."

■ Got Him! Darren Huckerby, flanked by satisfied chairman Peter Ridsdale and manager David O'Leary, meets the Press after his £5million signing.

CHAPTER TWO

JIMMY'S DEMANDS

CHAIRMAN Peter Ridsdale came up with a plan that could have netted Jimmy Floyd Hasselbaink a personal windfall of £1.2million had he agreed to stay at Elland Road for the Millennium season. But the Dutch international striker turned it down flat – inside three minutes!

"In a bid to make Jimmy change his mind and stay at Leeds for one more season, I offered to make him the best paid player at the club," the chairman revealed. "I also promised that if we were to receive a bid of £10million or more for him at the end of it, we would let him go and he could have a 10 per cent cut of the transfer fee."

> # "His wage demands were at such a high level that I knew he had no real interest in staying at Leeds."
>
> Peter Ridsdale

With a £22,000 a week wage packet on offer and the near certainty of a £1.2million pay off at the end of the season, United had put Hasselbaink's commitment to the club to the test. I put that offer to his agent but he was back on the phone to me less than three minutes later to say he had spoken to Jimmy who had turned it down," the chairman said.

United feared the worst in Hasselbaink's case well before they opened talks on a new deal and were hardly surprised to see him move to Spain. "Whether it was the truth or not, it had already been indicated in the newspapers that Jimmy would be moving on," said Ridsdale.

"The first time I met his agent for talks I got the firm impression that Jimmy did not want to stay with us because his demands were so outrageous – and I don't mean just the financial ones either. "The conditions he wanted putting in were really quite amazing."

"One was that he ALWAYS had to be the highest paid player at the club. Another was that any bid we may get for him of £6million or more we had to accept, even if he had signed his new deal with us, and he also wanted a personal bonus scheme in addition to the team bonus, which was payable only to him.

"These were conditions that we just could not accept. In addition, his wage demands were at such a high level that I knew he had no real interest in staying at Leeds.

"His agent subsequently claimed that Jimmy had always wanted to stay at Leeds and that we could not offer a sensible contract but at no time did I believe his demands were aimed towards agreeing a reasonable contract – the sort we could accept."

Apart from the loss of Hasselbaink, United had a very successful summer, re-negotiating the contracts of six of their players and signing those David O'Leary had placed on his summer hit list.

"It has been a very satisfying time," said the

chairman. "I thought I would get a two-week break with my family, but as it turned out I managed only five days. One of those days was taken up sorting out Michael Duberry's transfer and I had calls on club business on the other four days as well!"

Such are the demands on present-day club chairmen, which makes it all the harder when, despite their time and effort, the criticism keeps on coming. It's a fact of footballing life these days that club chairmen are regarded as targets for criticism, no matter how successful a team might be.

Ridsdale, a lifelong United fan who was among those hardy supporters who camped out all night at Elland Road to make sure of a ticket for the 1965 FA Cup final against Liverpool at Wembley, is the most popular chairman Leeds United have had for many years. Indeed, perhaps the most popular ever.

But that hasn't saved him from criticism – as some letters that arrived in his summer postbag underlined in no uncertain manner.

spend," he added, pointing out that United had splashed out some £40million over the past three years.

"Sometimes there are things that you just cannot say publicly. You may want to but you just have to keep your own counsel. We believed that we were handling things appropriately and I believe that in the end we have delivered," he said.

Since he took over as chairman of the club from Bill Fotherby three years ago, Ridsdale has made a point of visiting the various supporters' club branches up and down the country.

But he let himself in for a rough ride when he attended a meeting of the London branch shortly before the start of the season. "I got a fair amount of criticism from them," the chairman admitted.

"At that stage Michael Bridges was purported to be on his way to Tottenham and though we were interested in him we had not then been given permission to talk to the player."

> "Whatever people may have felt about our naivety in the transfer market we delivered and raised a few eyebrows on every player we targeted last summer."
>
> Peter Ridsdale

"I had hundreds and hundreds of letters that summer accusing the club of not backing our manager, claiming that that was the reason George Graham left and that David O'Leary would go for the same reason," Ridsdale recalled.

"I had to try to remind everyone that I was only the man who went out to buy the players – I did not select them. That was the job of the manager and that is what happened with George and we have the same arrangement now with David."

Criticism, however, does have an effect on people and the United chairman is no different. "I am a Leeds fan and I'm doing the job as best I can. It hurts when I am criticised but it hurts even more when the criticism is unfair," he said.

"And one of the most annoying things aimed at me was that we as a club didn't have money to

The London branch members felt the United chairman's openness and honesty was causing the club to miss out on players they wanted, the suggestion on this occasion being that George Graham had beaten them to the punch for Bridges.

That assumption, of course, turned out to be wrong. United, not Spurs, won the race to sign Bridges. "I am what I am and I try to do my job as well as I can," the chairman stressed. "Yet whatever people may have felt about our naivety in the transfer market we delivered and raised a few eyebrows on every player we targeted last summer."

MICHAEL DUBERRY, who knew there would be strong competition for central defensive places when he left Chelsea to move north, had had to be

content with a place on the substitutes' bench for United's opening game against Derby County.

But he was given his debut when United travelled to the south coast and David O'Leary opted to take on Southampton with three central defenders and use Ian Harte and Danny Mills as attacking wing backs.

United enjoyed an eventful flight to Southampton aboard a plane which the club were trying out with a view to hiring it for trips into Europe later in the campaign.

They were scheduled to take off at 10-15am from Leeds-Bradford airport on Wednesday, August 11, but the flight was delayed for half an hour so that the players and club officials could view the eclipse of the sun while flying at 25,000ft.

At one stage of the eclipse, the view out of one side of the aircraft presented a dark and eerie picture while there was brightness and blue sky from the other side.

But the general consensus of opinion was that the eclipse, or what little could be seen of it from the small windows of the plane, was a bit of an anti-climax. Every time I close my eyes I can see it," quipped Nigel Martyn.

Peter Ridsdale is very much as a "hands-on" chairman. His enthusiasm for the job is second to none and there was evidence of this when the aircraft landed at Southampton airport. Taking over the microphone from the chief cabin crew attendant, he announced: "Welcome to Southampton. We hope you have had a pleasant flight."

Quick as a flash came a response from a player, who shall remain nameless for obvious reasons: "Crikey, don't tell me he's been flying the b----- plane as well!"

Having dropped a couple of points against Derby County, the need to take something from their visit to The Dell was all the more important. A draw might have been acceptable, but victory was the target O'Leary set his men.

And they duly obliged with Michael Bridges making his presence felt by scoring a hat-trick – and then gleefully claiming the match ball by stuffing it up his shirt at the end of the game.

"There was no way I was going to let that ball get away from me," Bridges said. "This was a first for me. I'd never scored a senior team hat-trick before."

He had, however, gone close the previous season while playing for Sunderland against Sheffield United. "I scored twice and then we were awarded a penalty, which I took. Unfortunately I put it wide," he recalled.

To accuse the young lad from Sunderland of being selfish would be quite wrong. He had someone else in mind when he grabbed that match ball. "I had it framed in a glass case and I've given it to Jack Hickson, the man who first brought me into football at Sunderland," Bridges revealed.

"I was about 16 years old and I shall always be grateful to him."

Bridges' opening goal for United at Southampton was a real gem, a cleverly worked set-piece move involving Michael Duberry bringing the reward. The goalscorer revealed: "We had worked hard in training on the set play move where Doobs knocks the ball back for either myself or Harry Kewell to have a go at goal and I have to admit that it hadn't worked once in training!

"So it was great to see it count against Southampton. When the ball came to me I noticed their goalkeeper, Paul Jones, was off his line so I lifted the ball over him and into the goal." Bridges followed that up with two more goals in the second half. "I managed to get on the end of two great crosses," he recalled.

The former Sunderland striker was still clutching the match ball as the United players arrived at Southampton airport for their return journey to Leeds and refused to use it in an impromptu midnight kick-about!

As the players waited on the Tarmac for the skips to be loaded on to the plane, United's Operations Director, David Spencer asked Bridges if he fancied a kick-about with the match-ball. "He just was not having any of that. He wasn't letting go of that ball at any price," Spencer said.

United had an old score to settle at The Dell. A 3-0 defeat there the previous season had been a rude awakening for David O'Leary's side.

Complacency or not, that reverse came after United had scored ten goals in their three previous games, while Southampton had been struggling in the depths of the Premier League.

"We let ourselves down in that game," said the United boss. "For the first time since I took over as manager we were out battled."

That poor showing by United was recalled in O'Leary's team talk before the match on August 11.Whatever he said had the desired result as United, courtesy of that Bridges treble strike and a fine all-round team display, won 3-0.

DARREN HUCKERBY'S £4million transfer from Coventry City came close to having the skids put under it – literally!

While United were on the south coast preparing for their match against the Saints, the lightning fast striker was at Thorp Arch and as chief physiotherapist, David Swift, was with the first team, United's second physio, Alan Sutton, was overseeing Huckerby's medicals.

"He had had part of his medical at Thorp Arch and I then had to drive him to Morley to see the club doctor for the heart test," Sutton explained.

"I drove on the A1 - M1 link road but as we attempted to come off on the slip road at Stourton we had a crash. I had begun to move into the roundabout but a car came flying round and I had to stop, at which point there was a bang as the car following me hit us.

> ## "I thought 'Oh no, this is the last thing we need in the middle of a medical'"
>
> Alan Sutton

"It wasn't a serious knock but it was sufficient to give both me and Darren a bit of a jolt."

Sensing an opportunity to give his driver a shock, Huckerby immediately grasped his neck and complained of pain. "He said his neck hurt," Sutton recalled. "And I thought 'Oh no, this is the last thing we need in the middle of a medical'."

By this time the lady driver of the car that had run into the back of them had got out to apologise. "I remember saying to her that I had a £4million player in the car and that we were in the middle of a medical.

"I don't think she was a Leeds United fan but later on when I rang her to re-assure her that everything was all right she told me she had heard the news of the transfer deal on the radio about an hour after the accident," Sutton added.

Said Huckerby: "I wasn't really hurt. I was just having Alan on when I said my neck had been injured. There was no real damage to either car and we continued on and I got through the medical, thankfully."

The Huckerby deal had been signed, sealed and delivered, by United chairman Peter Ridsdale – without any "assistance" from David O'Leary.

Club policy dictates that the manager selects the players he wants and the club attempt to get them. However, an exception was made when the Bridges negotiations took place with Sunderland chairman Bob Murray. But the United manager's efforts cost his club £125,000!

"Because David had a very good relationship with Bob Murray I agreed that he and I should go together to finalise the deal," said Ridsdale "At one stage we were sticking on the fee. There was some £250,000 difference between us.

"It was part of the transfer discussion tactics and I felt we would get the player without having to pay the extra £250,000 but David suddenly suggested we should split it down the middle. I reckon he cost us £125,000 but we had a laugh about it afterwards – and David was happy enough because he had got another player he really wanted."

Perhaps it's needless to say it, but the manager was not party to the negotiations that brought Huckerby to Elland Road!

United had first inquired about the young striker early in the previous season and been told firmly that he was not for sale. The situation, as it so often can - and does – in football, changed and United again were able to get their man.

O'Leary made it clear that Huckerby had not

been signed as a replacement for Jimmy Floyd Hasselbaink, but for reserve striker Clyde Wijnhard, who had joined Huddersfield Town.

Nevertheless Huckerby found himself thrown in at the deep end when United visited Old Trafford on Saturday, August 14, to tackle their arch rivals Manchester United.

United had not won a league game at Old Trafford since 1981 when little Brian Flynn scored the only goal of the game. It was a stiff challenge for O'Leary's young side – and for Huckerby.

Following their efforts of the previous season O'Leary's men could number Reds boss Sir Alex Ferguson among their admirers. "Leeds are an exciting team who, under David O'Leary, really caught the imagination last season," he said.

■ Darren Huckerby, pain in the neck!

O'Leary likes his team to be less than cautious - to attack well whenever the situation allows. He opted to take the game to the Reds, playing three up – Michael Bridges, Huckerby and Harry Kewell - with Alan Smith still out of the reckoning because of an ankle injury.

Training towards the end of the build up week had centred on this plan but it all went wrong when Bridges suffered an ankle injury in a second minute tackle by Henning Berg, which caused him to limp out of the game 18 minutes later.

With no other strikers available on the bench, United had to change their plans, midfield man David Hopkin coming on. Even so, O'Leary's side held their own and with Kewell choosing the stage to turn on the style they had the better of the first half.

The Australian forward missed a great chance to open the scoring after 66 minutes when Lucas Radebe's well-judged forward pass put him clean through. Kewell's low shot beat goalkeeper Raimond van der Gouw, but the ball struck the foot of a post and rebounded to be cleared.

When Dwight Yorke pounced in the 77th and

80th minutes it was all over, though many felt a draw would have been a fairer reflection of the play. Still, O'Leary summed the game up succinctly. "You have to take your chances at this level and they took theirs while we missed ours. Other than that there wasn't a lot between the two teams," he said.

CLUB secretary Ian Silvester suffered an embarrassing moment in the boardroom at Southampton, following United's 3-0 success at The Dell – and it was all down to chairman Peter Ridsdale, who seized on an opportunity he impishly felt was too good to miss.

Not surprisingly, Ian's nickname at the club is "The Cat" – after the long-suffering cartoon cat, Silvester.

In a lull in the boardroom conversation the United chairman suddenly revealed: "Ladies and gentlemen, I have an announcement to make. I thought you might like to know that our secretary Ian 'The Cat' Silvester is going to have the 'snip' tomorrow.

"Then we'll have a neutered 'cat' at the club," added the chairman, who later recalled: "Ian's crimson face was a picture but I just couldn't resist the opportunity."

Silvester admitted: "My face was red. I had no idea the chairman was going to do what he did. It took me completely by surprise and I recall being quite embarrassed at the time," added the father of two.

Boardroom chat also revealed that the United chairman cancels all his Sunday newspapers if his team loses – and so does Manchester United chief Martin Edwards.

This came to light after United had gone down 2-0 to their archrivals at Old Trafford. "We were talking in the boardroom and Martin Edwards came over to say hard luck on our defeat and asked our chairman if he would be cancelling his Sunday papers because of it.

"Peter replied that he always did if we lost and

Martin Edwards said that he did the same on the rare occasions Manchester United lost a game," said Silvester.

FORTUNE, they say, favours the brave, but United could claim that hadn't been the case at Old Trafford. David O'Leary's plan was to take the game to the Reds. "We set out to try to win every match and why should we think otherwise just because we were playing Manchester United?" he asked.

Sir Alex Ferguson's team may well have been regarded as the best in Europe following their triple success the previous season so maybe it was a measure of the progress O'Leary believed his team had made that he felt they could go to Old Trafford with such confidence.

"We have a fine young side with plenty of ability so I thought why not be brave and give it a right go," O'Leary recalled.

For a long time it looked as though the ploy might pay off. Had Harry Kewell being able to take full advantage of that superb pass from Lucas Radebe who knows what the outcome of the game would have been?

increased when they took on newly promoted Sunderland at Elland Road. Latest culprit was Darren Huckerby who, when put clean through the Wearsiders' defence, had only goalkeeper Thomas Sorensen to beat, yet failed to do so.

Alan Smith, fit again after an ankle injury and brought on as substitute, also got through Sunderland's defence, but he was prevented from scoring when hauled down from behind by Darren Holloway.

Amazingly, though, the "one-on-one" bug reared its head again when Kewell failed to beat the keeper from the resultant penalty!

Another ear bashing from the boss? Probably not, as United had recovered from the setback of a Kevin Phillips penalty in the 38th minute, awarded by referee Paul Alcock who adjudged Lucas Radebe to have brought the Sunderland striker down, with goals from Lee Bowyer and Danny Mills.

Former Charlton defender Mills can hardly lay claim to be tamong the top scoring full-backs, as his first goal for United was only the fourth League goal of his career, which at that stage had taken in more than 100 league games.

> # "I had a word or two with Harry about his finishing. I told him I expected better from such a talented player and that I wanted to see him score quite a few goals this season."
>
> David O'Leary

Although United's young Australian forward took the eye with some admirable play in the game, that didn't save him from a bit of an ear bashing because of his glaring miss. Having also failed to cash in on a one-to-one situation in United's opening day goalless draw against Derby County, his manager felt it was time to make a point.

"I had a word or two with Harry about his finishing. I told him I expected better from such a talented player and that I wanted to see him score quite a few goals this season," O'Leary said. "He knows how highly I rate him and when I criticise him he takes it on the chin and just gets on with things. He is always willing to listen to advice."

United's failure rate from "one-on-ones"

Spirits were naturally high after that victory and at least one player had a smashing time at Thorp Arch in the week that followed. Several first team players had taken to deliberately trying to annoy physiotherapist Alan Sutton.

"It was a lunchtime and a few of the lads were messing about in the medical room. Lee Bowyer was there and a few of the other lads and I was wanting to give some treatment to David Hopkin and Michael Bridges," Sutton said.

"I was trying my best to get the lads to leave but they wouldn't. I knew they were due to train again early in the afternoon and I just said to them: 'Sod you, I'm going' and locked the lot of them in. I

■ Sheer delight. A shirtless Danny Mills is ecstatic after scoring his first goal for Leeds in the 2-1 home victory over Sunderland. Ian Harte is also happy.

went off to the gym, thinking it was up to them to get out in time for the training session," he added.

David Batty came to the rescue of his teammates, though it has to be said, unwittingly. The midfielder wanted to get into the medical room and mistakenly thought they had placed a wedge underneath the door to keep him out. He hadn't realised it was locked.

"He just got his shoulder to it and the door burst open, splintering the woodwork near the lock and leaving a job for the joiner," said Sutton. At least the lads weren't late for the training session!

THE arrival of New Zealand international central defender Danny Hay for a fee of £200,000 from Australian side Perth Glory took David O'Leary's summer spending to around the £19m mark and further increased the competition for places at the heart of the first team defence.

Hay, 6ft 4in and 24-years-old, had impressed O'Leary during a short trial at Thorp Arch. The manager wanted to sign him immediately, but the near impossibility of the player, born outside the

European Union, being able to get a work permit was a major stumbling block.

But Hay came to his own rescue, or rather his girlfriend Diane did. Although born in Perth, Australia, Diane's father is German and holds a German passport, which meant that once Diane and Danny were married, Danny was able to come and work in Europe.

But any suggestions that this was a marriage of convenience could not be wider of the mark. "We had been living together for two years. We were engaged and had already planned to get married," explained Hay.

Hay had played his football for the previous two seasons in Australia with Perth Glory. "Playing there was good for me. It has provided me with a stepping stone and now I hope to be able to benefit from being with such a big club and with such a manager as David O'Leary," he said.

A regular member of the New Zealand national side for the past four years, Hay added: "I have played about 16 matches for New Zealand but as you can imagine being stuck out where we are, we don't play all that many games at international level."

"Now I am with a big club. I don't think I could have joined a better one. There is a big challenge in front of me and I hope things work out well."

Few New Zealanders have been seen in English soccer over the years and, hardly surprisingly, Hay's signing for one of the Premiership's leading clubs received major news coverage back home.

"It is unusual for someone from New Zealand to sign for a big soccer club in England and now it is up to me to make the most of it," Hay said.

"I have no regrets about leaving home and then Australia. Coming to Leeds is a big opportunity for me.

"I have joined a club where there are a lot of very good defenders so I know I will be a difficult job trying to break into the first team."

ANY sportsman worth his salt has to be able to take the rough with the smooth and David O'Leary's side were given a rough ride when Liverpool arrived at Elland Road, played to a specially prepared plan and went back to Merseyside with three points from a 2-1 victory.

Manager Gerard Houllier's decision that he needed to formulate a plan specially to beat a United team he genuinely believed to be one of the title contenders, was a compliment to the progress O'Leary's team had made in less than 12 months.

Playing with just Robbie Fowler up front, packing midfield and breaking out with power and pace and precise passing, posed all sorts of problems but on a night when few United players did themselves justice, the United manager did not pull his punches.

"The better team won. Ours was a disappointing performance and the players knew it. Liverpool ran the show from start to finish and I delivered a few home truths to my players," O'Leary revealed. The United boss was, however, looking for some good to come out of the defeat.

"Maybe this will bring a few people, within the club and outside it who think we will win the title, down to earth a bit. Maybe it will take some of the hype out of the situation. We have a lot of very young players in our side and they still have things to learn," he added.

Time off for United players was cancelled for the week as extra training was put on the schedule but it was not all doom and gloom. Howard Wilkinson, selected five of O'Leary's players in the England Under-21 international squad to prepare for games against Luxembourg at Reading on September 3 and Poland away four days' later.

Forwards Alan Smith and Michael Bridges, midfielder Lee Bowyer, right-back Danny Mills and goalkeeper Paul Robinson were the players in demand.

■ Reserve goalkeeper Paul Robinson works on his fitness in pre-season training.

AS THE intriguing meeting with George Graham's high-riding Tottenham side loomed large, there was the distraction for United of the draw for the first round of the UEFA Cup, which paired O'Leary's side with leading Yugoslavian side Partizan Belgrade.

Chairman Peter Ridsdale and club secretary Ian Silvester had to interrupt their normal weekly schedule of running the club to undertake the "onerous" task of mixing with the jet-setters in Monaco for a couple of days while the draws for the various UEFA competitions were made.

As they say, it's a hard life for some!

This top duo, however, were hardly welcomed back to Elland Road with open arms. After the delights of previous European trips to Madeira and Rome, the prospect of going to Belgrade flipped over the other side of the coin and left United facing not only one of the more difficult ties but also an administrative nightmare.

The problems were obvious – and many. A decision as to whether United would be able to fly into Belgrade for the away leg of the tie rested initially with the European Union of countries, who had banned flights into Belgrade during and because of the Kosovo crisis.

UEFA would also be involved, of course, and United were instructed to speak with the British government as well before a final decision on whether the trip could be undertaken or not was made.

Waiting for the decision left United in a state of European limbo but at United's Thorp Arch training complex, the strength and potential of their squad was being underlined by a succession of international calls on O'Leary's talented players.

The final count ended at 16. Following the inclusion of five of their men in the Under-21 squad, Nigel Martyn, David Batty and Jonathan Woodgate were in the full England squad to prepare for a crunch Euro 2000 qualifier in Poland.

David Hopkin reported with Scotland, Eirik Bakke with the Norwegian Under-21s, Stephen McPhail and Alan Maybury with the Republic of Ireland Under-21s while Matthew Jones was in the Welsh Under-21 squad.

Australia selected Harry Kewell for the Olympic

■ Alan Smith - one of five Leeds players in the England U21 squad.

Under-23 squad, Martin Hiden was wanted by Austria, but the biggest surprise was Gary Kelly's recall to the Republic of Ireland squad for their European Championship matches against Yugoslavia and in Croatia and Malta.

Shin problems had kept Kelly out of first team action for the whole of the previous season and though he had proved himself fit for this season, O'Leary had not at that stage brought him back into his first team starting line up.

While Kelly was celebrating, there was only shock and amazement for his nephew and United team-mate Ian Harte, who, having been a regular member of the Irish squad, found himself omitted. There had been a time when Harte had been selected on a regular basis for his country while having been dropped into United's reserves by previous manager George Graham.

Harte's immediate attention, however, was being directed – as was that of the rest of the United squad - towards putting one over on George Graham's high-riding Tottenham Hotspur side.

Having played badly in their home defeat by Liverpool, United's visit to White Hart Lane had taken on an even greater significance. The fact that it was billed as Graham versus O'Leary – master against pupil – was understandable, though O'Leary, at least, had attempted to play that angle down.

Yet even he could hardly deny that an intriguing fixture was in prospect. United fans clearly thought so.

■ Thanks for the points pal. David O'Leary and his mentor George Graham shake hands after United's victory over Tottenham at Elland Road.

CHAPTER THREE

O'LEARY-GRAHAM RELATIONSHIP... THE TRUTH

ONCE the best of friends and a successful and happy management duo at Elland Road, relationships between David O'Leary and George Graham had been soured following Tottenham Hotspurs' snatching of Dutch midfield man Willem Korsten from United's grasp.

The two men were daggers drawn, didn't speak to each other and were now the greatest of enemies. Or so the story went.

Here, however, the United manager puts the record straight. There is no feud, no animosity and no ill feeling. "It is rubbish to suggest there is anything like that," he said. "The media had hyped things up before the game at White Hart Lane suggesting we were no longer friendly towards each other. But that is simply not the case," O'Leary stressed.

In a bid to keep the build-up to such an eagerly awaited fixture as low key as possible, O'Leary took the unusual step of banning the media from the Thorp Arch training complex and from talking to players. He also refused to talk about the game.

"I knew if I did my comments would be taken the wrong way and in addition I didn't want players being drawn into it. So we opted to keep the media out and go for an uninterrupted build-up to the game," he explained.

Naturally this went down like a lead balloon with the media but the decision had been made and it wasn't going to be reversed.

The sun was beating down and the temperatures had soared again when United arrived at White Hart Lane for their late August meeting with Spurs. A note was waiting in the visitors' dressing room for O'Leary. "It was from George inviting me to his office for a pre-match cup of tea and a chat with him," said the boss.

"I went up and spent a very pleasant half hour chatting with George and his daughter. We talked about things in general, about Harrogate and if it was as nice as ever, which I said it was. About the families and how the ground was at Elland Road. Things like that.

> "He is responsible for having brought me to Yorkshire, where me and my family are so happy and for me having the job I love so much."
>
> David O'Leary

"It was all very pleasant but he knew that once the game started I would be trying as hard as I could to kick his butt and I knew he would be doing everything he could to kick mine.

"That's the nature of the business we are in – the jobs we have demand that. But that doesn't mean to say we aren't friends any more. Okay, so he leads his own life and I lead mine but I owe George a lot – and I'll never forget that.

"He is responsible for having brought me to Yorkshire, where me and my family are so happy and for me having the job I love so much. If it weren't for him I would very probably not be back in Yorkshire now and enjoying my life so much," he added.

The two men present a different public image but both have similar goals. Both of them hate losing, both are determined to be winners. That, as David himself might say, is the bottom line.

Graham has been the best – his trophy winning days at Arsenal underline that forcibly – and while O'Leary has just kicked off his career as a manager, he has designs on becoming the best.

When Graham was at Elland Road, players quickly found out he was not a man to be messed with. His word was law. He wanted respect, commanded it and if he didn't get it it was too bad for the individuals concerned.

By comparison, O'Leary appears to be much more amenable and approachable. But he can be just as ruthless as his mentor, when there is need to be, as several players have already found out. The major difference between the two is that while Graham's heart was in London, O'Leary's is very much based in Yorkshire and centred on Elland Road.

When the two went head-to-head at White Hart Lane in August it was O'Leary who came out on top - a victory for the pupil over the master - and as the referee's final whistle blew to signal United's win, there followed the customary handshake between the two managers. But even that didn't satisfy some.

It was interpreted as cursory and lukewarm. "What did they expect. Did they think I should have thrown my arms around him, hugged him and danced around?" the United boss asked me.

A free kick by Ian Harte, struck so ferociously that one-time United hot-shot Peter Lorimer would have been proud of it, settled the issue in O'Leary's favour on this occasion. Harte's rocket shot in the 81st minute after Alan Smith's well taken 53rd minute equaliser to Tim Sherwood's first half opener for Spurs, must have been like a bullet to the head for Graham.

The young Republic of Ireland international was not exactly Graham's favourite player when he was manager at Elland Road. The youngster had been dropped from the senior side while being a regular at international level.

Returning from international duty to train with United's reserves was hard to stomach. But patience paid off and when he got his first team chance again he took it. Scoring a goal against Spurs the previous season to earn United a fifth round FA Cup replay was sweet revenge but to blast in the winner in the White Hart Lane league meeting this term was more 'take that' stuff.

Understandably, spirits were sky high as the team returned to Leeds and then put league ambitions on the back burner for a couple of weeks as the Premiership closed down for the weekend of September because of international calls on many of its players.

Activity off the pitch, however, was intense. The debate was on as to the dangers of an English team visiting Belgrade so soon after the conflict in the Balkans.

Eventually UEFA decided that the Belgrade leg of the tie should be played on neutral territory and chose Heerenveen in northern Holland. But the decision came late – leaving United with just six days to prepare. A "bit of a nightmare" for United's administrative staff, was how club secretary Ian Silvester described the situation.

As far as manager David O'Leary was concerned there was the substantial concern that while Partizan officials were able to get to England to see his side in action at Tottenham and Coventry, he was unable to watch Partizan because there were no direct flights from England to Belgrade.

Organising the trip to Holland, however, got under way as soon as possible. "We are a very professional club and we had quite a few people working long hours to try to see that everything was in place for the safe transportation of the team and supporters," Silvester said.

He revealed that not long after the draw paired United with Partizan Belgrade he received phone calls from parents of the younger players who were worried about the prospect of their sons having to go to Belgrade.

"We were always going to be guided by the Foreign Office and when the decision was made by the EU not to lift the ban on flights into Belgrade we knew we would not be going to Yugoslavia," he added.

HEAD physiotherapist David Swift has one of the most important jobs at Thorp Arch – seeing that injured players are given the correct treatment and returned to full fitness as quickly as possible.

Like all jobs, though, it has its down side - especially when Lee Bowyer happens to be one of the "patients" in his treatment room. The England Under 21 international midfielder is "Mr Perpetual Motion" on the field of play but when he's on the injured list, he's a pain in the backside for Swifty.

"If I had to choose a player who I would least like to have in my treatment room for a day it would be him. Players don't normally like to be in the treatment room anyway but Lee really hates it," he explained.

"When he's in for treatment he moans about

■ Physio David Swift regards Lee Bowyer as Leeds United's biggest treatment room moaner. Here Lee has suffered an injury playing for the England Under-21s but thankfully it proved to be nothing serious.

everything and that's simply because he gets so frustrated at not being able to play. I suppose that underlines his commitment. On the field he's the type of player who just wants to be involved all the time."

Slight of stature and small in height Bowyer may be, but he possesses what the coaching staff at Elland Road refer to as a great engine. In other words the ability to cover every blade of grass on the pitch throughout the 90 minutes of a match and have energy in reserve at the end.

There is more to Bowyer's game than mere stamina, of course, as was evident the previous season when he showed a keen eye for goals.

While Bowyer ranks as a far from ideal patient when injured, the United player classed as the best by Swift is Dutch defender Robert Molenaar, who for much of the previous season and this one, was fighting a hard battle to recover from a ruptured cruciate knee ligament.

"Robert, I would say, is the model patient. He's had a serious injury and all his attention and effort was focused into recovering from it," said Swift. Each programme he was given, he stuck to diligently. If he was supposed to have achieved a certain amount of progress by a certain day and he wasn't able to, then he wanted to know the reason why not."

Molenaar had begun to make his mark in the Premiership forming a formidable central defensive partnership with Lucas Radebe that had conceded only one goal in the first six League games of the 1998-99 season.

But in December of that season, he suffered his knee injury at Arsenal that left him facing a long road back. Worse was to follow, for after undergoing an operation to repair the damage, he ruptured the ligament a second time and had to undergo another operation.

While Molenaar had to battle on in search of fitness, team-mate Martin Hiden, who suffered a similar injury when playing at Old Trafford in the same season, recovered from his in time to undergo pre-season training. Weighing in at 11st 7lbs, the Austrian international is considerably lighter than Molenaar. Could this be a factor in the rate of recovery from such a serious injury?

"I honestly don't know," Swift said. "We are fortunate in that we have one of the best knee surgeons living within 20 miles of the club and we have talked to him a lot about this.

"Being the heavier of the two Robert was putting more weight on his knee than Martin was on his. And I think if you look at the history of players who have suffered with cruciate ligaments, the heavier guys tend to have taken a bit longer to get over the problem."

This was a thought Molenaar also had and he admitted he made a conscious effort to lose weight after the injury. "I lost about a stone and at one stage the manager asked me what was the matter with me because he thought I didn't look all that good," said Molenaar.

After the Dutch defender ruptured the ligament a second time he looked at things a little differently. "When all you can do is sit there

■ Gary Kelly made a 'much awaited' return to first team action after having missed the whole of the previous campaign with shin trouble. He looks in fine shape in this action shot.

resting with your leg in plaster, eating is one of the few pleasures left open to you. So I ate well," he recalled.

Once he was able to begin remedial work, Molenaar's attention was focused very much on that – and also on helping care for his newly born son, Jeroen, after his wife Karin gave birth to their first child in early September. While Molenaar remained the model patient United's head physio came up with further evidence of the tremendous spirit at the club.

Gone are the days of the treatment room malingerers – players who preferred the warmth and comfort of the indoors to the rigours and cold and wet of the training ground during the week before making a remarkable recovery in time for a game.

"To be honest, I don't think there is anyone at the club now who would be keen to miss training, and that may not always have been the case here in the past," said Swift.

GARY KELLY'S 12 month frustration during which he saw the four walls of the treatment room almost daily, apart from a couple of stays in hospital, ended at White Hart Lane when he was called into first team action as a second half substitute.

His task on re-entry to Premiership football could hardly have been more testing. Keep David Ginola quiet, was the order from his manager.

The enigmatic Frenchman, who had given Danny Mills a taxing time, was Tottenham's dangerman but "Kels" immediately got to grips with his opponent whose effectiveness was diminished and United went on to win the game.

As he strode on to the White Hart Lane pitch, the Republic of Ireland international had cause to think of a 'drill' exercise that had put him on the road to recovery.

No end had seemed in sight to Kelly's shin problems until it was suggested that drilling holes into the tibia might provide a solution. "We felt that if that was done it would relieve the pressure, so three holes were drilled into the tibia and that, followed by rehabilitation work, did the trick," head physio David Swift revealed.

Packard Bell

■ Leeds United official team group. Back left right Robert Molenaar, Michael Bridges, Jonathan Woodgate, Nigel Martyn, Michael Duberry, Paul Robinson, Eirik Bakke, Alfie Haaland, and David Hopkin. Middle: Sean Hardy (kit manager), Bruno Ribeiro, Ian Harte, David Batty, Gary Kelly, Danny Mills, Jimmy Floyd Hasselbaink, Eddie Gray (assistant manager), David Swift (physio). Front: Stephen McPhail, Alan Smith, Harry Kewell, Peter Ridsdale (chairman), Lucas Radebe.
David O'Leary (manager), Lee Bowyer, Matthew Jones, Martin Hiden.

■ Darren Huckerby in serious mood as he answers media questions.

■ The rush is on. Fans run into Leeds United's superstore at Elland Road to be the first to purchase the new first team strip.

■ Lee Bowyer seems
to be enjoying the
pre-season training.

■ Top: **A winner!**
Michael Bridges
salutes his goal
that gave Leeds
United a 3-2 home
success at the
expense of
Newcastle United.
High riding Lee
Bowyer and Harry
Kewell were also
on the scoresheet
that day.

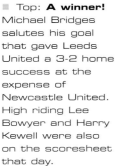

■ Centre: Harry
Kewell celebrates
his goal against
Middlesbrough.

■ Bottom:
It's a goal mate!
Alan Smith wheels
away in delight
after scoring
against Sheffield
Wednesday. Peter
Atherton's appeal
for offside was in
vain.

■ Top: **Well done Ian!**
Full-back Harte gets the
congratulations after
netting the only goal of
the game against West
Ham at Elland Road.

■ Centre: Alan Smith is
congratulated after
scoring in the 4-1 home
victory over Lokomotiv
Moscow.

■ Bottom: **Hitching a
ride!** Stephen McPhail
leaps onto Michael
Bridges to celebrate a
goal against Bradford
City.

■ Manager David O'Leary spells out a message before the game against Lokomotiv.

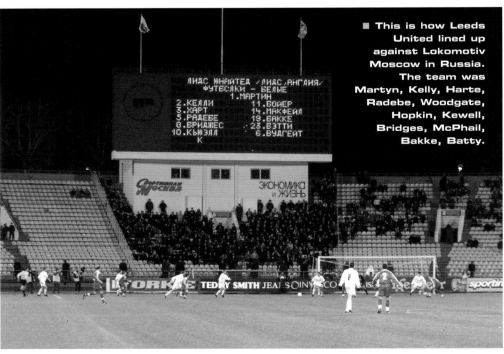

ЛИДС ЮНАЙТЕД /ЛИДС,АНГЛИЯ.
ФУТБОЛКИ - БЕЛЫЕ
1.МАРТИН
2.КЕЛЛИ   11.БОЙЕР
3.ХАРТ   14.МАКФЕИЛ
5.РАДЕБЕ   19.БАККЕ
8.БРИДЖЕС   23.БЭТТИ
10.КЬЮЭЛЛ   6.ВУДГЕЙТ
К

■ This is how Leeds United lined up against Lokomotiv Moscow in Russia. The team was Martyn, Kelly, Harte, Radebe, Woodgate, Hopkin, Kewell, Bridges, McPhail, Bakke, Batty.

■ Moscow in November.
David O'Leary holds a
pre-match Press
conference.

■ No fingerprints here –
just footprints as Michael
Bridges and Harry
Kewell, both wearing
gloves as protection
against the cold of
Moscow, attack against
Lokomotiv.

■ Darren Huckerby challenges a Spartak Moscow player for possession at the sparsely populated stadium in Moscow.

■ Altogether now – Harry Kewell, Michael Bridges and Eirik Bakke make up a happy threesome after Bridges hit the target against Southampton.

■ Harry Kewell puts an arm around Danny Mills after what turned out to be Mills' only league goal of the season, against Sunderland.

■ Fans salute a goal from Ian Harte.

■ Lucas gets in on the act. Leeds United 's skipper helps ballet dancers Colin Wilkinson and Pauline Hines promote the Ballet Rambert company's show in Leeds.

■ Top: **If you're Irish...**
Some of Leeds United's
Irish contingent,
Stephen McPhail, Ian
Harte and Gary Kelly
share a joke with Father
Ted star Ardal O'Hanlon,
who played Father
Dougal in the hit TV
show.

■ Right: Chairman Peter
Ridsdale pops into Leeds
United's Cyber Café at
Elland Road, where the
public can get an
introduction to the
internet.

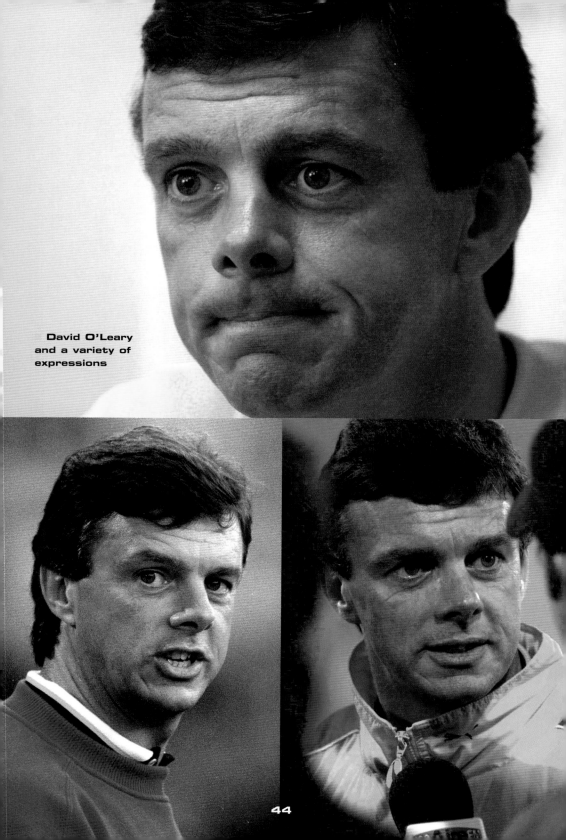

David O'Leary
and a variety of
expressions

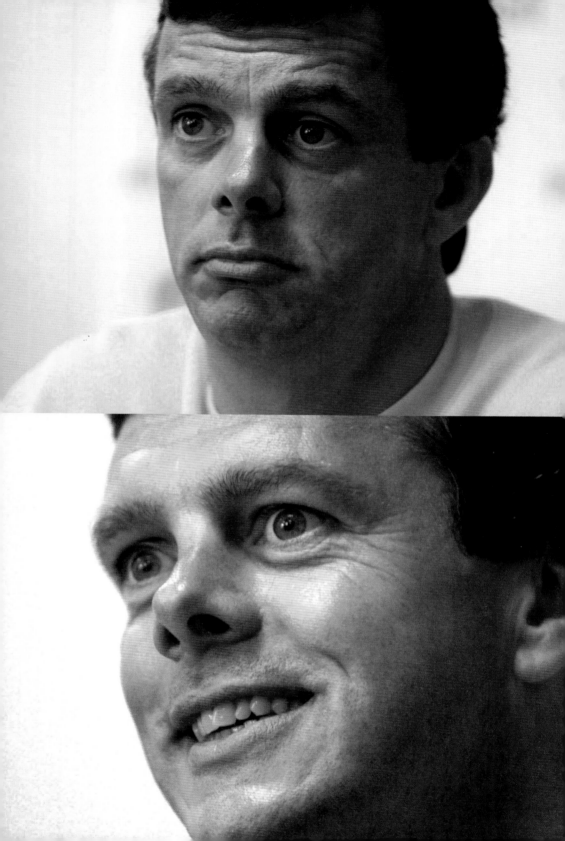

■ Who wants a game
of footie then?
The kids are alright
at Thorp Arch!

Harry Kewell and Michael Bridges - sophisticated men about town.

"It was great to have a bit of the action again," said Kelly who, despite being fit at the start of the season, had waited patiently for his recall. "You could say it was like having a new start to my career. I had non-stop football for five years before it was halted by shin trouble. Then I missed a whole season so it was like starting from scratch all over again this season," Kelly said.

"You have to win back your place in the team and establish your reputation all over again. A lot of people have had long injury lay-offs and had to fight hard to prove themselves again. The important thing is to impress in training and once you think you have done that you need to have patience. I had.

"Although I certainly didn't think so at the time, being out for so long could well prove to be beneficial to me in the long run. I had had so much football but after a year out I think I am a lot hungrier," he added.

United manager David O'Leary, who hailed Kelly's return as being "like signing a new player," agreed. "It's fantastic to have him back but I think we saw a new Gary Kelly – a different Gary Kelly on the training ground and in how he looked after himself. We had a fitter Gary Kelly and that came about for one reason only – there was a big threat to his place.

"It's all down to competition for places – and I was brought up on that at Arsenal. Gary knows that if he plays well enough he stays in the side. If he doesn't then there's Danny Mills to take over and Gary is well aware of that.

"Gary battled back really well. He bided his time and I was totally and utterly impressed with him. But in the end it comes down to competition. Ian Harte found himself in a similar situation when Danny Granville was signed and he too rolled up his sleeves and won back his place," O'Leary pointed out.

After a trip away on international duty the young Irishman got another taste of first team action, coming on as substitute in the goal-crazy clash at Coventry that had managers, David O'Leary and Gordon Strachan tearing their hair out. "It was good to have a taste of first team football in the games at Tottenham and Coventry and then to be

in from the start in the UEFA Cup tie against Partizan in Holland was fantastic," Kelly added.

As a spectacle the game was top class entertainment and fever-pitch excitement, but it was United's fans who had the greater satisfaction as their side edged through to win 4-3.

A great advert for the game? Of course, it was. But managers never like to see their teams conceding goals – especially to that extent. No surprise, then, to see the emphasis put on defence when next United trained.

I WONDER if supporters ever think how effective verbal abuse of an opposition player is. Few players are intimidated by it. For most it serves only to make them more determined. David Batty is a prime example of this. By the very nature of his game, the combative midfield player has had more than his fair share of abuse from crowds. But he has thrived on it.

His sending off in England's Euro 2000 qualifying game in Poland three days' earlier, made him Number One target for the Coventry boo boys but Batty responded in the best possible manner – with a man-of-the-match performance.

> "My game is a physical one but the stick I get just spurs me on — I react positively to it. In fact I enjoy it."
>
> David Batty

"It doesn't bother me – and it never has," said Batty as relaxed and assured as he has ever been. "When I am on the pitch nothing worries me. My game is a physical one but the stick I get just spurs me on – I react positively to it. In fact I enjoy it."

Involvement in two of United's goals was only a part of what was a sterling all-round contribution to the victory. But Darren Huckerby, who also had to take some "stick" from Coventry fans on what was his first return to Highfield Road, had cause to thank Batty for creating the chance for him to open his goal account for United. Another perfect response to the boos and jeers.

There was little time to bask in the joy of that high scoring victory as United looked to launch their bid for European glory.

You could almost hear the sigh of relief when it was finally confirmed that O'Leary's 'babies' would face Yugoslavian champions Partizan Belgrade at Heerenveen in the north of Holland in the first leg of their first round UEFA Cup tie. It was a step into

Placing an English club with one from Yugoslavia in the initial first round groupings seemed unwise, to say the least, and when the draw actually paired the two of them together the wisdom of it was questioned even further.

"It may sound strange but when the draw was made I was thinking only about football and my initial reaction was that despite the fact we were seeded in our group we had drawn the hardest tie of the group," chairman Peter Ridsdale said.

"What I was slightly confused about was that

> "The British government's view was that they would not allow or advise us to travel to Yugoslavia because they could not guarantee our safety."
>
> Peter Ridsdale

the unknown as O'Leary admitted he had been a little "scared" at not knowing much about the Yugoslavs but decided attack would be the best course of action.

Confidence was all around the camp as United flew out to Holland. Almost as soon as they arrived in Heerenveen they were training at the neat 13,500 capacity Abe Lenstra stadium. Chairman Peter Ridsdale was with them, combining business with pleasure.

Kitted out in a United track suit, he demonstrated his skills (strictly limited!) with the ball at the same time as taking calls on his mobile phone relating to the Sky TV deal which was to gross United £14million.

A small number of Dutch-based Serbs had gathered outside the main entrance to the stadium on the day of the game, a couple of whom taunted the media with hostile chants about the Elland Road club and also questioned the sexuality of Prime Minister Tony Blair.

If it needed doing, this highlighted the anti-British feeling that existed and gave backing to UEFA's decision not to play the game in Belgrade. United's players found the ideal way to silence the chants, an excellent display which opened up a 3-1 first leg lead.

we, as a seeded team, found ourselves drawn against a team who had played in the Champions' League qualifying round. I would have thought that a seeded team would not have played a team of such stature.

"It was only when the media started asking me if we would be prepared to go to Belgrade that I began to think about the implications. That set the alarm bells ringing and I realised this was a hot potato we were going to have to deal with," he added.

UEFA had announced prior to the draw that the Yugoslavian team would have to prove there were proper commercial air links with the country of their opponents by a week after the draw.

"The British government's view was that they would not allow or advise us to travel to Yugoslavia because they could not guarantee our safety, given the possible ramifications, and that they believed UEFA would acknowledge that, which indeed they did," said Ridsdale.

When the talking was over it was down to action on the field. O'Leary said: "All I had seen of them was a video. The night before the game I shut myself away in my hotel bedroom and thought long and hard about the best way for us to play it."

The coffee pot was emptied and filled up again before he decided on his plan of action. Not surprisingly for a manager who favours a refreshingly positive approach to all games, he decided to be bold and adventurous. "I drank cup after cup of coffee before deciding on our plan of action," he said.

The result, a five man midfield, worked well as a couple of goals from Lee Bowyer and a collector's item strike from skipper Lucas Radebe overcame the 20th minute set-back of Partizan's opener, to leave United with a handy 3-1 advantage for the Elland Road return leg.

Lucas Radebe has been such an infrequent visitor to the opposition penalty area, it was said he needed to stop and ask teammates for directions to it!

So rare had been his visits to the box that United's head physio David Swift has struck a bet each season with the South African that he couldn't score three goals in a single campaign. And "Swifty" has been quids in. "I've had this bet with Lucas for a few years and it has paid off very nicely for me," he said. "In fact if I take the money from him again I'll have to declare it on my tax form as regular income."

Radebe did get his name on to the scoresheet in the home defeat by Liverpool but unfortunately that was an own goal. "He tried to claim it towards his three goal target but I told him own goals didn't count," the physio added.

Radebe, however, did manage to open his account with a goal against Partizan – and what a strike it was too. "It's got to be a contender for goal of the season," United's happy skipper said afterwards as a broader than usual smile stretched across his face. The fact that Radebe had ventured into the Partizan penalty area for a free kick had been a shock in itself.

Jonathan Woodgate headed Ian Harte's free kick high into the air and Radebe, in his determination to put in a challenge, fell to the ground but looked up to see the ball dropping and promptly hooked it in with an overhead kick. "What a goal," he enthused later. "I know I don't score too many but you have to agree that when I do, people remember them. But they all count."

His goal, which put United 2-1 up, following Lee Bowyer's 25th minute equaliser, was only the second goal he had scored since joining United in August 1994. His other goal was in the 4-0 FA Cup third round victory against Oxford in January 1998.

■ One for the scrapbook. Goal celebrations for Lucas Radebe are rare so it was not difficult to understand his feelings after he scored against Partizan Belgrade.

Radebe does take a bit of stick from some for not scoring more often, but he points out that as a central defender his job is to prevent goals from being scored. "Always my first option is to defend. If I get that right that's my main job done," he said.

"I am not a goalscorer and I had always been the one to stay back in defence whenever we got free kicks so I did not have the chance to go forward all that often."

So why was he suddenly to be seen in the Partizan penalty area for that Harte free kick? "For that game and the one before it, at Coventry, the Gaffer had told me to move up for set-pieces," he said.

"So maybe there'll be more to come for me this season – and Swifty might just have to pay up for a change."

Bowyer's second strike, enabled United to return from Holland with a 3-1 first leg advantage over the Yugoslav champions – no wonder the champagne flowed on the flight home.

United had another hero at Heerenveen in goalkeeper Nigel Martyn who, after making a mistake when Partizan scored their goal, redeemed himself with a great penalty save – thanks to some extent to David Batty's indecision!

When Jimmy Armfield managed United in the late 1970s it was often said of him that his indecision was final. The same might have been said of Batty in this instance.

The United midfield man had played against Partizan a couple of seasons back when the Yugoslavs beat Newcastle with the aid of two penalties. As Vuc Rasovic prepared to take the spot kick against him, Martyn asked Batty which way the Yugoslav had put the kicks in the past.

"He told me he couldn't remember. I said 'Thanks for that' and then "Batts" came back and said he thought he favoured putting them to the keeper's right. I made up my mind to go that way and it paid off," Martyn said.

Having kept the scores at 1-1 Martyn then saw Radebe's strike and a second goal from Bowyer establish a 3-1 advantage for United to take into the Elland Road leg of the tie.

DAVID O'LEARY and his players had little time to bask in the glory of their European escapade before they turned their attention to Middlesbrough. In any case, their Euro first round assignment was only half accomplished, as the United boss was quick to point out.

Would Paul Gascoigne return to action for Boro? Would talented Brazilian Juninho, re-signed by Boro on loan, be back, too? These were questions pondered publicly in the build up to the Sunday afternoon meeting with United at Elland Road.

Not that these were questions that concerned O'Leary. Having assembled a side capable of beating most, he was entitled to feel confident as they faced up to the challenge of Bryan Robson's side.

Neither Gascoigne nor Juninho made it for Boro, but with England international midfield battlers Paul Ince and David Batty in opposition, the scene was set for an interesting game.

Michael Bridges scored his fifth goal in nine games to put United into a 14th minute lead before Harry Kewell hit the target for his first goal of the campaign. Having endured a miserable time in front of goal in the previous eight games of the season, Kewell had reason to be relieved when he put his name on United's scoresheet for the first time in six months.

The young Australian has impressed many people within the game but putting the ball in the back of the net was something he was keen to improve on. "Maybe I should score more and if I could end up with say 15 goals and the team finishes in the top three it will have been a good season," he said. "But I always work hard at my game and I've done that ever since I first came to the club."

The 2-0 victory over Boro hoisted United into the lofty position of second in the Premiership – a position not previously experienced in O'Leary's managerial career.

Asked if it meant anything special to him to see his side as high as that, the United manager said: "Having gone into second place at this early stage doesn't really mean a lot to me. You get nothing for being here now. Our league position at the end

■ Preparing to punch the air in delight. Harry Kewell is chuffed to bits after netting against Middlesborough.

dog yet" attitude Robson, who I first came into contact with when he was building Ipswich Town into a force in the 1960s, had to be admired for taking on such a pressurised job.

"It's not something I would want to do at that age – when I'm 66 I would want to be at home with the grandchildren and playing a bit of golf," O'Leary quipped.

"All the same, I admire him for taking on such a job at his age but I think he just wants to be in football. He obviously feels fit enough and he has the enthusiasm as well, of course, as a lot of experience."

The questions as Robson and his team arrived at Elland Road centred on whether Newcastle's rejuvenation under their grandfather manager would go on and if Shearer's excellent record against United would continue? No to the first... and yes to the second.

Shearer showed his goalscoring skills, bagging a brace to bring the Magpies level after Lee Bowyer and Harry Kewell had opened up a two goal advantage.

But David O'Leary's vibrant young side halted Newcastle's mini revival under Robson and sent home fans away happy after Michael Bridges fired in a 77th minute decider to cut Manchester United's lead at the top of the Premier League to just two points.

Bridges might not have been at Elland Road had it not been for Shearer. The Newcastle and England striker was the man Bridges listened to when the opportunity of a move out of Sunderland cropped up last summer.

The 21-year-old Bridges could have gone to Tottenham Hotspur where George Graham was desperate to sign him but he plumped for Elland Road and David O'Leary's emerging young side – after a brief chat with Shearer when the two met by chance at an airport.

"I had admired Alan as a player for a long time and as far as I am concerned he's still the best. He was a hero of mine and it was just a privilege to find myself on the same pitch as the player who had been my idol for years," said Bridges. "I want to play for England at full international level –

of the season is how the chairman will judge me, not at this stage."

ASK Alan Shearer which team he had enjoyed playing against the most over the years and he would probably say Leeds United. Unlike Southampton's Matt Le Tissier, who had never scored against the Elland Road club, Shearer had totted up more goals against United than any other team.

When the England striker arrived at the ground with Newcastle in late September he was suitably buoyant after having scored five times in his side's 8-0 drubbing of hapless Sheffield Wednesday.

Yet, Newcastle had been in such dire straits that they had seen fit to enlist the experience of 66-year-old Bobby Robson, striking a clear blow against ageism. And with a "there's life in the old that's my ambition and as I play the same role as him, my aim is to try to take that England Number Nine shirt from him."

Having fluffed several good first half chances, Bridges had to look on as Shearer, given just two chances, made both count to pull Newcastle level but he persevered and was rewarded with his 77th minute winner.

But that didn't spare him some good-natured ribbing from the master striker afterwards. "He had a bit of a go at me over those missed chances," Bridges recalled. "But that was my sixth goal in ten games for Leeds so I am proving that I can score goals in the Premiership."

David O'Leary watched as Bridges squandered those first half chances. "The game would have been finished at half time had Michael taken those chances but I wouldn't criticise him for that. I thought the movement and the play in getting into those situations were tremendous," he said.

■ David Batty had to endure a season of frustration because of injury but here he is in UEFA Cup action against Partizan Belgrade at the end of September.

"At least he was there to miss them so he was where he should be. And he didn't let it get to him. He just stuck at it and got us the winner, which we deserved."

O'Leary has no qualms about Bridges admiring Shearer. "He could hardly have picked a better player to look up to. Shearer is fantastic. He had two chances and he tucked them away, though our marking was shocking," he confessed.

United turned their attentions back to Europe and the second leg of their UEFA Cup first round tie against Partizan Belgrade - and prepared with an impromptu game of cricket. Or to be more precise, Nigel Martyn did. The United goalkeeper wielded the willow with great aplomb as he took the bowling of young Aussie Jamie McMaster apart in an unscheduled session at Thorp Arch.

"Not just Jamie. I gave them all a bit of stick – until we lost the ball on the roof," he said.

As the ball belonged to Bella, the black Labrador owned by United's kit manager Sean Hardy, it had to be retrieved, but United's multi-million pound rated keeper was "chewed up" by his manager when he caught him attempting to climb on to the roof of the training complex!

Martyn, who had to give up playing league cricket to guard against breaking a finger – which, of course, would not have helped his goalkeeping - abandoned his attempt and watched Chris Drury, a member of United's ground staff, get Bella her ball back.

Entry into the second round of the UEFA Cup was the ideal way for David O'Leary to complete a year since he was put in charge of team affairs at Elland Road in the wake of George Graham's departure to Tottenham.

What a year it proved to be, too, with United having finished fourth to qualify again for Europe and following that up by having made a brilliant start to his first full term in charge. I doubt there was a brighter young manager in the Premiership.

Bold and forthright in his views, brave and positive in his footballing philosophy, with good player judgement and an understanding nature. Yet ruthless enough when the need arises. Ingredients, surely, for success in the highly competitive world of top class soccer management.

Darren Huckerby's 55th minute goal in the second leg against Partizan was the one score on a night that promised more only for some poor finishing to stand in the way of a higher scoring victory. Still, a 4-1 aggregate scoreline against a team who had qualified for the Champions' League wasn't bad at all.

> ## "It is very encouraging to know that these young players, who are some of the most promising in the country, want to stay and play for the club."
>
> David Batty

THE week leading up to the Partizan game had seen Lee Bowyer finally put pen to paper on a new contract designed to keep him part of O'Leary's side for another four years. His signing was significant as it completed the club's determined efforts to secure young players, who had shown such promise the previous season, on longer contracts.

"At the start of the summer we set out to sign our most promising young players on longer term contracts and I am delighted to say we achieved what we set out to do," said the chairman.

"It is very encouraging to know that these young players, who are some of the most promising in the country, want to stay and play for the club."

Having duly qualified for the second round of the UEFA Cup, United chairman Peter Ridsdale and club secretary Ian Silvester linked up with their Newcastle counterparts for the flight to Geneva, where the draw was made. "Newcastle had chartered a six seater Lear jet and they asked us if we would like to travel with them so we hitched a ride," said the chairman.

A second round tie against Russians Lokomotiv Moscow was United's "reward" for beating Partizan. Not perhaps the tie - or the location - they might have picked had they been offered the chance. More immediate business, however, saw United kick off the month of October with a visit to Graham Taylor's newly promoted Watford.

Having closed the gap behind Premier League pacesetters Manchester United to just two points, O'Leary's side needed a victory at Vicarage Road to keep up the pressure on the Reds, who had a Sunday date at Chelsea. What a day it turned out to be.

O'Leary's side had been stung by the Hornets in the 41st minute when, after Lucas Radebe had been stretchered off with a thigh injury, Mark Williams took full advantage of space allowed him on the six yard line, to turn and volley in following a free kick.

Despite a temporary numerical disadvantage, it was slack marking on United's part. But dismay lasted only three minutes before Michael Bridges raced to the rescue, moving well on the left before cutting in to hit a terrific right foot shot out of goalkeeper Alec Chamberlain's reach.

His seventh goal in 12 outings for United underlined his form and prowess as a striker and when Harry Kewell grabbed the winner with a 30-yard swerver that fooled Chamberlain, United had extended their winning sequence to seven league and cup games.

The longest winning sequence since the Revie days was greatly satisfying, but the third day of October became even more notable when the events at Stamford Bridge unfolded.

Chelsea's clash with Manchester United had kicked off an hour later than the game at Vicarage Road and news filtered through that Manchester United were two goals down. When that game ended Chelsea had triumphed 5-0.

A wondrous result for Elland Road followers and even more so because O'Leary's boys moved into top place in the Premiership – for the first time under his management. They had topped the league briefly under George Graham's management in the previous season, after a victory over Southampton in early September, but that lofty placing lasted only 24 hours before Aston Villa, kicking off a day later, went back to the top.

United's rise to the top on this latest occasion prompted media questions as to the chances of O'Leary's lads winning the title this season. The United boss, predictably cautious, wasn't about to be drawn into any bold predictions.

"It's better than being at the bottom of the league," said a delighted O'Leary. "But there's no prize for being top in October. We've only come a short way, so don't let's get too carried away. Young sides, however promising, will make mistakes and have their ups and downs so we have to be patient," he added.

For Leeds United to have marked 12 months of David O'Leary's management by going to the top of the Premiership was amazing – a triumph in itself for a young and, to use his own description, naïve manager.

He continued to play down the achievement and even had a spat with his chairman, whom he felt had put pressure on his players by talk of winning trophies and qualifying for the Champions' League. Yet there was no disguising the fact that United's fame had spread far and wide and nowhere was this felt more than in Press Officer Dick Wright's office.

One of his tasks was dealing with sacks of correspondence from followers of the club outside the United Kingdom. Interest from Scandinavia has been high for many years and more recently correspondence from eastern European countries had increased greatly, with Romania, Bulgaria and Poland topping the list.

But Wright revealed that the latest converts to United's cause were in China. "We get a lot of letters from followers in China who are desperate to receive anything they can connected with the club," he said.

His dedication in keeping these faraway fans happy landed him with an additional duty. One Chinese supporter who had been in correspondence with him on footballing matters suddenly turned to him for advice on personal matters. "We had been in touch quite a few times and I had sent him some club literature and

posters but in October I got a letter in which he poured out all the troubles in his personal life," said Wright.

"He told me his parents had divorced and that he had quarrelled badly with his mother, whom he was living with and that his girlfriend, after promising to comfort him at school the following day had not done so. She had also refused to go out with him because she preferred to play volleyball."

In his letter, the young fan wrote: "I really need the comfort of my lover but she doesn't give any and it's breaking my heart. And I haven't spoken to my mother since we argued. Can you understand my heart, Dick, and tell me what I should do?"

So what advice did United's Agony Uncle offer? "I told him to make things up with his mother and forget his girlfriend. I pointed out you have only one mother and that he could always get another girlfriend," said Wright. In anticipation of receiving advice, the fan had enclosed a Tibetan protective talisman for the Press Officer. "I hope it will bless you," he wrote.

Further indication of United's standing in English football came at the beginning of October when the club was selected for a fact finding mission by Sheikh Mohammed bin Marhoon Al-Ma'Amari, Oman's Minister for Sport.

The Sheikh, whose official title is the President of the General Organisation for Youth Sport and Cultural Activities, was accompanied by his Director for Sport, Abdula Nassir Mansoor, Director for Public Relations Mohammed Sa'ad and private secretary Murad Karim Bakhsh.

"He was in England to learn about British sports administration and youth development and he wanted to visit a top football club to see how the youth Academy worked," explained United Operations Director David Spencer. The visit to Thorp Arch, however threw up another story.....

CHAPTER FOUR

REVIE, SMITH AND...
SADDAM HUSSEIN!

THE Sheikh and his right hand man were pleasantly surprised when they dropped in at Thorp Arch. There waiting to welcome them was a close friend – George Smith, United's Under-16 team coach who spent a number of years in Oman where he successfully coached both at club and national level.

Arabic speaking Smith spent 17 years' coaching abroad where he enjoyed a great deal of success and earned plenty of respect – nowhere more so than in Oman and Saudi Arabia. On his visit to Thorp Arch, Sheikh Mohammed said of Smith: "He is an Omani. He speaks like us and acts like us."

Smith had two stints in Oman, the first a four-year contract as national coach and his second, which kicked off in 1989, after he accepted an invitation from the Omani FA to go back as technical adviser for football.

"I ran the league, the cup and his Majesty's Cup, all the coaching courses for referees and coaches and dealt with all legal matters concerning FIFA and the Asian football confederation as well as the Omani Under 17 side," he recalled.

"It became a bit too much for me and when I made my feelings known, Sheikh Mohammed insisted that I concentrate solely on coaching matters. I went on to win the Asian championships and took the Under-17s to the World Cup finals in Ecuador where we beat Germany and world champions Nigeria and drew with Brazil. The result was that we finished third in the world – an achievement unheard of for Oman."

Smith was voted Asia's coach of the year but in July 1989 he suffered a heart attack and underwent

> "I ran the league, the cup and his Majesty's Cup, all the coaching courses for referees and coaches and dealt with all legal matters concerning FIFA and the Asian football confederation as well as the Omani Under 17 side,"
>
> George Smith

a five-times bypass operation. The medical costs rose to £25,000 but afterwards he was sent for by the Sultan of Oman, who said he would foot the bill.

Smith was with Manchester United as a youngster, but moved out to Oldham and then Birmingham City where he suffered a fractured skull. On recovery from that he was informed he should not head a football again. "I was only 22 and you can imagine it was a devastating blow to me," he recalled.

His days as a central defender were over and he drifted out of League football but made a playing return at non-League level after a friend suggested that, having such big hands, he should try his luck as a goalkeeper.

He went on to play in goal for Altrincham for 10 successful years and later coached the club. His overseas coaching career began when he went to Iceland in 1974 to coach Keflavik. "In the year I was there we won the league and the cup but then I went to Saudi Arabia to train the Halal club, who were their equivalent of Manchester United, though they hadn't enjoyed the same success.

"When we trained we got as many as 3,000 people there to watch us and when we played matches we had crowds of between 30,000 and 40,000. I won them their first League championship and the King's Cup," he recalled.

It was during one of his spells with Oman that Smith met Don Revie. The meeting – and subsequent ones – were bizarre to say the least.

"The day after the treaty was signed we were told we would not be allowed to train. We remained in our hotel and suddenly I heard the roar of cars. When I looked out of the ground floor window I saw several big black Mercedes cars stop outside the hotel entrance," said Smith.

"Guys with machine guns jumped out. My first thought was that they were going to come in and kill us. Then a great big guy got out of a car and, although I didn't know it at the time, it was Saddam. Soon afterwards I heard banging on the doors of the hotel bedrooms and these guys with the machine guns were shouting in Arabic for us to come out.

"They got all of us coaches together. Don was there too and so was Jimmy Hill. Then Saddam entered and said: 'You will go back to the countries you work for and you will inform them we do not accept this treaty and if any of the

> ## 'You will go back to the countries you work for and you will inform them we do not accept this treaty and if any of the countries support it we will come and destroy them.'
>
> Saddam Hussein

Both men were in Baghdad for the finals of the Gulf Cup, Revie in charge of the United Arab Emirates and Smith the Omani side. "The teams from Bahrain, Yemen and Saudi Arabia were already there and when I arrived with the Omani side all the Saudis immediately stood up, came over to us and started kissing and shaking hands," he said.

It was a clear enough measure of Smith's popularity in the Gulf. He carried on the tale: "Don was sat at a table just behind and as I turned round, he said to me: 'Who the hell are you?' "I replied: 'I might ask you the same question' and, believe it or not, that was the start of a very good friendship."

While the two men were in Iraq, a treaty between Israel and Egypt was signed. This was not well received in Baghdad and threats were issued to the two men from Saddam Hussein in person.

countries support it we will come and destroy them.'

"I looked over at Don and as you can imagine we were all in a state of shock," said Smith. However, another shock was in store for them half an hour later. There was more banging on Smith's bedroom door. This time it was his players who were clearly worried.

"They all came into my room and when I asked what was wrong they told me that Oman had decided to support the treaty. I asked to see the ambassador and he told us to relax, play the tournament and then get out.

"There were some demonstrations at the games but when it was all over we headed for the airport to return to Oman. When we arrived at the airport Don, whose party had got there before us, told me there was a problem with the luggage on my plane.

"The baggage was being taken off our charter plane and when I spoke to the pilot, who was British, he asked me if it had been checked through as normal and I said it had. But he wasn't taking any chances. As Oman were supporting the treaty he felt there had been the opportunity for someone to place an explosive device in the luggage if they were of a mind to. So he had every bag opened to check it out.

"That set Don thinking and he then insisted on all the bags in his party being examined before he boarded the Emirates plane."

George's admiration for Revie remains undiminished. "I have to say he would have forgotten more about football than I ever learnt," he said.

"He was in my view the best manager I ever saw. A month with him was worth a lifetime's knowledge. I picked up more from him than anyone else in the game. Now to have been asked to work at the club he was so successful at is wonderful for me.

"At the age of 65, I can't believe how lucky I am to have a job and especially one at such a wonderful club as Leeds United."

A COUPLE of old codgers is how David Batty describes himself and goalkeeper Nigel Martyn. At 31 and 33 years of age respectively, Batty and Martyn were the elder statesmen of O'Leary's young side.

But don't run away with the idea

> "Football is full of jokers and I love the whole crack of football off the park as well as on it."
>
> David Batty

that the age difference means they are left out in the cold when it comes to dressing room banter. Nothing could be further from the truth. "When I'm playing I room with Nige on away trips – two old codgers together you might say. But we're probably the most immature of the lot of them. So it works well," Batty said.

"I certainly don't feel out of things. Ask the younger lads and I'm sure they would be quick to say I am as daft as any one of them. Football is like that. It keeps you young and I like to think I muck in with them all. Football is full of jokers and I love the whole crack of football off the park as well as on it.

"It is good for team spirit and it has helped to give me a new lease of life. When I have made moves in the past they have always given my career a timely boost and it's certainly been the same with my move back to Leeds.

"I actually enjoy being the oldest player out in the middle. I know Nige is older than I am, but goalkeepers, being so far back, don't have a lot to say."

Batty believed he was likely to remain as one of the father figures of David O'Leary's talented team. "I doubt the Gaffer will bring in any new players who are older than I am. It is not his style. But I like it the way it is and I hope to be able to remain the elder statesman and one who maybe the younger players will continue to look up to a bit," he added.

Batty showed that he had lost none of his effectiveness after returning from a lengthy absence the previous season caused by three broken ribs – an injury that caused complications as it affected his breathing for quite a time.

"You can imagine how frustrating it was for me

picking up such an injury so soon after returning to Leeds," he said. "Because of that I had to wait a long time to get going. I played a few matches towards the end of that first season when I was quite pleased with my form. But it was like a new lease of life for me when this season began.

"I didn't feel as fit as I was hoping I would in the first few games but after playing with England early on I suddenly felt my fitness was back," he added.

There is a feeling in football that you should never go back to your old club. Batty did and he has had no regrets.

"Leeds were the only club I wanted to leave Newcastle for. I told Ruud Gullit that at the time and I think he appreciated my honesty," said Batty, who found the Elland Road club vastly different to the one he had left five years earlier to go to Blackburn.

"It's like a new club. The past club was not a patch on the present one, from the training complex up to the playing staff, he said.

Being among so many promising young players is refreshing for Batty. "You get everything you would expect from a young side. Great enthusiasm, a willingness to learn, and plenty of pace in the side, which causes the opposition endless problems," he explained.

"In addition we are getting a good name for the way we are playing. We are often the neutrals' favourites. Everyone is confident and in any sport confidence is the main thing. Just now we are full of it and from my own point of view I have felt very positive and full of energy."

JUST how much street cred Leeds United enjoy these days could hardly have been any better illustrated than by the two very lucrative deals that linked first BSkyB and then Nike with the Elland Road club.

It wasn't so much a question of United seeking out these two companies - more a case of companies lining up in a bid to get a share of United's action. In BSkyB's case the cost was £13.8million and Nike's kit involvement over a five-year period could add a further £10million to that total.

"For once big companies felt it necessary to come to us. We did not have to go out searching for sponsorships – and that was unusual. I cannot recall being in such a situation before," chairman Peter Ridsdale said.

David O'Leary's excellent team re-shaping efforts and refreshing brand of football aligned to Ridsdale's foresight, determination and business acumen made United one of England's most sought after clubs for the business world.

"I found it very gratifying that so many companies wanted to be associated with us. BSkyB are leaders in the field of sports media and I am delighted we shall be working with them. The Nike kit deal is a record for the club and puts us in and among the elite," the chairman said.

> ## "For once big companies felt it necessary to come to us. We did not have to go out searching for sponsorships — and that was unusual. I cannot recall being in such a situation before."
>
> Peter Ridsdale

United made it clear from the outset that the money coming in from BSkyB would be made available immediately for team strengthening, should the manager be ready to spend, so he found it frustrating to read some newspaper reports suggesting that had not been the case.

"One article which particularly annoyed me reported that the manager had won a battle with the chairman to get the money for players which was very definitely not the case. As a club we had stressed from the beginning that the money was for transfer market activity," said Ridsdale.

"The article was incorrect but the trouble is people tend to believe them," he said.

Another report that caused problems for the chairman was one suggesting shareholders were set to throw out the Sky deal. When it came to the voting the deal was regarded as good for the club and rubber-stamped inside 15 minutes!

United had talks with several companies before agreeing the deal which gave Sky just over 9 per cent of Leeds Sporting's share capital, a non-executive seat on the board and the power to negotiate lucrative media and commercial rights on behalf of the club.

Proceeds from such deals would be shared 70 per cent in favour of United with 30 per cent going to Sky. The agreement with Sky was described by the United chairman as "a further exciting step" in the club's declared strategy of developing Leeds Sporting as an integrated sports, media and leisure group capable of delivering enhanced shareholder value.

Shortly before the completion of the two deals, United had announced a set of excellent financial results for the year ended June 30, 1999, showing turnover had increased by nearly 30 per cent – to £37million.

Operating profit before amortisation of players had increased by 47.2 per cent to £6.4million, there was a big boost in football revenue to over £9million with average gates increased and season ticket sales up 12 per cent.

The importance of fees from television was illustrated with a 40 per cent increase to £11.5million, while commercial income went up by 38 per cent to a little over £13million.

"I think this set of figures shows that we have a quality business but the aim now is to see that these profits continue to grow," the United chief said. "It is important we do a good job behind the scenes but our responsibility always is to see that we make the club successful on the field."

**"TAKE a picture of this – you won't see it too often on the same pitch this season."
The scene was the Elland Road pitch at Leeds United's Press-day and the words were Alan Smith's as he stood alongside new signing Michael Bridges.**

United's young striker, who made such an

impact when he forced his way into the senior side the previous season might well have had an eye on the increased number of strikers who would be battling for first team slots as the season unfolded.

With Harry Kewell, Jimmy Floyd Hasselbaink, who was still a United player then, Clyde Wijnhard, and Bridges all available - and rumours linking Darren Huckerby with the club - Smith felt there might not be too many opportunities for himself and Bridges to operate in tandem up front.

Manager David O'Leary had been keen to expand his first team squad and maybe make full use of the squad system in these overcrowded seasons.

Smith's fears appeared to have been unfounded when the season got under way. O'Leary selected both players to start the game against Derby, but an ankle injury took Smith out of the game and he missed the next two because of it.

Once he recovered and returned to the side his partnership with Bridges looked promising. Smith has the ability to hold the ball up perhaps better than any other United striker and although he is not the most powerfully built of players he has the strength to hold off opponents.

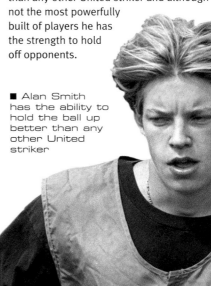

■ Alan Smith has the ability to hold the ball up better than any other United striker

His vision is good and of course he has the ability to find the target. His display in the 3-2 victory over Newcastle United caught the eye of former England defender and United manager Jimmy Armfield.

Jimmy was there in his role as radio summariser and as we walked into the car park together after the game he could not stop talking about the young striker. "For someone so young he has a lot of intelligence. He makes good runs off the ball, he retains possession when necessary and some of his touches to put Bridges in were a delight to see," Armfield told me.

Like any striker Smith wants to see the goals mount up against his name but he's not too unhappy to see teammates scoring, as was the case in the first quarter of the season. While Bridges knocked in seven in 12 appearances Smith's return was one from nine outings.

"I may have scored only once in that time but I feel my partnership with Michael is developing along exciting lines. We are working well together," he said.

"People tend to judge strikers on the goals they score and that's how I will be judged but there is more to playing up front than that. Michael is a great finisher but I don't always like playing as a target man. I prefer dropping off into midfield, making runs and perhaps creating something for someone else and when he plays I can do that a bit more," Smith explained.

The potential of the Bridges-Smith partnership was recognised at international level when Howard Wilkinson brought the Under-21 side to play Denmark at Bradford City's Valley Parade ground. The former Elland Road manager pitched the two of them in against the Danes, along with three other United players - Lee Bowyer, Danny Mills and goalkeeper Paul Robinson – but on this occasion it was Bridges who turned goalmaker.

First he put Smith in and the 18-year-old marked his Under-21 debut by scoring the opening goal and then gave Bowyer his chance to make it 2-0 before England went on to clinch a 4-1 success, an under-hit back header from Mills paving the way for Denmark's consolation goal.

Rothwell-born Smith, who also supplied the

crosses from which Carl Cort and David Thompson scored the fourth and fifth goals, was naturally delighted to have made such an impressive debut. "It was superb to do that – and to play at Under-21 level with Michael as well was great. We really enjoy playing alongside each other for Leeds," were his comments after the game.

Bridges echoed that feeling and added: "I was delighted to see Alan get a goal on his debut. It just shows the ability he has when he is playing - and scoring for the Under-21s at the age of 18."

While United's young England stars were going through their paces, watched by manager David O'Leary, operations director David Spencer and club secretary Ian Silvester were heading a delegation to Russia where arrangements for the UEFA Cup clash with Lokomotiv Moscow were discussed.

A near four hour flight and a further half hour to the hotel the players were to use was undertaken by the delegation, who then toured the 24,000 capacity stadium which left something to be desired in respect of dressing room facilities and amenities for supporters.

One unusual feature they noted was the absence of doors on the cubicles in the toilets. "I think that could be a bit of a problem for our fans," David Spencer told the Russian club officials. "I suggested doors should be fitted before our game there and they said they would see to it. But they hardly seemed convincing and I had my doubts the work would be done," he added.

United's pairing with the Russian side left United's club secretary with another tricky trip to organise. "Our first one against Partizan Belgrade was a problem because of the doubt as to where the first leg was to be played," Silvester recalled.

"When it was decided, we had only a short time to arrange travel and everything. The one to Russia threw up different problems such as sorting out visas and organising the vaccination we were advised to have before travelling to Moscow." That was for diphtheria and almost everyone making the trip had the jab. Chairman Peter Ridsdale was one who refused it.

The pairing with Lokomotiv was regarded as a

tough tie and nothing that David O'Leary witnessed when he went on a spying mission to Moscow to see the Russians play a cup game against St Petersburg changed that. "It was a long trip and the weather was very cold and bleak," said the boss.

When asked if he had learnt anything from that game, the United boss replied: "Sadly, I saw a very good team. Not that that surprised me because any team that qualifies for the UEFA Cup and reaches the semi-finals for two years running can't be all that bad."

Lokomotiv knocked five goals past St Petersburg, conceding only one, and O'Leary added: "They are a young side who love to score goals and I saw them score five very good ones. If we get through this round we will have done very well."

O'Leary made his trip a day before United entered the Worthington Cup but was back in time for his side's third round clash with Blackburn. After an unusually less than entertaining battle with Rovers it was cruelly suggested he might have been better taking his time to return!

A 90th minute free kick from Danny Mills gave United a 1-0 entry into the fourth round and a visit to Leicester City. Blackburn's tactics of keeping as many men behind the ball as possible didn't help, but much of what had gone on before that late, late winner had been eminently forgettable – David Batty's man-of-the-match performance apart.

O'Leary, however, was in no mood to make apologies. He admitted to breathing a sigh of relief at the end, but said: "We're through to the next round and in cup ties that's all that matters.

"You can't go on week in and week out performing brilliantly. Football is not like that. Cup games are all about getting into the next round. And that's where we are. If you play brilliant stuff in winning that's a bonus."

Managers – even those, such as O'Leary, who may be working wonders at their respective clubs – are not immune from criticism from supporters and there was some for the United boss during the derby clash with bottom-of-the-table Sheffield Wednesday.

For the second time in four days United were struggling against lesser opponents and when the decision was made to send on Darren Huckerby in place of Michael Bridges in the 62nd minute with the game still goalless, it was greeted with a chorus of boos from some fans.

Many supporters had felt Alan Smith, who had been well held by the Wednesday defence, should have been the player to come off. Not so the United manager and his decision was clearly vindicated as it had a distinct bearing on United winning a game they hardly deserved to.

Huckerby played a part in the moves that brought United two goals. And Smith, the player O'Leary decided to leave on the pitch, showed his predatory instincts to score both of them. "I heard the reaction from some of the crowd when I took Bridges off and not Smithy but I make the decisions as I see them and this time it worked well. Maybe it was lucky but I was vindicated on this occasion," O'Leary said.

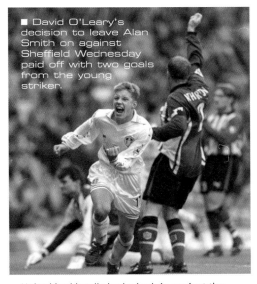

■ David O'Leary's decision to leave Alan Smith on against Sheffield Wednesday paid off with two goals from the young striker.

United had hardly had a look-in against the Owls, who had most of the play but failed to cash in on a number of chances. Most were squandered, but Nigel Martyn showed true class to bring off two superb saves to deny first Niclas Alexandersson and then Andy Booth.

Those two saves in the 64th and 65th minutes were, for me, the turning point of the match. Not long afterwards Smith gave United the lead when Pavel Srnicek spilled a shot from Huckerby and he wrapped it up for United with another close-range effort after Lee Bowyer, taking a pass from Huckerby, had hit the post with a 14-yard shot.

"He reminds me a lot of how my old pal Ian Wright used to be at that age," Martyn said of United's budding young forward.

"He hasn't got the pace Wrighty had but when I watch Smithy in the penalty area it takes me back to the days when I was at Crystal Palace and Wright was there too. Both have that knack of being in the right place at the right time and as far as finishing off chances goes, I believe Smith to be in the same class," United's goalkeeper reasoned.

Smith's double kept United on top of the Premiership and extended their winning run to nine games in all competitions – a record that even surpassed the achievements of Don Revie's great side and equalled the club record established way, way back in 1931.

This latest victory stung the Owls – and they weren't the only ones. A bill for £7,000 was to drop through the Elland Road letterbox for a car the club had offered as a prize in a half time shoot-out competition.

award the prize after I was told what all the booing was about," the chairman said.

With a tough UEFA Cup second round first leg meeting with Lokomotiv Moscow looming large, there was concern on the playing side for United, following two relatively poor displays in their past two victories. But United gave themselves and their supporters a real Elland Road tonic with an impressive 4-1 first leg victory over the Russian side.

What a tremendous performance it was – and what a way to shatter a record nine-match winning sequence that had stood the test of time since it was set in Division Two in the 1931-32 campaign.

A crowd of nearly 38,000 loved every minute of a thrill-packed match in which Lee Bowyer showed his liking for European games by scoring twice before Alan Smith and Harry Kewell added second half goals.

The tenacious little midfielder, who also bagged a brace against Partizan Belgrade in the first round away game, had the fans chanting "Bowyer for England" with another all-action gutsy show.

Everyone played his part to the full but for my money you needed to look no further than David

> ## "He hasn't got the pace Wrighty had but when I watch Smithy in the penalty area it takes me back to the days when I was at Crystal Palace and Ian Wright was there too."
>
> Nigel Martyn

Confusion had arisen over the rules of the competition that required contestant Terence Potter to kick a football through three holes in a sheet erected across the goalmouth – but in a certain order. At the time it was not clear in which order he was supposed to undertake the challenge but with the crowd booing amid the confusion, chairman Peter Ridsdale ruled: "Give him the car."

As the rules of the competition were not strictly adhered to, the insurance did not cover the cost of the car, so United paid up. "I took the decision to

Batty for the man-of-the-match display. His tackling was superb throughout and his distribution excellent.

Re-writing the record books with a tenth successive victory was, quite naturally, a main talking point among fans and media alike, though O'Leary refused to allow himself to wax lyrical over it.

"I went home after the game and I honestly did

not think about breaking the record. I thought about our performance and that we had beaten very good opponents 4-1. That is what was on my mind," said O'Leary.

"But I am delighted for the club and the players that we have established a new record. Don Revie was a great manager and we have some way to go before we equal his achievements.

"Winning ten games in a row takes some doing but it hasn't won us a trophy. My aim here is to win trophies, though maybe in years to come it will be nice to look back on the record and say, yes, that was quite an achievement, and not least because of the way we went about breaking the record.

"We haven't been boring. We have played to try and win every game," he added.

When United, managed by Dick Ray, set their winning sequence in season 1931-32, they were attempting to bounce back at the first attempt after having been relegated from the top flight the previous season. Their nine match winning sequence, all in the league, was:

Sept 26	Bristol City (A)	2-0
Oct 3	Oldham (H)	5-0
Oct 10	Bury (A)	4-1
Oct 17	Wolves (H)	2-1
Oct 24	Charlton (A)	1-0
Oct 31	Stoke (H)	2-0
Nov 7	Manchester Utd (A)	5-2
Nov 14	Preston NE (H)	4-1
Nov 21	Burnley (A)	5-0

United's ten match winning sequence under David O'Leary, achieved at a higher level but including cup games:

■ Bowyer for England!

Aug 28	Tottenham (A)	2-1
Sept 11	Coventry (A)	4-3
Sept 14	Partizan Belgrade (A)	3-1
Sept 19	Middlesbrough (H)	2-0
Sept 25	Newcastle Utd (H)	3-2
Sept 30	Partizan Belgrade (H)	1-0
Oct 3	Watford (A)	2-1
Oct 13	Blackburn (H)	1-0
Oct 16	Sheffield Wed (H)	2-0
Oct 21	Lokomotiv Moscow (H)	4-1

TOP football players are, in the main, usually regarded as dedicated followers of fashion and Leeds United's young stars are no different – but there are exceptions.

One who qualified as an exception was Michael Bridges, who came in for a bit of good-natured ribbing from his manager as he arrived for training prior to United's visit to Everton in late October.

"He's a bit of a mess isn't he," quipped the United boss as the baseball capped Bridges walked from his car. "No, I wouldn't say he was the worst dresser here – perhaps one of them.

"I told him I was willing to give him some advice and even take him round the shops if he thought it would help!"

Bridges took the ribbing with a smile, but there was nothing at all shabby about the talented striker when he pitted his skills against Everton and knocked in a couple of smart goals to take his tally to nine in 16 first team appearances.

His latest goalscoring exploits were not, however, sufficient to extend United's record breaking winning run to 11 games as Everton gave as good as they got in a swashbuckling 4-4 draw.

Entertainment of the highest class was the order of the afternoon at Goodison Park and while both O'Leary and his Everton counterpart, Walter Smith, would have wished for better defending, both agreed the game had been an edge-of-the-seat cracker for the crowd of over 37,000.

Heavy rain had fallen overnight and continued throughout the day of the game, but the pitch offered a good surface for attacking football and both teams utilised the conditions to the full.

Former Arsenal striker Kevin Campbell, singled out by the United boss as potentially the biggest danger to his side, cracked in a goal after less than five minutes only for Bridges to capitalise on excellent approach work from Harry Kewell by knocking in the equaliser ten minutes later.

So open was the game and so attack-minded were both teams that further goals seemed certain. And so it proved. Campbell was causing United's defence a lot of concern and he scored a second after 28 minutes. Everton's lead lasted seven minutes before Kewell pulled United level again, with a cross-cum-shot that deceived goalkeeper Paul Gerrard as it dropped into the far corner.

Back came Everton and Don Hutchison restored his side's lead with a 37th minute goal. But the Evertonian was far from convinced he had scored what would be the winner. He told Lee Bowyer his thoughts as the teams left the field at half time. "This is a 4-4 match and that's how it will end," he remarked to United's battling midfield man.

It seemed as though he would be proved wrong as another goal from Bridges and the first of the season for Jonathan Woodgate gave United a 4-3 advantage. His strike was followed by a prompt inquiry from one admirer who wrote to Press Officer Dick Wright to inquire if the young central defender had an official fan club.

"I shall be writing to tell her that he has and that the meetings are held in the telephone box at the end of the road," he quipped.

Unfortunately Woodgate's goal was not

> ## "This is a 4-4 match and that's how it will end."
>
> Don Hutchison

sufficient to give United victory for with just seconds left on the clock, this crazy game took another turn as full-back David Weir came up to head in a last gasp equaliser. A fair result maybe, but it brought to an end United's remarkable ten-game winning sequence.

United would have lost the leadership of the Premier League had Sunderland managed to win at West Ham. Though Peter Reid's men were leading for most of the game they, like United, suffered a last minute equaliser, which left O'Leary's boys on top – a point ahead of Arsenal.

United's draw at Everton left them understandably disappointed, though far from downhearted. O'Leary smiled and told the Press contingent: "I'll settle for ten wins and a draw from our next 11 games."

His side had demonstrated their powers of recovery on three occasions to claw their way back against Everton and he added: "I never really doubted that we had the ability to bounce back each time we went behind.

"I'm sure that Everton couldn't have felt too secure at 3-2 up because we always looked like scoring, but considering the way we defended I didn't feel too safe when we went 4-3 up. It was one of those games."

The enthusiasm and confidence of youth is not easily subdued and United's young players remained brimful of confidence after the 4-4 draw, as Harry Kewell revealed.

"We have a lot of young players in our side – eight under the age of 23 – and though it may just be the optimism of youth, the players are beginning to think we might just be able to upstage such as Manchester United, Arsenal and Chelsea," he said.

Kewell's talent and ability to unsettle defences is well known and respected throughout the Premiership but the young Aussie seems to be happier – and more effective – when Ian Harte, a relatively unsung hero of the United side, is playing behind him.

As natural left-footers the two of them link up effectively on the left flank and Kewell acknowledges the part the Irishman plays, as do United's management. "I wouldn't say that Hartey makes Harry a better player," assistant boss Eddie Gray said. "But he certainly helps Harry to be more involved and effective.

"Being a left-sided player, Hartey's first intention when he gets the ball is naturally to look to knock it up the left side so consequently Harry gets the ball quicker than if, say, Gary Kelly plays at left back.

"Gary did well when he stood in in that position but being right-footed his first touch was always inside to get the ball under control with his right foot. But it works the other way round as well. Harry is good for Ian because he can pull people towards him and create gaps for Ian, who likes to go forward himself, to run into.

"In fact with Stephen McPhail in the side and doing well we are very fortunate to have three naturally left-sided players who are all capable of making an impact on the game," he added.

Like Kewell, Harte signed a new four-year deal with United at the start of the season which means, all things being equal, the pair of them will be able to continue with their productive left flank partnership.

"It looks like we are going to be around together for a few years yet and that's good to know. All of us at the club hope we can win something in that time," Kewell said.

Yet a couple of years earlier Harte's future at Elland Road looked far from assured as George Graham suddenly left him out of the team. Those unhappy days are now very much a thing of the past for this likeable Irish lad.

Hard work and the shedding of some excess weight played a part in his fight back to first team status as he saw off the challenge of former Chelsea full-back Danny Granville and Scottish international David Robertson to become an integral part of the United side.

Harte did force his way back into the side before Graham left for Tottenham but he could be excused if he felt some relief at the manager's

departure. Not a bit of it, though he will admit to enjoying his football more under present boss David O'Leary.

"I think I have to say that George helped me in the defensive part of my game. He gave me advice on how to deal with different types of opponents while David O'Leary has made me into a better all round player because he allows me to attack more," Harte explained.

Fitness, of course, is vital to any sportsman and Harte pays a great deal of attention to keeping in trim these days and enlisted the help of Buddy, an Austrian Weimaraner dog he bought with his girlfriend Laura.

A dog in need of almost daily long walks, Buddy provided the ideal opportunity for Ian – and Laura – to top up their fitness routines. I found the seven-month old dog a real friendly bundle of bounding energy when I called to take a picture of master and dog.

"We take him on walks as often as we can – usually to Roundhay Park – and walk perhaps a mile or so with him each time. I suppose it does help keep us fit," said Harte.

As United prepared for the visit to Elland Road of West Ham at the end of October, Manchester United manager Sir Alex Ferguson was claiming that O'Leary's side was too young and inexperienced to last the pace of the championship race.

■ Hard work played a part in Ian Harte's return to first team status.

Sir Alex's comment was construed by some as purely psychological but it was also one that was duly noted by United's confident young players who, quite frankly, feared no one. It might also have been interpreted as one to spur them along though, as Jonathan Woodgate, echoing the feelings of his team-mates, pointed out: "We go into every game thinking that we can win it."

That is the confidence of youth, but when you possess as much footballing talent as these United youngsters, comments like that have a greater meaning.

BBC Match-of-the-Day pundit Alan Hansen, arguably the most interesting and entertaining of the "expert" panel, might well have been putting on weight as Harte continued to make him eat his words.

Hansen had once suggested the Republic of Ireland defender had only one good foot – his left. But Harte continues to prove him wrong – and his right foot shot that produced the winner against the Hammers was just another example.

"My left foot is my best foot and my most accurate but I can actually hit a ball harder with my right," Harte revealed.

His 57th minute 18-yard winner deservedly earned him the adulation of United fans in a 40,190 crowd but he had to share the cheers on this occasion with United chairman Peter Ridsdale, who chose half time to announce a freeze on season ticket prices for the 2000-2001 season.

"There has been a lot of criticism of football clubs for their pricing polices effecting the ability of supporters and their families to attend matches on a regular basis," said Ridsdale.

"Our ticket prices, in my view, are at a level now where, given the income coming in from elsewhere, such as the Sky, Nike and Strongbow deals, we had the opportunity for a freeze on season ticket prices on this occasion," said the chairman.

"We took that opportunity so that as many people as possible could come and watch us."

The offer was for supporters who committed themselves to a season ticket by the end of March 2000, with the club making available a six months interest free payment scheme.

CHAPTER FIVE

UNITED GO EAST AND MAKE HISTORY

MOSCOW was United's next destination as David O'Leary's side took on Lokomotiv Moscow on the Elland Road club's first ever visit to Russia. Not even in the years of United's pioneering European days were they ever drawn to play in the former Soviet Union.

Numerous trips were made behind the old "Iron Curtain" – to East Germany, to Czechoslovakia, Yugoslavia, Romania and Hungary - but draws for the various competitions had never sent United to Russia before.

Strange then, as things were to turn out, that they should find themselves having to make a second trip to the Russian capital inside three weeks.

Visiting countries such as Russia are rarely as straightforward as you might want them to be. Visas are required and the Russians insist you account for every article of value you take into the country and state how much money you have.

Currency most valued in Russia is the US dollar and the United party was required to complete individual forms stating how many dollars they were taking into the country and again how many they were bringing back with them.

Any discrepancy had to be accounted for, as United chairman Peter Ridsdale discovered when he and club secretary Ian Silvester left Moscow early on Friday morning to fly to Geneva for the UEFA Cup third round draw.

The chairman had 600 dollars with him and as he had signed his entry form three days' earlier stating he had not taken any dollars into the country, the Russian authorities wondered how he had got them.

Sensing some inconvenience at least, the chairman was quick to pass the buck. "He just handed them on to me saying they were mine, not his," club secretary Silvester revealed later.

> ## "I had plenty of talking to do to convince them that a lot of the money was to pay for the tickets we had sold."
>
> Ian Silvester

Silvester himself had had plenty of explaining to do when the United party first arrived in Moscow as he had been carrying 20,000 dollars. "It was quite a sizeable sum to be taking into the country and when I declared that amount on my entry form I was viewed rather suspiciously," he recalled.

"I had plenty of talking to do to convince them that a lot of the money was to pay for the tickets we had sold. Lokomotiv would not accept a bank transfer from us. They wanted the money in US dollars.

"The rest of the money was to pay for other expenses on our trip and eventually my explanation was accepted and we were allowed to enter the country."

After he was unexpectedly handed those 600 dollars by the chairman as they attempted to go through customs on their way out of the country, United's club secretary found himself with more explaining to do and more forms to fill in. But everything worked out well in the end.

Before boarding United's chartered plane that also carried a large media party in addition to a number of corporate supporters, some photographers were keen to record a Russian flavour for their first pictures.

A Russian imitation fur hat was produced but Alan Smith was quick to turn down the chance to pose in it. Jonathan Woodgate also refused, saying: "Are you asking me because you think I'm the daft one?"

Dick Wright assured him that wasn't the case at all. "It's because you are a fun-loving lad," he replied. But that didn't change the young defender's mind. It was left to Lucas Radebe to give the photographers what they wanted. "Well, he HAS to do it because as captain it's his place," Woodgate added.

The United players were understandably in high spirits. They had the comfort of a 4-1 advantage from the home leg of their second round tie to cushion disadvantages caused by a long flight out to Moscow and a three hour time difference, not to mention anticipated sub zero temperatures.

■ Training is a serious business as David O'Leary demonstrates during a session before the second leg of Leeds United's UEFA Cup tie against Lokomotiv Moscow.

Because of the need to adjust to the time change, O'Leary felt the need to have his players in Moscow two days before the game rather than the usual one.

Not surprisingly most of his players were hoping to be able to see some of the sights Moscow has to offer, Alan Smith being one of them, only to be told by the manager that there would be no free time.

"We are here to do a job not to go sightseeing," O'Leary said. The United boss did relent, however, to allow his players to take a coach trip to Red Square.

Extra time on this trip meant more hours of hotel life for the players – but for the media contingent and the corporate fans who also flew out on the team's chartered aircraft, there was more time to take in the sights and savour local delicacies while investigating Moscow's night life!

To borrow a famous line – it was all done in the best possible taste!

Visits to Red Square, the Kremlin, Lenin's tomb and St Basil's Cathedral were top of the sightseeing agenda and at night local hostelries were frequented and much sleep was lost.

For those of us who made it to the hotel breakfast room the morning after there was the attraction of smoked salmon, caviar and champagne to tickle the taste buds before moving on to the more traditional English breakfast and completing the first meal of the day with pastries.

At least it fortified those who chose to go on the organised trip around Moscow and came up against a formidable Russian lady guide who, for over four hours, insisted on informing her captive audience of Russia's history.

"Auntie Edith", as Dick Wright christened her, was also the interpreter on the media coach when it fought its way through Moscow's horrendous traffic congestion on its six-mile journey to the stadium.

Fervent pleas from United's public liaison officer, Liz Dimitrijevic, to begin the journey earlier because of the traffic problems – Moscow has some 18 lane highways, all jammed with traffic – fell on deaf ears.

"Auntie Edith" insisted the plan was to set off at the same time as two other coaches carrying supporters so that a police escort could guide all three coaches through the traffic chaos. With eight lanes completely blocked by cars how can a police car guide three coaches through?

The answer was with difficulty - great difficulty.

Flashing blue lights, wailing sirens and gestures from police for other rush hour vehicles to move over are all well and good – if there are spaces for them to move into. Most of the time there wasn't.

Broken down or overheated vehicles, not to mention a number of minor shunts and bumps, added to congestion that made the dreaded M25 around London seem like a nice place for a pleasant Sunday afternoon drive.

With time running out and serious doubts as to our ability to get to the game in time for kick off, "Auntie Edith" attempted – but failed - to put minds at ease.

Her voice boomed out over the microphone: "Don't worry. They won't start without us." Somehow the scenario of UEFA officials delaying the kick-off because the British media had not arrived in time appeared doubtful to say the least.

As luck would have it we arrived 20 minutes before kick-off, our journey time cut following a hair-raising ride along tram tracks which took us past a large chunk of the traffic that was jamming the roads.

Suitably protected against the freezing temperature – thermal underwear and extra jumpers with some of us looking a shade (?) ridiculous in those imitation fur hats the Russian street salesmen pester visitors to buy – the Press corps finally made it to their seats five minutes before kick-off.

When the real business of the trip got under way United were under expected early pressure as Lokomotiv went close to scoring on two occasions. But once Ian Harte had fired United into a 15th minute second leg lead from the penalty spot, the tie was as good as over.

United then had a 5-1 advantage and when the magical Michael Bridges struck twice before half time to take his goal tally for the season to 11 and

establish a 7-1 aggregate advantage, Lokomotiv, who had been shunted into the sidings in the first leg, were de-railed.

The second half, a mere formality, was dull and the final whistle must have come as blessed relief to the Russians.

For United there was only one blot on the night – the booking of Radebe, who picked up his third yellow card of the competition which meant an automatic one match ban and put him out of the first leg of the third round tie, against Moscow Spartak.

With Martin Hiden injured, New Zealander Danny Hay having dislocated a shoulder in a practice game and Michael Duberry recovering from a thigh injury, United were thin on the ground for central defenders.

"It is very disappointing to miss any game but it's not a disaster. I knew when I went into the second game against Lokomotiv that another booking would bring a suspension," Radebe said.

"But I could not afford to let that situation affect the way I play. You just have to accept the situation. Anyway I am confident the lads will get along fine. We've got good players at the club and I won't be missed."

While Radebe was left to contemplate his fate, chairman Peter Ridsdale was given the job of writing out a cheque for £150,000 to send to Sunderland – a task he was more than delighted to undertake.

Part of the deal that brought Bridges to Elland Road in the summer involved a payment of £150,000 when the young striker reached a double figure goal tally with United.

Such a big aggregate victory against a Russian side that had reached the semi-finals of the UEFA Cup in the two previous seasons and who were due to finish as runners-up in their own league championship again, produced a feeling of satisfaction and achievement in the camp.

"When I first went out to Moscow to watch Lokomotiv I thought we would do very well to scrape though 1-0. Yet we have finished miles in front of them and that is fantastic," said David O'Leary.

He was, however, keen to see that everything was kept in perspective. "Winning in the way we did exceeded all my expectations. It was a magnificent victory but Europe is still an adventure for us," he added.

"I don't know if teams will fear us after our big win over Lokomotiv but I honestly don't think we will be a force in Europe for another couple of years."

It was no secret he did not agree with UEFA's decision to allow losers from the Champions' League group matches to have their fall from grace cushioned by a place in the third round of the UEFA Cup.

"It's now on to the Champions' League," he said with a tone of sarcasm in his voice. "One of the Champions' League boys will win the UEFA Cup - that's the way it's set up. But I hope they don't."

"I just hope we don't get one of them in the third round. They're better than we are - that's the reason they were in the Champions' League in the first place. Knowing our luck we'll draw somebody big from the Champions' League," he added.

How true – as less than 24 hours later the draw paired them with Russian champions Spartak Moscow.

It meant another difficult administrative challenge for United – and a third trip to the Russian capital for club secretary Ian Silvester, who headed the team that supervised plans for the team's second visit to Russia in such a short space of time.

A snow-covered runway greeted their arrival – "When I looked down and saw that I didn't like the look of it," Silvester admitted. But the landing went well. "The snow wasn't deep but there was a good covering and the temperature was much colder than it was the last time we were in Moscow," he said.

The Dynamo Stadium in Moscow lacks cover but has undersoil heating that is supposed to keep the pitch playable in extreme weather conditions. "When we got to the stadium there was snow all around but the pitch was clear and we were told that should there be a heavy fall of snow they would get enough people from the army to shift

it," he said.

While travel plans were being discussed for a return visit, the United manager was quietly concerned about the fitness of his side as they faced a demanding Premier League game against hard-running, hard-working Wimbledon at Selhurst Park so soon after the Lokomotiv game.

"Playing in Russia on Thursday night and taking into account the time change, a long flight home and all the travelling, I think we will be tired for the Sunday game at Wimbledon," predicted O'Leary.

United flew direct from Moscow to Heathrow to allow the players to stay in London to rest up for the Wimbledon game and the United boss added: "If we have a fresh team we have a great chance of winning there.

"But we really don't have the capacity to cope with a game in Moscow on a Thursday night and a top game in England on the Sunday," he warned.

Prophetic words these turned out to be as United were beaten for the first time in 11 weeks during which time they had won 12 and drawn one of 13 games in league and cup.

"It was a tired performance - there wasn't the same sparkle or cutting edge about our side. But it's hard competing on several different fronts and that's why Manchester United have such a massive squad," said O'Leary.

"They have virtually two good teams – and even they are not competing on all fronts this season, having pulled out of the FA Cup."

Michael Bridges missed the game with a back injury while several other players turned out with slight strains, Harry Kewell and Lee Bowyer being the most notable among them. "That's football life for you. We have a punishing schedule and we just have to try to cope," said the United boss.

"I don't know how we'll do when we go back to Moscow to play on a Thursday night, then tackle Southampton at home on the Sunday and visit Leicester in the Worthington Cup two days after that.

"When I look at that ten day schedule I have to admit that I am anxious about our ability to deal with it," he confessed.

■ Leeds United fans are hardy souls as some of them proved when they peeled off their shirts – but kept their Russian hats on - at halftime in the away leg of UEFA Cup tie against Lokomotiv Moscow.

■ The names aren't recognisable but they are actually Leeds United's goalscorers as displayed on the scoreboard in Moscow during United's 3-0 win. Ian Harte was first to score and Michael Bridges scored the other two.

Defeat by the Dons knocked United off the top of the Premiership for the first time in five weeks, Manchester United moving back up, but O'Leary said: "I am happy to see us in second place. Having such a young side I am delighted with that."

At least those United players who were not called away on international duty as the Euro 2000 play-off matches were undertaken had the chance to have a breather in readiness for the visit to Elland Road of near neighbours Bradford City.

There was another episode in the long running club-v-country row for the injured Kewell who, despite an injury, was required by Soccer Australia to fly to Melbourne to report for a friendly international in which, because of his injury, he would not be playing.

> "When I look at that ten day schedule I have to admit that I am anxious about our ability to deal with it."
>
> David O'Leary

When Harry failed to catch the flight out, the wrath of the Socceroos was incurred and they reacted by asking football's governing body FIFA to invoke a rule, which in effect banned him from playing in the 'derby' match against Bradford.

After it was initially reported the way had been cleared for Kewell to play, FIFA announced they had, after all, backed the Aussies and stopped him from playing.

Disappointed though he was, United managed to take three points from City, who were left still wondering when they would win for the first time at Elland Road.

Yet it took almost an hour for United to get their noses in front and even then there was debate as to whether the goal that did it was a lucky one, Alan Smith sticking out a leg and diverting a Michael Bridges shot over stranded keeper Matt Clarke.

Suffice it to say, Smithy confirmed it was a fully intended action on his part. It was his fifth goal of the season and with Bridges at that stage having totted up 11, it was small wonder that Smith enthused about the partnership.

When Ian Harte stroked in an 80th minute penalty after Clarke had brought down David Batty, United seemed home and dry. But they were relieved when Jamie Lawrence missed a great chance for City four minutes before Dean Windass knocked in City's 90th minute consolation goal.

David O'Leary's men had not been at their best. But former Elland Roader, Lee Sharpe, who appeared at left-back for City, had no doubts about his former club's ability to win something.

"Leeds have a team that can win the title," he said. "In many ways they remind me of the Manchester United team I grew up in. There is the same buzz and feel about them."

Although United were not at their best against City, the ex-Manchester United winger knew enough about David O'Leary's side to be suitably impressed. "They have strength throughout the team and I see no reason why they cannot win the championship if not this season then next," he said.

"If they continue to make progress in the various competitions this season, then a build up of fixtures towards the end of the season could be the stumbling block."

Having safely tucked away three more precious points to retain top place in the Premiership and keep Manchester United at bay, David O'Leary's side focussed attention on their UEFA Cup challenge again - and a return trip to Moscow.

Red Square tradesmen who pester visitors to buy Russian imitation fur hats were doubtless rubbing their hands with glee again and they certainly did a roaring trade.

Those who had not succumbed to the sales patter on the first trip were easier prey this time as the numbing cold took its toll. But the happiest trader of all must have been the one who sold Eddie Gray 11 hats. "I bought them to take back for the family," Eddie explained.

CHAPTER SIX

FROZEN OUT IN MOSCOW

UNLIKE the first visit to Moscow, when the temperature hovered above freezing, the Russian capital this time proved to be inhospitable in the extreme – and in more ways than one.

Freezing temperatures of minus 20° C were something none of the United players had experienced before and as if this wasn't bad enough, United ran into what was dubbed a dirty tricks campaign from the Russian champions, which left both O'Leary and his chairman, Peter Ridsdale, fuming.

When United turned up at the Dynamo Stadium for training the night before the game they found the pitch frozen rock hard, despite the under soil heating. Ice had formed in parts and it was obvious the pitch was in a dangerous state.

The United manager did not mince his words. "It's a joke. The pitch is unplayable – just like concrete and there is a real threat of injury to players if we play on that surface," he said.

His players trained on the pitch for only ten minutes before O'Leary, on the advice of the club doctor and physiotherapist, called an end to it. "We couldn't do any ball work. All we could do were a few runs. It would have been stupid and dangerous to carry on," he said.

So concerned were United that chairman Peter Ridsdale attended the UEFA meeting which is normally held on the day of a game. "On this occasion I thought it necessary that I went along to voice my concerns," he said.

As things turned out, commonsense prevailed with Swedish referee Anders Frisk refusing to be

swayed by the Russians, who wanted the game to be played. The official deemed the pitch unplayable and postponed the game.

That didn't stop the Russians aiming a broadside at United – accusing them of being softies for not wanting to play on the frozen pitch.

> "The referee was strong and positive and no one was going to influence him. He was quite right to call it off."
>
> David O'Leary

Grigory Yesaulenko, Spartak vice president, claimed United's management had "behaved in the unfairest of manners."

He went on: "The day before the game should have been played, Leeds began to create tension saying they were cold and that the pitch was bad. If they don't like it, let them go play in Africa."

The pitch, however, was definitely not fit to play on and O'Leary could hardly disguise his relief when the decision was made to postpone the game. "I was sorry for the fans who had spent hard earned money to make the trip," he said.

"But the surface was a disgrace. Had the game gone ahead there would have been a big risk to players. The referee was strong and positive and no one was going to influence him. He was quite right to call it off."

So United – and the 500 or so fans who followed them into the cold – had had a wasted round trip of some 4,000 miles at a time of the season when the fixtures for O'Leary's trophy hunters were beginning to come thick and fast.

After further discussions at which both Liverpool and Sofia in Bulgaria had been mentioned as a neutral venue for the postponed game, UEFA decided the Georgi Asparuchov stadium – home of Levski Sofia should be the venue.

Even though the game was retained in an eastern European country that did not stop a further verbal outburst from the Russian camp. There was the ludicrous suggestion that United had attempted to bribe Spartak, who were due to spend ten days in England to prepare for the second leg, with a cash inducement to play the first leg at Anfield.

Needless to say this was strongly denied by United. "The possibility of switching the first leg to a venue in England did not even cross our minds until Spartak put it to us," Ridsdale said.

Determined to stress that such allegations, who ever made them, were untrue, United made an official complaint to UEFA. "I was not really worried what action, if any, UEFA would take but it was necessary to make the complaint. The allegations were libellous and wholly untrue but people would have read them and we needed to put matters straight," he said.

O'Leary, who described the allegations as nonsense, refused to become involved in a war of words with the Russians. His more immediate attention was seeing his players shake off their travel weariness in time for the home league clash with Southampton at Elland Road.

"I was actually more concerned over the Southampton game than I was by our trip to Moscow," O'Leary confessed. Mindful of what happened when his side lost at Wimbledon after their first trip to Moscow, the United boss feared there might be a similar adverse effect from the long mid-week trip this time.

"We struggled, lacked sparkle and looked a tired side when we played Wimbledon," he recalled.

He needn't have worried on this second occasion. His players were well up to scratch – and none more so than Jonathan Woodgate, whose form earlier in the season had dropped below the high standards his manager expected of him.

O'Leary's public image is of a 'Mr Nice Guy' but he can be as tough as teak when the need arises – as Woody found out. "My standards are a lot higher than many people think and having played centre-half myself I feel I am well qualified to judge what is needed to be a top quality central defender," O'Leary said.

"Woody had fallen below the standards I set, though he knew that himself, and while I have so much respect for him I found it necessary to have some harsh words with him in private. The answer was to work him hard on the training pitch and we had extra sessions with him in the afternoons for a while," he added.

"I was happy to do it," Woodgate said. "People might have thought I was doing okay but my form had slipped below the high standards we set at this club. I had no idea why that should be. I was going out for every match thinking I was the best... and I was not playing as well as I should.

"Right from the start of the season I felt I wasn't up to the form I showed in the previous season. It was the sort of spell a lot of players go through and when that happens you have to knuckle down and work your way through it.

"The boss and Eddie (Gray) and the rest of the lads all helped me and I am now much happier with my form."

Woodgate's display against the Saints was potentially a vital one. Lucas Radebe's duties with South Africa had taken him out of the equation and Michael Duberry, having picked up several bookings in reserve games, was suspended.

That left Woodgate as the only recognised centre half in United's side – his partner at the heart of the defence on this occasion being full-back Danny Mills. "That didn't worry me in the least. When you have someone like Danny Mills coming in and Gary Kelly and Ian Harte as full-backs you have a very good back line," he said.

"We all have a good understanding whether Lucas is playing or 'Doobs' (Michael Duberry), who is a fantastic lad and a good player. We all have a fair bit of experience behind us now."

"It was against Southampton that I began to feel I was beginning to play more like I did in the previous season."

Woodgate's partnership with Mills against the Saints worked well enough, as a clean sheet suggested, but United saved the best until last... the very last in fact as Michael Bridges hammered in the only goal of the game in the last minute.

That sent United up again to the top of the Premiership and put them in good heart for the re-arranged meeting with Spartak in the Bulgarian capital of Sofia. The night temperature in Sofia was only minus 3deg C, which compared to that experienced on the recent Moscow trip was positively mild!

O'Leary felt Spartak, who had dropped out of the Champions' League, should not be in the UEFA Cup at all, and he knew his young team would be in for a difficult night. There was little in the first half-hour to suggest that, as United, with Michael Bridges and Harry Kewell prominent, made their presence felt.

And when the Australian international nipped in smartly to take the ball past goalkeeper Alexander Filimonov to score in the 13th minute all looked well for United. An injury to Bridges, however, disrupted their flow and Spartak took full control; subjecting United to arguably their most difficult time of the season to date in the second half.

With David Batty and Lucas Radebe both missing, United struggled to contain the Russians. Alexander Schirko had levelled matters in the 37th minute but all Spartak had to show for their second half domination was a goal from Luis Robson.

United were fortunate to get away with a 2-1 first leg deficit and O'Leary knew it. "We missed Batty in that second half but we can't really complain because I know we can play better than we did. We gave away two silly goals," he remarked.

Having lost only once in their previous 16 matches, defeat was something United were not used to. Disappointed though they were at this second set-back, United's players were certainly not too downhearted and spoke confidently about pulling it round in the second leg.

"Spartak will find it very different when they come to Elland Road," said Nigel Martyn. "They finished the stronger of the two teams in this game

■ You can't keep Michael Bridges out of the picture. Here he is again celebrating another goal - this one was the only goal of the game against Southampton at Elland Road.

but we'll play with two up at home and put them under a lot of pressure."

The matches were still coming thick and fast for United's upwardly mobile young side and before getting to grips with the Russian champions for a second time, they had the challenge of Derby County at Pride Park to negotiate.

Having seen Manchester United return to the top of the Premier League the day before, O'Leary's men knew they must beat Derby to regain pole position. Although United dominated the game it was another late, late show that brought victory.

Ian Harte looked as cool as a cucumber when he stepped up to take the last-gasp penalty kick and duly scored to give United a 1-0 win. But beneath that cool exterior, however, there lurked a fear.

"I was nervous before talking the penalty," he admitted. "So much rested on it and it was vital

Not surprisingly, the rival managers had differing views, Derby's Jim Smith claiming that video evidence had shown there was no contact made while David O'Leary said: "That was Harry at his best and if you lunge in when he is in full flow there is always a risk."

Kewell himself maintained there had been contact, his back foot being caught.

Going back to the top put United in good heart for the return European clash with Spartak – and what a sizzling game it turned out to be.

Having been privileged to watch United in action dating back as far as the Don Revie era I have experienced some great European nights at Elland Road. I have to say, however, the clash with Spartak Moscow ranks right up there with the best of them.

It was a real nerve-tingler from start to finish with both sides playing football, as it should be

> ## "I had put my recent penalties either wide to the right or left of the goalkeeper. This time I decided to hit the ball more or less straight and that is what I did."
>
> Ian Harte

that I didn't fluff it. I shudder to think what sort of reception there would have been on the team coach for me afterwards had I missed it."

Horacio Carbonari's lunge at Harry Kewell as the final seconds of the game ticked by was responsible for the penalty and Harte rose to the occasion.

"I made up my mind what I was going to do and where I was going to put the ball. I had put my recent penalties either wide to the right or left of the goalkeeper. This time I decided to hit the ball more or less straight and that is what I did," he recalled.

The penalty incident was strongly contested by Derby who claimed that Kewell had conned referee Paul Alcock by going to ground when Carbonari lunged in at him.

played. Attacking football at its best, scares at both ends and excellent saves by both Nigel Martyn and Andrei Smetanin and a tremendous atmosphere in the ground made for high level entertainment.

Either side could have snatched the win but in the end the more experienced Russian side were beaten by a late and rare header from skipper Lucas Radebe to a superb inswinging corner from Stephen McPhail six minutes from the end.

What a goal...and what a night!

"It was a great night for us," agreed United's beaming skipper. "I don't score that many goals but I am sure this one is one that people will remember for a long time.

"At that stage of the game we had nothing to

lose. We had to get forward and score the first goal. When the corner came over I went in with the goalkeeper, stuck my head in and knocked the ball in. It was a brilliant feeling. I really enjoyed it."

This tie-clinching goal was Radebe's second of the season, his first also coming in Europe when he scored the second goal as United beat Partizan Belgrade 3-1 in Heerenveen. O'Leary said: "The 'Chief' doesn't score too often but when he does they're usually important ones."

Coming so near to the end of the 90 minutes, United demonstrated for the third game in a row their staying power, as a goal in the last minute of the victories over Southampton and Derby County clearly illustrated.

Similarities between the famous Revie side and O'Leary's emerging young team are growing all the time. Revie's men never accepted defeat until the final whistle. O'Leary's young bucks possess that same creditable attitude.

"We are still on a learning curve as far as Europe is concerned. We hope to be a force in a season or so but right now this is an enjoyable adventure for us and one we are learning a lot from," said the United boss.

The bear-hug that chairman Peter Ridsdale gave his manager on the pitch at the end of the battle summed up the tension, relief and pure joy of the evening. United had beaten a very good side and the European adventure continued... until March at least.

It was small wonder that the manager was not in for treatment for bruised ribs the following day! But he did admit: "I'm sore all over and hoarse from all the shouting I did. But it was a wonderful night. I am delighted for the fans who supported us so well and I have nothing but admiration for all my players."

What a pity that Spartak's assistant coach Vyacheslav Grozny should be so ungracious in defeat, choosing the after match Press conference to attack United with a comment or two that, frankly, smacked of sour grapes.

"Why did they cause such a fuss in Moscow," he said of United's reaction to the solidly frozen pitch that was ruled unplayable by Swiss referee Anders

Frisk. "Their tactics meant that we had to play both legs of the tie away from home. Nothing was to our advantage.

"In the first round Leeds did not want to play in Belgrade and in our third round tie they did not want to play in Moscow. Only one team wanted to play in Belgrade but were not allowed to do so while in Moscow one team wanted to play and the other did not.

"Are Leeds United on another planet or what"

Vyacheslav Grozny

"Are Leeds on another planet or what?" he asked before stressing that the criticism was not levelled at the United players but at the management.

When it was pointed out that the referee had decided the pitch was unplayable and he was then asked if the undersoil heating at the stadium had been switched on or off he chose not to answer and instead began to talk about the game.

David O'Leary had steadfastly refused to become embroiled in a war of words with the Russians, stating that he hoped United would do their talking on the pitch – as indeed they did.

The bribery allegations made by the Russians led to the indignant United chairman writing officially to UEFA with a strongly worded denial and complaint. "The way the Russians reacted saddened me – and I have to say that I feel their actions were premeditated," he said.

"I felt more sadness than anger. You try to conduct yourself in a manner that befits your club. We had met the British ambassador for lunch and I felt proud to be over there in Russia as part of an English team playing in the UEFA Cup.

"Then you find you have to respond to comments that frankly were so stupid as to be a joke. But they were so serious that you could not take them as a joke.

"That is why I felt I had to respond on behalf of

the club. Frankly I find it despicable that in a game of sport where UEFA's ideals are about countries playing together in the spirit of sport that we get some people who feel this is not the normally accepted practice.

"I can only assume Spartak were fearful of our reputation and were trying to put us out of our stride. I was delighted to be able to say that from start to finish they failed.

"But funnily enough their officials who we entertained in Leeds before the second leg actually apologised to us about the comments only for us to find out later that the comments were repeated by another of their officials.

"But we had a lawyer with us and an independent interpreter and they could confirm that the remarks Spartak officials alleged we said were never made," Ridsdale added.

"We had a very, very good response back from UEFA. The words they used in their reply implied that they were not surprised at the situation and that this was not perhaps the first time they had experienced this from this particular club.

"I felt re-assured that having taken the step of writing to UEFA their response was an extremely positive one and as far as I am concerned nobody – but nobody – in their right minds would believe any of the aspersions made against us," he added.

Under the circumstances United's success at Spartak's expense was all the more satisfying. Ridsdale's decision to write to UEFA had deliberately been taken and completed before the outcome of the second leg.

"We didn't want it to sound like sour grapes on our part had we not gone through," the chairman explained. He need not have worried on that score, though there was concern for the chairman and club secretary Ian Silvester the morning after the game.

"The chairman had hired a private plane to take us to the draw for the next round and as I got up at 5am snow, which had been forecast, was already falling," Silvester recalled.

"As I got nearer to Leeds-Bradford airport the weather was getting considerably worse. Peter arrived and so did Adam Pearson and David

Spencer and as we got on to the plane the snow was coming down in bucketloads," he added.

With concerns in the United camp having increased considerably the plane taxied to the end of the runway. "I think we were all very nervous as we looked out of the plane windows – I know I was," Silvester said.

Just as the plane was about to prepare for take off, the decision was taken to close the runway. "It was obvious there was not going to be an immediate improvement so we called the flight off altogether," he added.

> # "I was booked making my first tackle for Leeds and I felt a bit embarrassed about that."
>
> Eirik Bakke

LEEDS UNITED fended off strong interest from Manchester United – among others – to sign Eirik Bakke, the young Norwegian midfielder who made an instant impression on David O'Leary when he came over for a trial.

"I want him signed," was the manager's message to his chairman, who duly obliged by negotiating his move from Sogndal.

"He's one for the future," added O'Leary as the Norwegian Under-21 captain signed in, but because of injury problems the young midfielder had to be pressed into first team action – and he made another immediate impact!

"I was booked making my first tackle for Leeds and I felt a bit embarrassed about that," recalled Bakke.

He made his debut for United when he came on as a substitute in the second game of the season. Two more substitute outings followed in tough away games at Manchester United and Liverpool before he was given his first start in the home game against Newcastle at Elland Road.

He immediately stood out with his vision and commitment and it was not difficult to see why O'Leary and his coaches have high hopes for Bakke. "When I bought him I was not looking to put him into the first team immediately," the United manager said.

"He was one we had planned to develop but we had to put him in at the deep end and there's no doubt he's done very well. He has all the ingredients to become a top class player."

Bakke's preferred role is the right side of midfield. "I think that is my best position," he said. "But with competition for places at Leeds high I will play anywhere to get a game, though I would hope eventually to be able to settle down at right midfield. I am new to the club and still learning but I am happy at the way things are going for me and the way I am playing."

United were certainly happy with – and indebted to - the Norwegian for their third round FA Cup home victory over Port Vale. He opened his goals account for United by scoring twice in the second half to sink the Valiants.

"We started well but Leeds wore us down with their quality. That's what did us in the end," confessed Vale manager Brian Horton. "Leeds have some very talented players and I think they will go on to win something this season."

David O'Leary was naturally delighted to see his side progress to the fourth round but he took a verbal swipe at the Football Association for having placed the third round ties at the end of a European week. "The FA Cup, for me, is still the greatest cup competition in the world and it used to be the case that clubs were given a whole week to prepare for their ties. Not so this season," he complained.

"We had played a very taxing UEFA Cup tie against Spartak on the Thursday night so in effect we had little more than a day in which to prepare for the FA Cup game. That is not enough."

But Bakke rode to United's rescue with two second-half goals – his first for the club – to sink Brian Horton's battling side and put O'Leary's men into a fourth round tie against resurgent and promotion hunting Manchester City at Maine Road.

"It was a great feeling to get those first Leeds goals under my belt but really I just managed to get on the end of two very good deliveries," said the modest Norwegian.

With one cup game safely out of the way, O'Leary's men had no time to relax before turning their attention to a Worthington Cup fourth round tie at Leicester - and what a Filbert Street fiasco it turned out to be.

Having fallen to Leicester in the same competition the previous season O'Leary's men, keen to keep up a four-pronged assault on honours, were on a revenge mission.

David Batty made his long awaited comeback after an Achilles tendon injury but United's problems began after only 20 minutes of the game when the England midfield man suffered a recurrence of the injury. But it was Lucas Radebe's clashes with Leicester striker Emile Heskey that sparked controversy that was to overshadow the result, which went Leicester's way following a penalty shoot-out.

United's skipper, booked for a first half challenge, was ordered off in the 91st minute when he tangled with Heskey, who went down very easily for a big man. Referee Graham Barber produced the yellow card and then the red, leaving United to battle for half an hour of extra time with ten men.

The dismissal left a nasty taste in Rabebe's mouth and the South African skipper felt so bad that he could not resist claiming that Heskey's reaction had got him sent off.

■ Lucas wasn't laughing at Leicester.

"I could hardly believe it when he threw himself to the ground," Radebe said. "Heskey was aware that another yellow card for me would mean me going off and he made a meal of the incident."

Although Radebe's teammates managed to survive the extra time period without conceding a goal, the penalty shoot-out was a disaster for United, Gary Kelly and Lee Bowyer both missing their spot kicks after Jonathan Woodgate and Ian Harte had converted theirs.

A plea from United to referee Barber to have a second look at the incident – and also the booking of Lee Bowyer who clearly got the ball in the tackle for which he was booked - fell on deaf ears.

But with Martin O'Neill's side due to visit Elland Road on Boxing Day, United – and Radebe – had only 11 days to wait for another crack at revenge against the Foxes. Before then, however, United had a very tough looking trip to Stamford Bridge to undertake.

An air of tension bordering on the threatening, some very physical challenges, verbal abuse and plenty of ill-feeling. Life in the Bronx can be difficult and dangerous. But the scene on this occasion was not the notorious district of New York. It was Stamford Bridge where the so-called aristocrats of the Premier League had a real 'go' at David O'Leary's side in a bid to get the victory they so desperately needed to resurrect their hopes of making a serious tilt for the title.

With this scenario it was perhaps fitting that the match-winner should be United's graceful young midfielder Stephen McPhail – who once lived in the Bronx for four years.

The Irishman, who was actually born in London, went to New York when his parents moved there to work with his uncle who had a construction business in the Bronx. "I was very young at the time and I did not really know too much about it. But I remember not being able to go out on my own. Whenever I went out there was always someone with me," he recalled.

Chelsea manager Gianluca Vialli had lit the blue touch-paper on the eve of the game by calling for his players to rid themselves of the so-called 'southern softies' tag they are often labelled with.

"We are trying to be the best team at playing football but we also must try to be the best at fighting. People identify us as 'the foreign team' and when they play against us they think they are playing a continental team. So we must be able to handle the physical side of things," Vialli said.

The game had been in progress for only a few seconds when Lee Bowyer was unceremoniously bundled to the ground by Dennis Wise. Less than a minute later Bowyer was booked for a foul on Wise.

There is obviously no love lost between the two clubs – a situation dating back to the days of the 1960s and 1970s, when United were last at the height of their powers and fought some tense and difficult battles against the Blues.

On this latest occasion, O'Leary's young musketeers, as he christened them, showed maturity beyond their years and kept their heads while Chelsea, particularly Frenchmen Frank Lebouef and Didier Deschamps, lost theirs.

After watching his side lose a bad tempered battle 2-0 to second half goals from young Macca, Blues boss Vialli admitted his side had lost the plot – and that O'Leary's young guns had the capability to win the title.

After the game it was difficult to single out anyone in the United camp as being the happiest chappy. But McPhail probably edged that one as a result of scoring the first senior goals of his career. "It was a great feeling to get them and I enjoyed the first one the most," he said recalling how he finished off a great move involving Harry Kewell and Lee Bowyer in the 66th minute.

His second, three minutes from the end, came from a totally unrehearsed dead-ball situation. United practice their set-piece moves to near perfection but McPhail just saw his chance and fired the free kick goalwards and in it went as Eirik Bakke stepped over the ball.

"We didn't practice that one," O'Leary said. But he wasn't complaining... and neither was McPhail!

At four years of age McPhail was too young to realise what was going on when he lived in the Bronx. "So I wasn't frightened, though when I look back now it was a real eye-opener. We lived very near to a hospital so it was noisy with all the ambulance sirens blaring," he recalled.

Now though, his thoughts are centred on doing well for Leeds United. "All of us at the club have a belief that we can be the best," he says.

With Chelsea trailing to McPhail's first strike, Lebouef was given his marching orders by referee Jeff Winter, for the second of two bookable offences on Kewell. To make matters worse he followed up the second challenge by treading on the prone figure of the young Australian. The red mist had certainly formed.

When the heat of the battle had subsided, United were given widespread media praise and manager David O'Leary was understandably proud of his side. "We had eight players aged 23 or under while they had nine aged 29 or over. We had to 'dig in' but it was a tremendous victory for us."

■ Stephen MacPhail doubled up at The Bridge.

The United manager was told in no uncertain terms by some writers to stop playing down his side's title chances. "Look," he said, "we won't be scared to win the title but whatever people say we are still learning our trade. I have no idea where we will end up. When the pressure increases we might just 'bottle' it but we'll have to wait and see," he added.

Lebouef later apologised to Kewell for having stamped on his ankle saying he had lost his temper. "I was frustrated and it was a spur of the moment thing," he said.

Vialli, who had seen his side squander some chances, joined the growing band of admirers who thought O'Leary's side were genuine title challengers. "Yes, I really think they can win it," he said.

"Leeds seem to have everything, They are quick to turn defence into attack, they can score goals from anywhere and everywhere on the field and they don't shirk the physical side of the game," he reasoned. "They seem to have that little bit of luck

going for them as well but they are a joy to watch - probably the most exciting young team in England," he added.

O'Leary had made a surprise swoop to sign £3million winger Jason Wilcox from Blackburn a couple of days before the visit to Stamford Bridge and he was quickly into match action with his new club, coming on in place of the injured Michael Bridges early in the second half.

Despite having to endure injuries, suspensions and international calls to his relatively small squad, the United manager had stuck true to his word not to rush into signings until the players he wanted were available.

Wilcox, he said, had been on his wanted list for some time but when the deal was done it was completed rapidly and without any Press speculation. "I had been trailing him for some time and when we found that Blackburn would sell we went about it in a quietly efficient way," O'Leary recalled.

The 28-year-old Wilcox, who before his move to Leeds was the last player from Blackburn's

> "Leeds seem to have everything, They are quick to turn defence into attack, they can score goals from anywhere and everywhere on the field and they don't shirk the physical side of the game."
>
> Gianluca Vialli

championship winning side still at Ewood Park, has set his sights on further honours... with Leeds. He said: "My move here happened so quickly that I don't think my wife knew anything about it until it was done!

"The move came right out of the blue. But once Blackburn made it clear they were happy for me to leave and that the interested club was Leeds United there was really no decision for me to make," the left-sided midfield player said.

Seven days after their Chelsea triumph, United were back in match action – and on song, too – as they extracted revenge against Leicester City for their recent Worthington Cup defeat. A Boxing Day crowd of 40,105 – the biggest of the season to date at Elland Road – saw United serve up some fine festive fare, even though they had only two goals to show for their efforts.

■ Michael Bridges put the finger on Leicester City when he scored in the 2-1 Boxing Day victory over the Foxes.

Radebe was still smarting at having been sent off following his clash with Heskey in the Worthington Cup game, and had gone on record before the game to ask the referee to keep a close watch on the burly striker.

Not surprisingly, Heskey was hardly flavour of the month with United fans, but any personal clash was lost in a match that delighted the home fans. United even gave away the first goal, scored by Tony Cottee after just ten minutes.

Harry Kewell ran the show for United. "He's an absolutely outstanding player," said Leicester boss Martin O'Neill. But the game saw a return to form for Michael Bridges, who scored the equaliser in the 29th minute and then set up what proved to be the winner for Lee Bowyer just before half time.

"We played superbly from start to finish and we could have scored five or six goals," delighted manager David O'Leary said.

There was barely time for United's players to catch their breath before they were on the road to London for their final game of the century, where Arsenal, O'Leary's former club, were waiting for them.

An injury to Darren Huckerby during the Leicester game had left United with Bridges as their only recognised striker for the game at Highbury. The signs were not good – and even O'Leary admitted that he had sensed his players were tired on the train journey to the capital.

Attempts weeks earlier by O'Leary to have the game moved to a Wednesday, in a bid to ease fixture congestion, had been swiftly turned down by Arsene Wenger. "He would have none of it and it proved to be a wise decision for him," said the United boss.

Alan Smith though still not over an ankle injury, was brought back, but United had lost their sparkle against an Arsenal side who took all the honours and won 2-0 with goals from Fredrik Ljungberg and Thierry Henry. Those writers who had gone over the top with their admiration of United following that great win at Chelsea had to eat some of their words as caution crept in.

Arsenal defender Tony Adams immediately cast doubt on United's title chances, claiming he felt they would not last the pace. "It's not because they don't have good players but because of the size of their squad," he argued.

O'Leary would not be drawn into a public debate with his one-time roommate other than to add: "Arsenal have still to come to our place in April. It is no good me spouting off about it. Let's see what happens then, whether he is right or wrong."

United's place at the top of the Premiership was under serious threat now from Manchester United, who were playing at Sunderland that night and who needed to win to regain the coveted top spot. Having gone two goals down very early, the Reds battled back and a goal from Nicky Butt four minutes from time earned them a draw – which wasn't sufficient to knock O'Leary's side off the top rung.

CHAPTER SEVEN

'BACK ME OR SACK ME' ULTIMATUM

ENTERING the new Millennium as top team in the country left everyone at Elland Road with a feeling of great pride and satisfaction. Quite right too, when consideration of the immense progress that has been made, was taken into account.

The Whites had so far managed to give the richest and top club in the world their biggest challenge. "I'm not going to pretend any other. I love it. Being on top of the Premiership is a fantastic feeling," manager David O'Leary admitted.

A time such as this was most opportune to take stock of just what had been achieved at Elland Road in such a short space of time. No one was happier, of course, than chairman – and long standing fan - Peter Ridsdale, who had been so instrumental in bringing about the resurgence.

Yet the progress had not been all plain sailing. Ridsdale revealed that he had deliberately plunged himself into rough waters at one point over his insistence that the club should appoint David O'Leary as manager.

It even got as far as the chairman issuing a 'Back me or sack me' ultimatum, which had its roots in the 1-0 defeat against Roma in Rome's Olympic Stadium.

The chairman explained: "The most outstanding memory of that night in Rome for me was that it convinced me David O'Leary should be the next manager of Leeds United. The way in which the team played, the way in which the crowd responded to both the team and to David left no doubt in my mind.

"At half time in that game I turned to Jeremy Fenn (then United's financial director) and said this man is going to be our next manager. I was so convinced it was the right decision to make that when we arrived back in Leeds after the Roma game, Jeremy and I went to David's house that night and offered him the job there and then," he said.

However it was not quite as straightforward as that.

"Being a public company I had to clear it with the plc board but there was one non-executive director, who shall remain nameless, who, as he was quite within his rights to do, questioned whether I had thought the matter through.

> "At half time in that game I turned to Jeremy Fenn and said 'this man is going to be our next manager'."
>
> Peter Ridsdale

"I turned round, and though it could have cost me the job I love, said: 'I am the chairman of this football club and I am saying we should appoint David O'Leary. You either back me or get a new chairman," Ridsdale recalled.

"The individual concerned replied: 'If that is

how you feel it's good enough for me. You clearly believe very strongly in him and I will support your judgement' and I went off and told David the job was his," Ridsdale added.

When George Graham upped and went to Tottenham, the United chairman admits that initially United did not know what to expect. "We thought it might even turn into a crisis," he said. "But I also thought – and said so at the time – that it could turn into a moment of opportunity and that is exactly what it did do."

It is common knowledge that United had wanted to speak with Martin O'Neill, the Leicester City manager. "We asked for permission but we never got the chance and anyway after that night in Rome I became convinced that the man we needed was already at our club.

"Needless to say, really, I have absolutely no regrets at all in appointing David," added the chairman who saw his first United game back in 1959 when he was seven years old and became a regular watcher three years' later.

"In my time watching the team, I cannot remember being more excited about our prospects as I am as we go into the new Millennium," he said.

O'Leary said. "We don't get owt for it at the moment but believe you me we are delighted to be there. When you consider what has been achieved in those games it is nothing short of fantastic.

"If we had been in fourth or fifth place at this stage I would have thought we were doing well. We are in top spot now so people will begin to nit-pick. What you wonder now is how our young players will cope in the remainder of the season," he added.

However, the United boss was in no doubt that Manchester United were still the team everyone else had to beat. "They are the yardstick. There is never a good time to play them but it would be nice to be able to play them at our place on the day they arrive back from Brazil," he joked.

"Arsenal will be up there fighting for the title as well and the team I have always fancied is Liverpool. I see them closing the title gap. They're out of the League Cup, they're not in Europe and they don't have the number of fixtures we have. And they have spent £36million so they are entitled to be up there.

"We don't have the capacity of some of those squads but we won't be ducking the issues," he warned.

> "As we go into a new year we've got Europe to look forward to, after coming through three hard rounds, we are still in the FA Cup and with 20 league games gone we are top of the tree."
>
> David O'Leary

O'Leary, of course, is the man charged with bringing success back to the club and, as he knows, United have made rapid progress under his guidance. Sensibly he made no rash predictions, though he could afford to look to the future with confidence.

"As we go into a new year we've got Europe to look forward to, after coming through three hard rounds, we are still in the FA Cup and with 20 league games gone we are top of the tree,"

O'Leary hit the nail firmly on the head when he summed up his side's home defeat by Aston Villa. "Manchester United in Brazil will be the team laughing the most after this," he said.

The Elland Road side's defeat by Villa ended a 12 match winning home sequence but with the Reds taking part in the World Club Championship tournament in Rio De Janeiro, O'Leary's men were looking to increase their points advantage at the top of the Premiership.

A crumb or two of comfort came with their nearest title rivals, Arsenal, Sunderland and Liverpool all dropping points. "All the other results went for us but the only team that will be truly laughing after this will be Manchester United," O'Leary said.

> ## "If you could have picked a day to play Leeds here at Elland Road then this would have been the day."
>
> John Gregory

Arsenal surrendered a lead to draw 1-1 at bottom-of-the-table Sheffield Wednesday while Sunderland went down 1-0 at Wimbledon and Liverpool lost by the same scoreline at Tottenham.

After their defeat at Arsenal, which gave ammunition to those critics who doubted their staying power, the Villa game gave United the opportunity to bounce back. But they were up against it before a ball had been kicked.

Referee Graham Barber had remained intransigent when asked to reconsider actions that led to Lucas Radebe and Lee Bowyer being suspended for the Villa game. With injuries also ruling out David Batty and Stephen McPhail, United went into the match without three first choice midfielders.

It was a situation not lost on Villa manager John Gregory. "We knew Bowyer and Radebe were going to miss the game and that gave us a lift," he admitted. "If you could have picked a day to play Leeds here at Elland Road then this would have been the day. In Bowyer I think Leeds have one of the most exciting prospects in English football at the moment. I think he is a great player.

"With David Batty out as well Leeds had one or two very influential players missing and we took advantage of it. But even so they still have an exceptional squad and it is never easy to win at Elland Road," he added.

Shoddy defensive work allowed Villa to take a 19th minute lead from Gareth Southgate of all people. "He goes forward for corners and free kicks but he's known as 'The Ornament' because that's about as much use as he is in those situations," Gregory joked.

O'Leary's men were not at their best but when Harry Kewell brought them level with a wonder strike from 35 yards in the first minute of the second half, they were given new hope. But it was a false dawn as 'The Ornament' struck the winner in the 62nd minute.

"Of course it's a blow – and a set-back. When we needed to bounce back after Arsenal we lost a complete midfield and it's very hard to cope with that, even Manchester United would have found that difficult and they are the best side in the league," O'Leary said.

"We are a young side trying to do the best we can. We'll be judged on what we do at the end of the season – it's as simple as that," he added.

His side retained leadership of the Premiership but with only one point more than the Reds, who had two games in hand, the situation left no one in the Elland Road camp in any doubt that there was no margin for error.

"It was a blow losing to Villa," admitted goalkeeper Nigel Martyn, whose two wonder saves in the second half kept the margin of defeat down. "We've a couple of tough looking away games coming up at Sunderland and Liverpool, and we are now going to have to look to win both of them," he said.

Before then, however, O'Leary's young guns had a tricky looking FA Cup fourth round tie at First Division leaders Manchester City to prepare for.

THE big debate had been running among Leeds United fans for a while. Which is Harry Kewell's best position? Is it left side of midfield or up front?

Manager David O'Leary – the man who really counts, of course - put in his contribution on the 'pros' and 'cons' of the issue after Kewell's two-goal man-of-the-match display in the 5-2 cup-tie hammering of Manchester City at Maine Road.

"Up front is where I see Harry playing,

eventually," said O'Leary, who revealed that he had demanded more goals from the young Australian, who for the most part had been used in a wide running role on the left.

"I need to get some more players in first but that is easier said than done. The experts think I should get them all the time and produce them out of thin air but unfortunately it's not quite as easy as that," he added. But O'Leary said that giving Harry more opportunities up front had been at the back of his mind when he signed Jason Wilcox from Blackburn.

"I thought the cup tie at Maine Road was the opportunity to give Harry a run up front and with Jason available it made that possible. There is no doubt in my mind that Harry will eventually become a really tremendous player.

"But one area where he needs to improve is his goalscoring. He has got to score more goals and I have been demanding more from him and he produced the goods at Maine Road," added the United boss.

Despite twice falling behind early on to efforts from Shaun Goater, albeit from an offside position, and a cracker from Ian Bishop, O'Leary's musketeers hit back in quite awesome fashion.

Eirik Bakke, Alan Smith and Harry Kewell all scored to give United a 3-2 half time advantage. Lee Bowyer added a tremendous fourth goal before Kewell tapped in his second and United's fifth a couple of minutes from the end.

Even then Kewell carved himself a chance to grab a hat-trick but though his low angled drive beat England Under-21 keeper Nicky Weaver, the ball rapped the far post and came back out.

It all left Blues boss Joe Royle high on admiration for O'Leary's team. "I thought Leeds were terrific... in fact quite awesome at times. And don't let David O'Leary kid you, this Leeds side can win the Premiership," he said.

"They came back twice after going behind in what was probably a tricky tie coming to Maine Road and for young kids that showed great maturity and belief. Though you don't like having to do it, there are times when you have to hold your hands up and admit you have been beaten by a much better side," he said.

"On the day Leeds were excellent. They are fast, they are fit, they are committed, they have lots of ability and they have internationals, or soon to be internationals, throughout the team.

"It didn't happen overnight for them. Two or three seasons ago people were saying Leeds would slide out of the top division but George Graham arrested the slide and David has taken it on from there," he added.

The United manager had repeatedly said he would not go in for short term fixes when looking to strengthen his squad but his most recent signing, left winger Jason Wilcox, showed his worth when he made his first start for United in the cup-tie at Maine Road.

Four successive substitute outings had not given him much of a chance to make an impact. But with Michael Bridges out through suspension and Kewell moved up front, the left wing berth was left vacant for Wilcox.

"When you come to a club who are top of the league it's a matter of waiting for your chance and then hopefully being able to make the most of it," said Wilcox, who enthused over Kewell's skills

"Harry has that individual brilliance that all successful teams need. Alan Shearer had it when he was at Blackburn. Harry is a great player no matter which role he plays his was a special performance when he played up front against City," Wilcox added.

■ Harry Kewell turned in a special performance at Maine Road.

Another of O'Leary's signings, Norwegian Eirik Bakke also showed the rapid progress he made since joining United at the beginning of the season. His goal against City was his third in the FA Cup and his display left O'Leary very encouraged.

"I asked the chairman a year back if he wanted me to buy for the present or with the future in mind. I am a great believer in developing things so I asked him if the club would back me if I bought a player or two who would perhaps not go straight into the team and he said they would."

Bakke first came to United's notice when a tape of a game in which he was playing was sent to O'Leary. "I liked what I saw and made the effort to go out to see him in a game in Athens. I liked him right away."

"I think Eirik will become a tremendous midfield player. He is quick, he glides over the ground, has great feet, is good in the air and is a fine athlete," added the United manager.

WHILE United were battling in the league, work was already going on behind the scenes to ensure the smooth running of United's return to Italy in early March for another UEFA Cup meeting with AS Roma.

But the backroom team had a laugh at the expense of United's stadium manager Harry Stokey, who arrived at the airport wearing slacks and a blazer. When asked by director and club secretary Ian Silvester where his coat was, Stokey replied that as their destination was Italy he hadn't thought it necessary to bring one with him.

"He said he didn't need a coat to go to Rome," Silvester recalled. "We thought he was joking and that he had a coat in his bag but he hadn't. Yet this was mid January and it was pretty cold in England and, according to the weather reports we had at the time, even colder in Rome.

"Roma had also invited us to watch their match

> ## "I liked what I saw and made the effort to go out to see him in a game in Athens. I liked him right away."
>
> David O'Leary

that night against Cagliari and Harry sat in the stand shivering. Fortunately it was a bit warmer the following day, but still not warm enough to be without a coat," he added.

United, of course, played in Rome the previous season and their impending return to the impressive Olympic Stadium had quickly captured the imagination of their supporters. "It became apparent very quickly that the trip to Rome was going to be a big operation for us. In no time at all we had 3,500 people booked on flights and the figures went quite a lot higher than that in the end," he said.

"People who have worked at the club for some time could not recall taking that many supporters abroad before," he added.

The two-week break United had after their FA Cup win over Manchester City saw manager David O'Leary sign highly rated Australian Under 21 goalkeeper Danny Milosevic. Dubbed 'down under' as 'the new Mark Bosnich' the 21-year-old Milosevic had made a big impression at Thorp Arch when he spent a month on trial.

His signing – on a three-year contract – put pressure onto United's England Under 21 goalkeeper Paul Robinson, who had shown his qualities when standing in for Nigel Martyn the previous season.

Competition for places is something O'Leary had been keen on creating for every position and United had been reduced to two goalkeepers after injury brought a premature end to Mark Beeney's playing career. "We really need three good goalkeepers and Danny's arrival brought us back up to that number," O'Leary explained.

Australian sources regarded Milosevic as the natural successor at international level to Bosnich – and in the near future too.

But it wasn't all plain sailing for United and the Elland Road 'ship' hit rough waters when Jonathan Woodgate and Lee Bowyer were arrested following an incident near to a Leeds nightclub that left another youth injured and in need of hospital treatment.

Even though the two were released without charge pending further inquiries, it didn't stop many jumping to conclusions. In this country people are presumed innocent until proved otherwise. The bad publicity heaped on to the club

brought up well and I believe in good values. So we will not shirk away from our responsibilities."

Referring to pre-match suggestions that neither Bowyer nor Woodgate should have played against Sunderland, O'Leary stressed: "I will not be told what team to pick. No one knows what team I pick, not even my Number Two, until a couple of hours before a game."

> # "These two lads were taken in and accused… nothing else. But everyone wants to pre-judge them."
>
> David O'Leary

made sales-boosting headlines for newspapers and did nothing for the club's image.

Preparing for a tough looking Premier League game against high-riding Sunderland at the Stadium of Light was not easy but United closed ranks and concentrated on training. There was never any doubt in my mind that David O'Leary would play both Woodgate and Bowyer against Sunderland, provided the players were in the right frame of mind.

But it was not until shortly before the game that the United manager made his decision public. Both played. "I never considered leaving them out. They are part of the team that has taken us to the top of the Premiership," he said after United had returned to winning ways in the league with a 2-1 defeat of Peter Reid's team.

Speaking of the incident near to the nightclub the United boss added: "I know in general what happened but I cannot say too much. What I will say is that it is right to keep on picking them and I will continue to do that unless I hear otherwise.

"These two lads were taken in and accused… nothing else. But everyone wants to pre-judge them. Some of the newspaper stories disgusted me and my only worry was how they would cope with all the rubbish that had been spouted but I was quickly satisfied that they were all right mentally to play."

The United boss went on: "What has happened and what has been said hurt me because I was

Although United were not at their best they had more craft than a Sunderland side who relied to a great extent on good honest graft. Predictably, both Bowyer and Woodgate, whenever they touched the ball or made a tackle, came in for verbal abuse from Sunderland fans.

If it worried them they certainly did not show it. Theirs was a thoroughly professional performance, though Woodgate, who reached his 20th birthday the day before the game, did make the slip that allowed Kevin Phillips to hammer in Sunderland's 52nd minute goal.

United had gone 2-0 up a minute before that response, when Michael Bridges cleverly turned in Jason Wilcox's left wing cross to score against the club he had left in summer. A case of Sods' Law as far as Sunderland manager Peter Reid was concerned. "It didn't really surprise me because these sort of things happen in football," he said.

Bridges, who was also given a dose of the 'verbals' by Sunderland fans, took his goal tally for the season to 14 with this latest strike and Reid added: "He's a smashing lad and a very good footballer in a very good team and there is no problem with him."

While the game was richly satisfying for the England Under 21 international on a personal level, it was also rewarding for Jason Wilcox, the former Blackburn winger who had only recently moved in at Elland Road.

Playing his second full game for his new club, Wilcox turned in an impressive left-wing display. In addition to creating the chance for Bridges' goal, he fired United ahead in the 24th minute with a blistering left foot shot from 20 yards that zipped past Sunderland keeper Thomas Sorensen at 72 mph.

"I knew I had hit it well," Wilcox recalled. "And naturally it's great to get my first goal for Leeds." He might also have added: "And in front of Kevin Keegan too" as the England coach was at the game.

The wide left position had been a problem for Keegan and after his man-of-the-match display against Sunderland, the 28-year-old Wilcox could well have thought he had pushed himself back into the international frame.

"My priority is to play for Leeds regularly. I have to try to keep my place, but like most players, I still have ambitions to play again for England. If anything should come along I'll take it with both hands," he added.

Wilcox could hardly believe his luck when he left a struggling Blackburn Rovers' side and walked straight into a club that was at the top of the Premier League. A bolt out of the blue was how he described it.

His signing raised more than a few eyebrows among United fans but David O'Leary had done his

■ Jason Wilcox scored his first goal fo the club at Sunderland.

homework and he further surprised many when he stressed that he hadn't bought the Lancastrian merely as cover for other players.

The planning was simple. "I see Harry (Kewell) as being given a freer role up front but to be able to try that out I needed to get in a left sided player. Once I had managed to get Jason the option was there for me to let Harry have a run as striker," the United boss said.

So far so good. Wilcox played a key role when United hammered Manchester City in the recent FA Cup fourth round tie and he carried on against Sunderland when given his second start.

Having spent 14 years with Blackburn, the transfer to Leeds was his first. "I have settled in very quickly but a lot of that is down to the fact that I have been playing on the left wing, which is the role I most enjoy," he said.

When he hammered the ball into the Sunderland net, following a superb pass from Stephen McPhail which left him with a clear run on goal, he must have felt a world away from the experience he suffered at Ewood Park earlier in the season.

"I was having to play in a variety of positions and that didn't help so I was delighted when David O'Leary said he wanted me to play on the left wing," said Wilcox who had had to endure jeers from Blackburn fans when things were not going so well.

There was further comfort for Wilcox when O'Leary spoke of how highly he regarded him as a player. "I have always rated him and particularly after I played against him. I was delighted to bring him to Leeds. He gives us great balance," said the United boss.

Though he is one of the senior players at the club, Wilcox, the proud holder of a Championship winners medal with Blackburn, doesn't agree that he is the finished article as a player. "I am still hungry to win things. I want success on a personal level and for the club and I want to improve as a player. I don't think you ever stop learning at this game," he said.

Coincidentally, after he had cracked in that superb goal against Sunderland, one area of his game he believes needs improving is goalscoring.

"Frankly I am disappointed with my career goal tally," he said. "I should score more often than I have done but if I can continue to play in my favourite position on the left then hopefully I can score quite a few more," he added.

A winger's priority is not to score goals but to provide openings for others and chip in with a goal every now and then. An intelligent player and an accurate crosser of the ball, Wilcox has made quite a few chances for Alan Shearer.

Early indications were that, given the opportunity and freedom from injury, he would make quite a few chances for the exciting young strikers in David O'Leary's side.

LEEDS UNITED'S Youth Academy enjoys a position of envy in this country and further afield too. Hardly surprising, you might say, in view of the success it has achieved in bringing through such talented players as Harry Kewell, Jonathan Woodgate, Ian Harte, Alan Smith, Stephen McPhail, Matthew Jones, Paul Robinson and the like.

It's fame and status now borders on that enjoyed by Manchester United who have long had one of the best youth development schemes. So it is only to be expected that budding young footballers from all over are queuing up to be admitted to the Thorp Arch academy.

Many, even if they show sufficient promise and have potential, will be disappointed. It's not the fault of the Elland Road club... more a case of them falling victim to FA rules which tie the hands of the clubs.

United are banned – as all clubs are - from signing any youngsters between the ages of nine and 12 who live more than an hour's drive from Elland Road and 13 to 16 year olds, who live more than one-and-a-half hours' drive away.

The Premier League legislation was well intentioned, aimed at giving smaller clubs a chance to sign the best players in their areas, but United's Academy Director, Alan Hill, a man who is never afraid to speak his mind, believes it should be scrapped.

"I don't think there is enough talented players to sustain a Premier League club in the areas we are allowed to extend to and Leeds United are not alone in thinking the restrictions should be lifted," he said.

"I believe we need a vehicle to be able to go outside those areas. We would probably need maybe up to ten players of various age groups from outside the area.

"Because of the quality of our facilities and the high standard of our coaching it is important for the benefit of English football that clubs such as ours should have the chance to sign the best English lads, wherever they live," Hill said.

■ United stars of tomorrow? Youngsters are put through their paces at Leeds United's training complex at Thorp Arch.

Initial outlay for United's Thorp Arch training complex was £5million but subsequent developments and more that are in the pipeline will double that figure and on top of that United are faced with an annual running cost of £2million.

"In the end I think it will have cost in the region of £10million. On top of that we have very high running costs each year. That's a lot of money to be paying out but when you compare that with the transfer fees asked for - and paid - in the Premier League it is cheap, though, of course, we have to keep on producing the goods."

Not all clubs can afford to spend so much on running an Academy so it is hardly surprising that those who can want the restriction lifting to enable them to have access to the best young English players – no matter where they live.

"The FA have asked clubs to invest these large sums of money in academies but they are restricting the young players we can bring in. It has been easier for us to go abroad and get kids, which is ridiculous," Hill said. The powers that be have, however, been keen to see that clubs abide by the restriction as was instanced in the case of one youngster who was desperate to join United.

"He and his family were very keen United fans and naturally he wanted to join us. His parents wanted that too. They lived on the Nottinghamshire border and it meant they were ten minutes outside the one-hour time limit. On a good day it was possible to do it, on a bad day, traffic wise, it wasn't.

So the Premier League, in their wisdom, decided to test it for themselves and actually sent someone to do the drive – which in my view was crackers. He found it was ten minutes over, so the rules meant we could not sign him," added Hill.

But the family refused to accept defeat in their attempt to have their son sign for club they wished. "Being avid Leeds United supporters over the years, they decided to move house that bit nearer so they could make the journey inside the hour mark.

"We have another player, Simon Johnson, who lived in Birmingham and who joined us before the restrictions were brought in. He has a younger brother we would like to sign.

"The parents want him to come to Leeds to join his brother, who they know is being very well looked after here, yet because of the travel limit he can't. It's a problem and one we feel needs sorting out," Hill added.

United's Academy director stressed he was not looking to take many from areas that are currently not open to them. "We will not be seeking to take 30 or 40 kids from outside areas," he added.

> "The FA have asked clubs to invest these large sums of money in academies but they are restricting the young players we can bring in. It has been easier for us to go abroad and get kids, which is ridiculous."
>
> Alan Hill

"What the FA are saying is that kids should sign for their local clubs and then it is up to us to identify them with the local clubs and go and pay them compensation. I don't agree with it. It would mean we could not get those young players and coach them in our way of playing. We would have to wait until these kids were 15 and by then they would be set in their ways.

"I am not being big-headed or disrespectful but we have some top quality coaches and clubs in the lower divisions can't afford to pay for those quality coaches and the kids then, maybe, do not get the type of coaching that would benefit them most," he added.

The Charter for Quality under the Academy scheme was the brainchild of former United manager Howard Wilkinson, who while he was manager of United, was instrumental in setting up the youth training facilities at Thorp Arch.

"Howard saw the value of youth development and his decision to have a training facility away from Elland Road – in a rural area and away from the city centre - was a brilliant idea. He put things into place but David (O'Leary) and his staff took things onward at a rapid pace.

"The success that Howard had at Leeds with such as Paul Hart and Eddie Gray working with the likes of Woodgate, Kewell and McPhail shows the value of youth policies. It is the best thing that has happened," he said.

Whether such players would have been given an immediate chance to show their talents and worth in senior football had George Graham stayed on at Elland Road is doubtful.

Listen to Alan Hill. "When I first came to the club I was asked by George to look at players and I made comments to him about Woodgate, McPhail, Kewell and Smith, people like that, but if he had stayed at the club I don't think he would have played them. David wanted to. He had said he would like to give them the opportunity and as soon as George left, David was true to his word."

Hill admits that having given so many young players first team opportunities handed United an advantage when looking for young players. "They have seen that youngsters, if they are good enough, get a chance at Leeds – and they do – and the desire to come to Leeds is all the greater. It is a big attraction," he added.

So far United's investment in youth has paid the richest of dividends with a high proportion of talented young players rolling off the production line. United's academy staff know there can be no resting on laurels. The name of the game is to keep up the good work.

That means bringing more youngsters through the ranks. "Our Under 17 squad is a very good squad - a talented one. Out of that side we have ten who are international players," he revealed. "The majority of them have already played in the

Under 19s and I think they will be the next group to produce players for the first team," he said. "We are competing for the best players and, because of the way the club has developed over the last few years, we're getting them."

Manchester United and Arsenal have always had first class youth policies but the one in place at Elland Road now ranks alongside those.

In recent years, United have pulled in scores of youngsters from Ireland – a productive area over the years for the Gunners and the Old Trafford club - and midway through the season a link-up with Home Farm, one of Ireland's best known, oldest and most successful youth clubs, was negotiated.

Johnny Giles, one of the Republic's and United's best ever players, played with Home Farm as did present United star Gary Kelly.

"This new link-up has excited United, whose actions were again taken with the travel restrictions in mind. United already had centres in Belfast, Coleraine and Derry as well as a base in Scotland."

Young players between the ages of nine and 12 will follow a coaching programme laid down by United. "Coaches from the centres will come to Thorp Arch and have some coaching education and from time to time our coaches will visit the centres to work with the youngsters.

"They will then be coached in the same way as we coach the young lads at Thorp Arch and the idea is to pick the best young players from the various centres and bring them together at least twice a year."

By doing that United believe they will get a quality squad together. And those young lads who are not taken on will have had the benefit of top class coaching which could help them get other clubs."

> # "They have seen that youngsters, if they are good enough, get a chance at Leeds."
>
> Alan Hill

CHAPTER EIGHT

BOOTED OUT... UNITED GET THE BLUES!

A PAIR of blue painted old boots helped Benito Carbone to a match-winning hat-trick as Aston Villa knocked Leeds United out of the FA Cup and if that wasn't bad enough in itself, David O'Leary insisted his players suffered the agony all over again by watching it on tape.

The video 'nasty' was on the agenda when United's players reported back at Thorp Arch for training a day or so later. "It wasn't very pleasant viewing," Nigel Martyn admitted afterwards.

"What came out of it was that only one player was left unscathed – Ian Harte. The rest of us got a telling off and we could hardly complain because we know we didn't perform in the second half," he said.

The defeat was a major disappointment and though we were 2-1 up at half time we hadn't played all that well but at half time we thought if we could go back out and play anything like we are capable of we could win the game.

"But as we got worse they got better and deserved their win. We were second to the ball and that was what baffled the manager, particularly as we are a team that closes down opponents so well and bearing in mind the amount of second ball we usually win.

"But we were second to everything all over the pitch and that was catastrophic. There was no obvious reason for it. Ten players felt hurt by their own performances and it is important to respond to that and bounce back. What we have to do is take it as a right kick up the backside and make sure we don't let it happen again," he added.

Martyn had to take his share of the criticism for Villa's second goal, when he was beaten by a stunning 35-yard effort from Carbone.

"I was trying to get a position where if he decided to clip the ball over the top or hit a diagonal shot I would be able to help the defence out. To do that I went further forward than I should have to get a view of him. When he struck his shot I soon realised I was in a bit of trouble. It was a great strike but there is no way he should have scored from that distance," he explained.

O'Leary had not pulled his punches immediately after the game either. 'We got what we deserved – nothing,' encapsulated his post match comments.

After leading 1-0 and then 2-1 at half time, United, having controlled the first half proceedings, must have felt they were on course for the quarter finals but the second half turned out to be a chilling experience for United players and fans alike.

"We deserved nothing and that's just what we got," he said. "In the second half hardly any of our players reached anywhere near their best. Too many of them were well below par and if you want to do well in the FA Cup you need better than that," he said.

"We were worthy leaders at half time, without having played to our usual standard, but you have to maintain that over 90 minutes and in the second half Villa were the better team and ran out worthy winners," he added.

Ian Harte's seventh goal of the season had given United a 13th minute lead and though Carbone equalised after half an hour, Eirik Bakke's fourth FA Cup goal of the campaign, following a superb left wing cross from Stephen McPhail, restored United's advantage.

"It was a wonderful cross but I think that was maybe the only time in the match that we strung three or four passes together," Bakke said.

"We were poor in the second half. For me personally and some of the other boys, it was not good at all. Personally I was very unhappy with my form in the last two games. I was terrible.

"Going in 2-1 up we were confident. We badly wanted to progress in the cup but in the second half we looked as if we didn't want to win the game. Aston Villa seemed to want to win it more than we did.

"But we are a young team and we have to learn a lesson from that. We are determined not to let the cup exit affect the way we approach the games we have left," he added.

Having lost the leadership of the Premiership the day before on goal difference to FA Cup-free Manchester United, who made the most of one of the league games they had in hand by beating Middlesbrough, it was the most disappointing week-end of the season for the Elland Road lads.

At least Villa manager John Gregory had some heartening words for the United camp. "I believe Leeds have enough quality in their side to remain up there with the best," he said.

"Having gone out of the FA Cup they are left to concentrate on the league and the UEFA Cup and I think they have enough bodies in their squad to cope with the challenge. Their exit from the FA Cup hasn't changed my mind on this," he added.

Manchester United's expected victory at Sheffield Wednesday, in their one remaining outstanding fixture, put the Reds three points ahead of David O'Leary's side who knew they faced a vitally important two week period if they were to stay on the heels of their arch rivals.

> ## "Having gone out of the FA Cup they are left to concentrate on the league and the UEFA Cup and I think they have enough bodies in their squad to cope with the challenge. Their exit from the FA Cup hasn't changed my mind on this."
>
> John Gregory

The diminutive Carbone completed his hat-trick with two second half goals – the first that super 35 yard shot that caught Martyn off his line – and then put it down to a pair of blue painted lucky old boots!

"Scoring had been a problem for me and I was lying awake one night thinking about the Leeds game and I suddenly remembered I had a pair of old boots in a cupboard downstairs. I got up, found them, tried them on and they felt good. I had done well in them in the past so I decided to wear them against Leeds – and they did the trick for me," he explained.

United, however, knew – and accepted – that they had only themselves to blame for such a disappointing cup exit.

The trip to fourth-placed Liverpool, a home game against George Graham's Tottenham side and the visit to Elland Road of Sir Alex Ferguson's team was a daunting prospect. But as Nigel Martyn stressed: "The young lads in the side fear no one. They believe they can go out and win every game, no matter who they are playing."

LIVERPOOL boss, Gerard Houllier surprised many after his team had beaten United in the second game of the season when he tipped David O'Leary's young side to be serious title challengers.

"I'm not too sure all that many people agreed with me but they have shown excellent form. I admire the job David O'Leary is doing at Leeds and admire the type of positive football Leeds try to play," he said.

But Houllier had his men fired up for the return meeting between the two teams at Anfield and Liverpool stormed their way to a 3-1 victory with three thunderbolt goals, from Dietmar Hamann, Patrik Berger and substitute Danny Murphy. Lee Bowyer's downward header to Jason Wilcox's bouncing left wing cross accounted for United's goal that had briefly put United back on level terms.

Manchester United's 3-2 defeat of Coventry at Old Trafford, meant O'Leary's side were six points adrift. But they held on to second place, courtesy of Bradford City, who beat Arsenal 2-1 at Valley Parade to prevent the Gunners from getting the three points that would have hoisted them into second place and dropped Leeds into third.

"Manchester United are the best team in the country and they clearly benefited from this set of results," O'Leary said. "In my view Arsenal are the second best and ourselves and Liverpool are trying to break up that monopoly."

Referee Mike Reed, not exactly a stranger to controversy, created more of the same and ran into trouble with the Premier League when he punched the air with apparent delight at Berger's stunning strike. Hardly the action you would want - or expect - to see from an impartial official.

But the Birmingham based referee explained he felt elated at having allowed play to continue when he could have halted it for a foul on another Liverpool player, Vladimir Smicer. "I punched the air somewhat in triumph at a successful advantage I played for the goal," he explained.

While the Premier League asked Reed to explain his actions, United were far from up tight about it. Chairman Peter Ridsdale said: "I think the best thing is to let sleeping dogs lie.

"In saw the referee punch the air and I think he did genuinely do it because he had let play go on and a goal was scored as a result. I thought the referee handled the game very well for both sides. Liverpool scored three excellent goals and were the better team."

Reed eventually suffered a rap over the knuckles from the FA, who felt his actions, however motivated, could be open to misinterpretation by supporters. He also had a televised match taken from him.

Liverpool certainly deserved their victory – a point conceded by United manager David O'Leary. They were quicker to the ball, channelled their aggression in the right direction and were the more positive side all round. They were particularly strong in midfield, too, which helped to establish their supremacy. How United must have wished for the presence of David Batty.

"We battled back into the game briefly but we are missing the likes of Batty and Lucas Radebe," the United manager admitted. "Those players are very vital to us and very experienced and the younger lads rely on them a lot. The sooner we have them back the better. When you go to a place like Liverpool those type of players count," he added.

The defeat at Anfield was United's fourth in six outings and writers and broadcasters, who not long ago had taken issue with O'Leary and criticised him when he warned against expecting too much too soon from his young side, were now changing their minds and writing them off!

"When we set out this season our target was to break into the Premiership's top three and qualify for the Champions' League and if we manage that it will be a great achievement for such a young side. We will have continued our progress," O'Leary pointed out.

His side had not given up on the title. Far from it. "Don't write us off," he warned. "There are still a lot of games to play. We are going to have 'dips' in form and results but we have shown we can bounce back before. We are not giving up on the title but any team winning it will have to top Manchester United."

Nigel Martyn echoed his manager's feelings. "Manchester United are going to take some catching. They have a great opportunity now to go on and retain the title. But I wouldn't say it's all over just yet. There might still be a few twists and turns to come.

"Both United and Arsenal can expect some of what we had at Anfield when they play Liverpool because they raise their game against top teams," he added.

Bowyer's goal, of course, meant nothing in the final analysis but it did demonstrate the creative ability again of young McPhail, whose excellent pass to Wilcox was a key factor.

The 20-year-old midfielder also provided the cross Bakke scored from in the FA Cup defeat at Villa and it was his superb pass that sent Wilcox clear for his goal at Sunderland.

"Since I got into the side on a regular basis it's gone well for me. Everything seems to be going to plan for me," McPhail said. "I had a very good pre-season but then I went with Ireland and injured my ankle which put me out for nearly three months. When I got over that I was back in the first team after playing just one reserve game and that was a welcome surprise.

"I hadn't expected to be back in the first team after just one reserve outing but I had worked hard during my injury lay off to keep as fit as possible and to make sure I kept my weight down and that helped me," he added.

His first team re-appearance was in the Worthington Cup victory over Blackburn Rovers in October but he had to wait 15 matches to put his name on the first team scoresheet with a brace against Chelsea at Stamford Bridge.

"It was good to get that first goal out of the way – it is probably the hardest one to get," he said. "Once I got it, it was a great feeling but I find it equally satisfying if I lay on a goal for someone else.

"We are all in the team to do various jobs and as a midfield player one of my main tasks is to try to set up goal-scoring chances. I get a real buzz if I can spot on opening and hit a pass that opens up a defence and puts one of our lads in with a scoring chance," he said.

Left-footed McPhail has a good understanding with left-back Ian Harte, which he points out is hardly surprising in view of the number of years they have played football together. "We have played together since we were 15 years old and we know what each other is thinking. He knows that I want the ball as much as I can," he said.

But McPhail also found little difficulty in forging a good working relationship with newcomer Jason Wilcox. "Jason is an all round great player and all good players are easy to play with. He wants the ball and whenever I get the opportunity I try to give him the ball because he is the sort of player who will make more goals for us from his accurate crosses or score some himself by cutting in and having a shot.

"Jason has a lot of experience. He has a championship medal with Blackburn and going into the last few months of the season I think we are going to need experience. We also need David Batty back in the team and Lucas Radebe to help us through. We are still chasing the title and hopefully we can progress in the UEFA Cup too," McPhail added.

> **"Once I got it, it was a great feeling but I find it equally satisfying if I lay on a goal for someone else."**
>
> John McPhail

The young Irishman, who played for his country at Under-15, Under-16, Under-18 and Under-21 levels and was selected in the full international squad for the friendly game against the Czech Republic before having to withdraw through injury, says he is indebted to United for his development.

He signed a new five-year contract with United at the start of the season and he hopes to play the whole of his career with the club. "I never want to leave here," he told me. "I have grown up here since I was 15 and I love the place. I don't ever want to leave and I think if you ask any of the young lads who grew up with the club, like Jonathan Woodgate, Alan Smith or Harry Kewell, I think they would say the same," McPhail added.

"If you have a lot of lads growing up together and coming through to the first team you have a great family atmosphere. Manchester United have done it successfully over the last eight years or so and if you ask the likes of Paul Scholes and Nicky Butt, I don't think they will want to leave Old Trafford," he said.

McPhail's loyalty – and chairman Peter Ridsdale's desire to ward off clubs seeking to prise talented youngster's away – led to the 20-year-old being called in for more contract talks during the season aimed at a financial upgrade. "When we gave him a five year contract the previous summer he was not a regular in the first team," Ridsdale explained.

"Since then he has managed to establish himself as a regular in the senior side and I felt he ought to be paid more money now that he is playing first team football. We try to reward people who do well for the club and the new deal will reflect that," he added.

ANOTHER return to Elland Road of former manager George Graham and his Tottenham side presented United's next hurdle and David O'Leary was having none of the 'George v David' hype which had accompanied the build up to more recent meetings between the two clubs.

THE rigours of the championship campaign were put aside for a few hours the night after the Liverpool defeat when United players old and new joined a gathering of 350 at the Elland Road banqueting suite to celebrate the club's 80 years of existence.

Players who donned the United shirt in the 1940s, Len Browning, Jimmy Dunn and Frank Dudley, right through to present-day stars Lee Bowyer, Nigel Martyn and Harry Kewell, were at the event, which was compered by TV commentator John Helm.

Ex-Liverpool hard man Tommy Smith, dyed-in-the wool Chelsea man Peter Osgood and ex-Arsenal and Leicester City defender Frank McLintock all recalled incidents when they played against Don Revie's United side.

Osgood, who spoke of many face-to-face confrontations with Norman Hunter - incidentally the two are truly good friends now! - recalled some bruising encounters but he said it had been a privilege to have played against one of the best teams in the world. Then he quipped: "I always thought that playing against Leeds was like taking on my mother-in-law and my wife because Billy Bremner and Jack Charlton never stopped moaning!"

Selecting United's team of the century was a task entrusted to chairman Peter Ridsdale, former manager Jimmy Armfield, life-long supporter Ron Deighton and the author of this book.

Not an easy task but after much deliberation we came up with the following: Nigel Martyn; Paul Reaney, Jack Charlton, Norman Hunter, Terry Cooper; Peter Lorimer, Billy Bremner, Johnny Giles, Harry Kewell, Allan Clarke, and John Charles. The subs chosen were: Paul Madeley, Tony Currie and David Harvey.

"It looks a great team on paper, doesn't it? Naturally, perhaps, players from the successful Revie era figure prominently in it but I was pleased both Nigel and Harry, from the present side, got in," said the chairman.

In all 36 United players – past and present – attended the dinner. They were: Len Browning (1946-1951), Jimmy Dunn (47-59), Frank Dudley (49-51), Harold Williams (49-57), John Charles (49-57 and 62), Albert Nightingale (52-56) Jack Charlton (52-73), Roy Wood (52-60), Bobby Forrest (52-57), Jack Overfield (53-60), Noel Peyton (58-63), Norman Hunter (60-76), Paul Reaney (61-78), Bobby Collins (62-67), Paul Madeley (62-80), Peter Lorimer (62-79 and 83-86), Johnny Giles (63-75), Alan Peacock (64-67), Mike O'Grady (65-69), Terry Yorath (67-76), Allan Clarke (69-78), Trevor Cherry (72-82), Roy Ellam (72-74), Tony Currie (76-79), Brian Flynn (77-82), Brendan Ormsby (86-90), John McClelland (89-92), John Hendrie (89-90), Gordon Strachan (89-95), Chris Fairclough (89-95), Lee Chapman (90-93), Gary McAllister (90-96), Tony Dorigo (91-97), Harry Kewell (95-), Nigel Martyn (96-) and Lee Bowyer (96-).

He made that perfectly clear in his pre-match Press conference. "Before you ask, yes, we are still friends. I rang George on Christmas day to wish him all the best. But that's all I am saying," the United boss told the assembled media.

That topic having been ruled out of order, talk centred on the importance of the game and the need for United, six points adrift following their defeat at Liverpool, to take maximum points to stay on the heels of Manchester United.

At the end of a very competitive match United had their three points and, with Manchester United going down 3-0 at Newcastle, the gap between first and second narrowed to three points. Harry Kewell's tenth goal of the season – a piece of individual skill in which he headed the ball over advancing keeper Ian Walker and then cut inside Sol Campbell to fire into the empty net - sank Spurs.

Passions, however, boiled over in a second half that was marred by some unsavoury incidents, and an unsightly melee when most of the players on the field got themselves involved. The melee, described by Spurs boss as a 'handbags' affair, followed an ill-judged and ferocious tackle on Spurs' Stephen Clemence by Lee Bowyer.

Inquests into the incidents resulted in the FA charging both United and Tottenham with failing to control their players and United full-back Ian Harte with an individual case of misconduct for his last minute clash with Chris Perry.

But as far as the melee was concerned most of the players appeared keen to prevent any trouble starting. No player was seen to throw a punch.

Referee Dermot Gallagher, who contented himself by showing Bowyer the yellow card when it was apparent that Spurs' players felt the red card had been warranted, booked four United men in all and five Spurs' players in the game.

The incidents provided welcome ammunition for those who maybe had found it hard to heap praise

■ Lee Bowyer supports the full weight of Tottenham's Sol Campbell.

onto a United side schooled by David O'Leary and Eddie Gray in the art of exciting open football.

With an eye cast back to the successful era of Don Revie, when United were the team the Press, particularly those with a southern base, loved to hate, the Daily Mail found it too good an opportunity to miss. "The snarling face of ugly old Leeds," said the headline on their match report.

The paper were keen to stick with the word 'ugly' and they repeated it in the same edition on a back page story titled: "FA to launch probe into ugly clashes at Chelsea and Leeds."

United chairman Peter Ridsdale reacted to the FA charges by immediately requesting a personal hearing for the club and for Ian Harte. "I was surprised at the charges in the sense that on Saturday after the game I didn't expect anything, on the basis that nothing took place in the match that the referee or his officials hadn't seen," the chairman said.

"I wasn't surprised once I saw the media hysteria on Sunday and Monday which was almost inviting the FA to charge us.

"But I think, having watched Leeds United for 38 years and without wanting to prejudice anything I had included in our defence, I was somewhat taken aback that the events on Saturday which were seen by all the officials, required the FA to intervene," he added.

> "I wasn't surprised once I saw the media hysteria on Sunday and Monday which was almost inviting the FA to charge us."
>
> Peter Ridsdale

of Leeds and Manchester prepared to go head-to-head in a crucial Premiership fixture at Elland Road. Reds boss, Sir Alex Ferguson, was shown in print appealing for match referee Paul Jones to 'be strong' when he refereed the game.

This was a similar ploy on the part of the Reds boss to one he used before his side played Inter-Milan at the San Siro Stadium the previous season. There was little doubt, though, that while the Reds had 'escaped' the wrath of the FA, the recent behaviour of some of their players had left them under scrutiny.

So the Elland Road stage was set for a tasty bit of Sunday lunchtime fare.

Before then, however, the Elland Road club had due cause for satisfaction when Howard Wilkinson included six United players – Jonathan Woodgate, Lee Bowyer, Michael Bridges, Alan Smith, Danny Mills and Paul Robinson - in England's Under-21 squad for the friendly international against Argentina at Fulham's Craven Cottage ground.

In addition Matthew Jones, was selected by Wales for their game in Qatar with Gary Kelly, Ian Harte and Stephen McPhail included in the Republic of Ireland squad to prepare for the Czech Republic while Eirik Bakke was called up by Norway, who were to play Turkey. Harry Kewell linked up with Australia for a European friendly.

There was also great satisfaction for Jason Wilcox, whose move to Elland Road from Blackburn Rovers and a return to his favoured left wing role, earned him a deserved call-up to Kevin Keegan's full England squad along, of course, with goalkeeper Nigel Martyn, for the friendly against Argentina.

The 28-year-old winger, who had two previous full international caps – one as substitute - to his credit, was delighted to have been included especially allowing for the fact that in the previous couple of months he had been faced with settling

Wimbledon and Chelsea along with Dons' coach Mick Harford, Chelsea midfielder Dennis Wise and Dons' defender Kenny Cunningham, also found themselves charged by the FA. Surprisingly though Manchester United, whose dissenting players had frequently been seen on television and in newspapers confronting referees in intimidating fashion when decisions had gone against them, were not.

It was against this background that the Uniteds

into new surroundings following his first ever transfer.

"It was a strange couple of months for me so being selected in the England squad was great news," Wilcox said.

"My world was turned upside down when I left Blackburn where I had played all my career but joining a club who were top of the Premiership was wonderful for me," he recalled.

"I had been at Blackburn such a long time and all of a sudden they agreed to sell me. I have to admit it was a bit of a jolt. There was a mixture of disappointment in that but also excitement because I was joining one of the best clubs in the country – Leeds are a massive club," he added.

"Leaving Blackburn was something I never expected to happen. Brian Kidd made me captain

can be ripped from under you," he said.

"There is no way I am going to get carried away after playing five or six games while I am not going to start taking any credit for the current league position. The most important thing for me is that the side wins. I am very much a team man.

"I have been very impressed with David O'Leary and Eddie Gray and if I get left out of the team I will be disappointed but there will be no complaints from me because football is a team game and there will be a reason for it. Leeds United are bigger than any one player," he said.

A married man, he and his wife, Joanne, have three children, eight-year-old Samuel, Emily (six) and Bethany (two), Wilcox remained in his

> "You rack your brains to think why you are suddenly not wanted but this sort of thing happens in football."
>
> Jason Wilcox

and I could even see me carrying on in football there after I had finished playing. Then, all of a sudden, everything changed. You rack your brains to think why you are suddenly not wanted but this sort of thing happens in football.

"I was really proud to have been captain and I had great and sad times there. I enjoyed everything about the club both on the field and off it.

"All that has gone now and I have absolutely no regrets about leaving because I have come to a club where things are on the up and where the manager, David O'Leary, and his assistant, Eddie Gray, have confidence in me. I hope that has translated on to the pitch," he added.

Bolton born Wilcox, who joined the Ewood Park club as a trainee, expressed his relief at the way he had slotted into life at Elland Road but after just a handful of games for United he was not taking anything for granted. "I have been in the game long enough to know that when things are going well for you there is always the chance the carpet

Manchester home preferring to make the journey to Leeds each day. "It's not much of a problem for me and if it became one then I would move. But the two oldest children are settled in and doing well at school and I did not want to move them," he explained.

As expected Wilcox retained his place in United's starting line-up for the big clash with the men from Old Trafford. Michael Bridges and Stephen McPhail failed late fitness tests and United were again without long term injury victim David Batty while Michael Duberry was unavailable because of suspension.

Lucas Radebe was back from African Nations Cup duty with South Africa and was pushed into action although not fully recovered from an ankle injury. Sir Alex Ferguson sensationally dropped David Beckham from the Reds' side following a reported training ground bust-up, which he refused to enlarge upon.

More than 40,000 spectators were in the Elland Road stadium for a game that was vital to both sides, Leeds because victory would put them level with the leaders on points and the Reds because it would put them six points in the clear.

A goal from Andy Cole in the 52nd minute settled the issue in the Lancashire team's favour, though David O'Leary's side hit the woodwork three times. Alan Smith was the last to do so, with an angled shot that saw the ball rebound to the unmarked Lee Bowyer who, to his great embarrassment, fired over from six yards.

It wasn't his, or Leeds' day, though Reds boss Sir Alex Ferguson admitted there wasn't much between the two sides on the day. "It was a very tight game but I thought we just about deserved to win it. The game was so condensed you always thought that whoever scored first would win. Fortunately it was us," he said.

The result left the Elland Road side with a mountain to climb in respect of winning the championship and while their initial target had been to finish in the top three and qualify for the Champions League, O'Leary and his boys pledged to keep the title pressure on the Reds.

"We've 13 games left with 39 points at stake – that's a lot of points to play for. No one here is giving up on it," Republic of Ireland international Gary Kelly said. "We're still in there with a shout."

With Arsenal strong enough to keep up their challenge, Liverpool making a determined late surge and Chelsea not yet out of things, O'Leary's lads needed to keep on picking up points in their bid to finish in the top three.

Welsh international Matthew Jones admitted that the mood in the home dressing room after the game was one of dejection. "It's much different to what it normally is after a match. We were very confident going into the game, we played well enough and had our chances but we felt gutted at being knocked back," he said.

If the victory had not yet assured the Reds of the title, it had certainly made them the overwhelming favourites. "It's going to be very hard for us now but with 13 games still to play we're not about to give up. It is an adventure for us and we'll give it our best shot, make no mistake about that," O'Leary said.

"I have said already that we'll make mistakes and have our set-backs but this season will only make us better for the experience. We really wanted to put one over Manchester United but it's not the end of the world because we didn't. We know, though, that we are improving and becoming mentally stronger," he added.

NO FEWER than 26 attempts at goal – yet not one that really counted. Rarely can a team that had so many strikes at the target have had to be content at the end with a goalless scoreline. Yet that was the bizarre story of Leeds United's goalless draw against Middlesbrough at the Riverside Stadium.

In an open game - Middlesbrough managed 12 attempts at Nigel Martyn's goal without success – David O'Leary's men allowed two precious points to get away from them and as Manchester United took only a point at Wimbledon, a great opportunity to close the gap at the top was missed.

> "We've 13 games left with 39 points at stake – that's a lot of points to play for. No one here is giving up on it."
>
> Gary Kelly

In the opening seconds Lee Bowyer had the ball in the Boro net for what should have been a goal but it was wrongly disallowed by the linesman's flag for offside but the battling midfielder had a great chance to snatch the points for United late on which he fluffed.

It was the second game in succession the England Under 21 man had missed a good opportunity late in a match. He had a great chance to grab an equaliser against Manchester United but failed to capitalise.

"We could do with a change of luck," Harry Kewell remarked after the Boro draw. "Nine times out of ten 'Bows' would have scored from one of his chances but we should have won the game. We hit the target so many times without getting one in.

> "I don't agree that this is a sticky patch for us, not when you see how many chances we have made in recent matches. If we keep on doing what we have been doing the points and the wins will come to us."
>
> Harry Kewell

"We should have scored from a couple of great chances but this was just one of those days for us. All the same it would have been nice to win when Manchester United drew. There was a real feeling of disappointment in our dressing room because we expected to get something more than we did from this game," he said

But the Australian striker was not too despondent. "I don't agree that this is a sticky patch for us, not when you see how many chances we have made in recent matches. If we keep on doing what we have been doing the points and the wins will come to us. We are still in a very strong position," he added.

O'Leary had Gary Kelly, Stephen McPhail, Eirik Bakke and Matthew Jones unavailable as well as long term injury victim David Batty, for the game against Middlesbrough but Alfie Haaland and David Hopkin provided the manager with a couple of major plus signs.

United opted to play with three central defenders, Haaland slotting between Lucas Radebe and Jonathan Woodgate, and the Norwegian, overlooked for much of the season, was outstanding. Haaland came in having played only a handful of first team games in the season amid rumours linking him with a possible transfer to First Division promotion seekers Manchester City.

He certainly did his stuff, with a no-nonsense defensive display while Hopkin, out of action for over three months following an operation, turned in a solid performance in a central midfield 'holding' role.

CHAPTER NINE

THE ITALIAN JOB

CHAMPIONSHIP demands and concerns were now put on the back boiler as attention turned once again to the UEFA Cup and in particular United's return to Rome for another meeting with the crack Italian side AS Roma.

Liverpool manager Gerard Houllier had kindly provided David O'Leary with a video of one of Roma's recent matches – a gesture much appreciated by the United boss – but viewing it served only to underline what a good side Roma were.

on their chartered plane the day before the game and were followed later by seven planeloads of supporters keen to see their side in action against the Romans in that ancient city. Estimations were that approaching 6,000 fans had made the journey to support their side – a quite amazing show of loyalty.

After what Alan Smith described as a 'choppy' landing at Rome's Ciampino airport, United journeyed to their five star hotel but not long after checking in, the players were on their way by

> "They are a class side. They are tremendous up front, have a great midfield and a very solid defence. Other than that, they're not much good!"
>
> David O'Leary

Asked by one Italian journalist what he admired about Roma the United boss replied: "They are a class side. They are tremendous up front, have a great midfield and a very solid defence. Other than that, they're not much good!"

The United manager had also made a couple of trips to watch Roma for himself and nothing he saw altered his opinion that here was great side – one he felt that could go all the way and win the UEFA Cup. "They'll take some beating but we've done marvellously well to get as far as we have and we'll give it a good 'go.' You can bet on that," he said.

United's players and management flew to Italy

coach to Rome's impressive Olympic Stadium for a training session.

Few who visit the stadium can fail to be anything other than impressed with its lay out and the facilities it offers players and spectators alike. It's an imposing place. On this occasion though the pitch left something to be desired, as Smithy pointed out.

"It wasn't the best pitch we've seen this season but with Lazio, as well as Roma, using it, maybe that had something to do with it," he said.

United trained for about an hour before David

O'Leary called a halt to the proceedings and made his way to give the customary pitch-side pre-match Press Conference and spoke of the enormity of the task he felt was awaiting his team 24 hours later.

The degree of difficulty was not lost on United chairman Peter Ridsdale either. As an incentive he even offered to loan his new Aston Martin DB7 to Michael Bridges for a week if the former Sunderland man scored the winning goal in Rome.

Having seen the bold policy of playing Haaland in a three man back-line work so well at Middlesbrough, despite the Norwegian having started only a handful of games this season, O'Leary kept faith with that formation for the first leg against Roma.

But United's side showed four changes in all, Gary Kelly and Eirik Bakke returning after suspension, Michael Bridges after injury and there was a recall for young Welshman Matthew Jones.

Danny Mills, David Hopkin and Alan Smith had to be content with a place on the substitute's bench. Winger Jason Wilcox stayed at home because of a two-and-a-half-year-old European ban imposed after he was sent off for two bookable offences in his last European game for his previous club, Blackburn.

"I wasn't too pleased at being forced to miss this trip," he said. "Having to serve a one match ban so long after the offence is a bit of a joke, in my view. Playing in a big stadium like the Olympic in Rome would have a great experience for me," added Wilcox, who had to be content with watching the game at home on television.

Smith, meanwhile, was disappointed not to be in the side from the start. "I'm always disappointed when I'm not in the side. All players are," he said. "But I got on for the last half hour and enjoyed it. Everyone worked very hard and Nigel had a great game and made some wonderful saves," he added.

Although United could not snatch an away goal, keeping the Italian side goalless left manager David O'Leary understandably proud of his players. "They did magnificently well in one of the biggest stadiums in the world and against some of the best players in the world. It was one of the proudest nights of my career," he said.

Although United had taken on and been narrowly beaten by Roma in the previous season's UEFA Cup competition, Roma had a new coach in Fabio Capello, a former Milan and Real Madrid star, and several new players.

■ Manager David O'Leary looks relaxed and in control as he supervises Leeds United 's training before the UEFA Cup tie in Rome.

A deal of £17million had brought in Japan's most famous player Hidetoshi Nakata, from Perugia, while £15million was shelled out to sign striker Vincenzo Montella from Sampdoria. Brazilian international midfield man, Marcos Assuncao had been signed and goalkeeper Francesco Antonioli had joined from Bologna.

French World Cup squad man Vincent Candela and Brazilians Zago, Aldair and Cafu remained from last season as did Totti, who many people rated as Roma's best player, and striker Marco Delvecchio, scorer of the goal that put United out of last season's UEFA Cup. A daunting prospect to say the least. No wonder Roma had impressed O'Leary with their class and power when he watched them.

His own players, however, had proved themselves to be an emerging side of talent and tenacity and they were not unduly perturbed by the prospect of facing such strong and highly rated opponents. "We have respect for every team we play against but fear doesn't come into it," Alan Smith said.

■ Nigel Martyn, the hero of Leeds United's 1st leg UEFA Cup tie in Rome with some tremendous goalkeeping, is rewarded with this hug from manager David O'Leary.

"I'm very proud of the way my kids held on."

David O'Leary

United went very close to giving the Romans an early shock when Eirik Bakke, who met Gary Kelly's right wing cross, got in a sharp downward header which Antonioli managed to block with a foot.

After that early encouragement it was mainly defensive work for United in the rest of the first half, with Nigel Martyn often in the thick of the action, though Harry Kewell, put through by Michael Bridges, fired wide from a good scoring opportunity midway through the first period.

Kewell was narrowly wide with another effort early in the second half but as the game went on, United were faced with more defensive work and again Martyn showed his class.

Relief at the end was etched on the faces of United fans. "I'm very proud of the way my kids held on," O'Leary said. "They were a real credit to themselves and the club. They are learning their trade on the front line and they battle for each other. We don't lack character - that was obvious from this display - but we did well to hold out against such a quality side," he added.

United had done the first part of their job and the tie was nicely poised for the return leg.

Roma boss Capello, who played for Juventus against United in both legs of the 1971 UEFA Cup final, which ended with a 3-3 aggregate score and gave United the trophy on the away goals rule, had become increasingly frustrated as the game went on. At one stage he angrily aimed a kick at the dug-out as his strikers failed to make the break-through.

His demeanour was altogether calmer and more rational when he conducted the after-match Press conference and paid tribute to Martyn's heroics in the United goal. "He was Leeds' best player and kept them in the game," Capello said. "Without him we would have won the game. The scoreline is false because we played better than Leeds," he added.

But Capello was not unduly worried by the state of the tie. He knew he had players in his side who were always capable of scoring a goal and if Roma managed one at Elland Road, then United would have to score twice to go through. "It's a 50-50 situation now and Leeds will have to be more positive than they were in Rome," he added.

The United manager did not attend the after match conference. He and his players made a quick getaway to catch their planned late night flight back to Leeds. Preparing for the home Premier League game against Coventry City was now high on the agenda.

Having taken only one point from the last six played for, O'Leary was well aware his side desperately needed to beat Coventry to keep the pressure on Manchester United and stay ahead of the clubs chasing a Champions League place.

Sir Alex Ferguson's side had been held to a home draw by their arch rivals Liverpool 24 hours before O'Leary's men faced Coventry but the points gap between first and second place had increased to seven.

The Elland Road side went into their clash with the Sky Blues on the back of a lean spell in relation to goals. A little matter of five-and-a-half-

before half time when Eirik Bakke found Kewell and he swept a superb pass into space for Bridges to run onto and round goalkeeper Magnus Hedman to score his 15th goal of the season. A dominant United should have had more goals to show for their superiority, but Jason Wilcox did make it 3-0 just before the end with his second goal for United and his first at Elland Road.

"It was satisfying to get my first home goal for Leeds though the important thing was that we won the game. I would far rather not score and finish on the winning side than score and end up losing," he added.

"Considering how tough our game in Rome was and taking into account all the travelling, the way we played against Coventry was marvellous," remarked O'Leary whose side were now only four points adrift of the leaders.

"I've been chasing teams as a player and with three points at stake for a win, which is a great thing, you can close a gap very quickly. It is up to us to keep on battling away. We'll go out to try to win every game and see where that gets us. We've not done too badly so far using that approach," he added.

The United manager, however, could not hide

> ## "Considering how tough our game in Rome was and taking into account all the travelling, they way we played against Coventry was marvellous."
>
> David O'Leary

hours playing time had elapsed since United last scored a goal – Harry Kewell's 23rd minute winner against Tottenham. Manager and players alike had made the same encouraging noises leading up to the game. "We're creating plenty of chances so there's not too much wrong," was the theme.

Ideally United needed a good start against the Sky Blues and they got it, Kewell ending the barren spell after 342 minutes without a goal with a successful fifth minute strike following Ian Harte's free kick.

Michael Bridges put United two goals up shortly

his delight at Bridges having netted his 15th goal of the campaign. But O'Leary stressed there would be no let up in efforts to turn the 21-year-old into an even more lethal striker.

"He possesses the attributes to eventually become the complete player but for the time being I will continue to be hard and demanding on him in an attempt to further improve his skills," said the United boss.

"I think eventually he can be a quality player for England because I liken him to Dennis Bergkamp.

He is that type of link up player. But he is still young with a lot more to learn but with his talent he has a great chance to become a tremendous player," he added.

The games were now coming thick and fast and no sooner had United accounted for Coventry, than the second leg of the UEFA Cup tie against AS Roma was looming large. Media applications for places at Elland Road had poured in, giving Press Officer Dick Wright a major headache. His problem was that the club had received far more applications than they had places.

Teams from such countries as Italy, Spain and France traditionally have a large media following and as the communications industry is rapidly expanding, football clubs receive far more applications now than they ever did.

Some clubs are able to cope with the problem better than others – Roma being one because they play in Italy's Olympic Stadium where their spacious and up to the minute facilities are second to none.

Underlining how widespread was the demand for Press tickets, were applications from 11 Japanese media representatives – their interest being in Roma's one Japanese player, Hidetoshi Nakata – while several Italian television and radio stations as well as 65 journalists covered the game. Demands on phone lines and seats were as high as they had ever been.

In all there were over 150 media applications for places and extra seats had to be found to satisfy demand. "It is a question of trying to keep everyone happy but I doubt I'll be able to please everyone," he forecast. But things went reasonably smoothly and no major problem was reported.

United fans had bought up all their seats for a game that was as big as they come and in anticipation of another great European night at Elland Road. Meanwhile, O'Leary primed talented striker Harry Kewell by reminding him of a private bet he had struck with the young Australian.

Having moved Kewell from a wide left role to that of striker, O'Leary was keen to see more goals from the player. "I've given him a certain target for the season and if he reaches it he'll win a nice little

wager," said the United boss. "He's a bit to go yet but I would be delighted to pay up."

Like all top players Kewell relishes the chance to perform on the big stage. "He enjoys playing at such places as Old Trafford and the Olympic Stadium in Rome. I thought he was wonderful out there in the first leg. Put him on the big stage and he revels in it," O'Leary said.

Inevitably with such a talented player there exists speculation that so called bigger clubs in Italy or other countries might be tempted to move in for him. And Harry himself had gone on record as saying that he might want to try his luck in Italy when he reached his mid twenties.

Keeping him happy at Leeds when he reaches that age might be difficult. But chairman Peter Ridsdale, who last summer had persuaded the young striker to sign a new four year deal reported to be worth about £18,000 per week, made it clear every attempt would be made to see the player remained at the club.

"There is little doubt in my mind that Harry, should he continue his progress, could rank among the top eight players in the country," Ridsdale said.

When it comes to another contract for the Australian, United are inevitably going to have to dig deep. If they don't, others undoubtedly will. But the United chairman does not see a problem in paying top money if the player in question has the skill and deserves it. "In my mind there is no problem making a player one of the best paid in the country if he truly merits it," he added.

The full-house signs were in place when the talented and wealthy Romans arrived for the second leg still confident of disposing of O'Leary's young European upstarts. With such talented forwards as Delvecchio, Totti and Montella, AS Roma were strongly fancied to get a goal – which would have left United needing to score twice for victory.

United might well have been regarded as novices in European terms but try telling that to O'Leary's players. Fear is a word missing from their vocabulary. And on what turned into one of the best European nights at the stadium down the years, United ran out surprise 1-0 winners.

Victory confounded O'Leary's pre-match comment that he felt his side had gone as far as they could in this season's competition. "Anything beyond this stage would be a wonderful bonus for us all," he had said.

The goal that sent United into their first European quarter-final for a quarter of a century was netted by Kewell though all the United players were heroes on a euphoric night which ended with the Italians having Candela and Zago sent off in the dying seconds. Roma found defeat particularly hard to take.

■ Early Bath Romans
It's scratch your head time for AS
Roma stars Vincent Candella (left)
and Zago as they head for the
dressing room after being sent off
in the UEFA Cup tie at Elland Road.

"It was a special goal but everyone knows what Harry can do," said Gary Kelly. "He's a world class player and I would make him man-of-the-match but there were ten other men out there behind him. Really it was an outstanding team performance crowned by Harry's goal," added the Republic of Ireland defender.

As Kelly said, United had ridden their luck in the first leg in Rome when Nigel Martyn was - and needed to be - in outstanding form but that was very much in the past as United and their fans celebrated a famous Elland Road triumph.

No one was more delighted with the outcome than Norwegian international defender Alfie Haaland, who threw his shirt into the West Stand at the end. "It was a show of appreciation on my part," he said.

"I had done so much warming up on the sidelines this season that I was actually on first

name terms with a lot of the fans there," he quipped.

Despite not having been a regular in the senior side this term, Haaland remained a very popular character with United supporters. He was given the sponsor's Man-of-the-Match award against Roma and I dare say few would argue against that.

Haaland had returned to first team action at Middlesbrough four games earlier in a three man back line and fitted in so well he held onto his place for the game in Rome. In both matches United kept clean sheets. He was back on the bench for the home game against Coventry but came in at half time when Jonathan Woodgate stayed off because of a calf injury and helped United keep another clean sheet.

A second meeting with Delvecchio and Co. was Haaland's lot in the return leg of the UEFA Cup when again United's defence held fast. "That's four clean sheets for us in the games I have played which is very nice and satisfying. It was a special night with a great atmosphere," Haaland said.

"Delvecchio is a handful but Roma have world class players up there. They are one of the best teams in the world and beating them was a brilliant scalp for us. We are not as good as Roma yet but we are trying to get there," he added.

It was Haaland's determined charge forward that laid the foundations for the all-important goal. "We knew we had to get a goal and we had had a couple of half chances. But it wasn't really happening for us. Everyone had to try to make something happen, including me. Maybe Harry would not have been allowed that strike if I hadn't got forward," he said.

The Norwegian's season had seemed to be heading nowhere and he had been linked with a move out of Elland Road. He admitted he had been uncertain about his future with United. "I wasn't getting picked for the team and when that happens to a player he begins to think his future may be elsewhere. Some weeks ago it didn't look too promising for me but suddenly it all turns around and you find you are back in the team," he added.

"Football is a squad game and the management

■ It's all over. Harry Kewell sinks to the ground (above) after scoring the goal that put much fancied AS Roma out of the UEFA Cup.

■ That's my boy! David O'Leary is as delighted as can be as he runs to congratulate Kewell (below) after his match winning goal.

pointed out to me that I would be needed at some stage and they proved they were right. If I hadn't have had a chance then it would probably have been better for me and for the club if I went elsewhere. But they haven't let me go yet and I like it at Leeds. The fans are great and have been very good to me," he said.

"The future of this club looks brilliant and I don't want to leave," Haaland added. But speculation about his future turned out eventually to have had more than grain of truth about it when the Norwegian was subsequently transferred to the Maine Road club in a £2.8million summer deal.

Kewell, all too often a man of very few words, seemed to take his vital goal against Roma well within his stride. "My aim is to try to be consistent and to score as many goals as I can. I don't get carried away," he said.

"I find it enjoyable to play against teams I have never come up against before but at the end of the day you have to go out and do the business – and that's what we did against Roma," he added.

His goal against the Italian Serie A side took his tally for the season to 12. It was his third in the UEFA Cup and was the ideal way to sign off for the

one match ban that kept him out of United's next fixture – a Premiership clash with near neighbours Bradford City at Valley Parade.

With just two days to rest up and prepare for what was always likely to be a hard and physical 'derby' clash against City, concern was expressed that disposing of Roma might have taken that bit too much out of the United players.

We needn't have worried. O'Leary's men rose to the challenge admirably to record their eighth away league win of the season with a 2-1 success, courtesy of a double strike from Michael Bridges. United's leading marksman put his side ahead after 12 minutes when he forced in an angled effort from an Ian Harte free kick and scored his second in the 67th minute when Alan Smith knocked the ball along the six yard line to him.

"It was a battle throughout and naturally it's nice to get two goals," said Bridges, whose double strike took his tally for the season to 17. "It would be great if I can end up topping the 20 goal mark this season and if I do I'll win a couple of wagers from people at the club."

Bridges said he felt the team played better when they were involved in two games a week. "If people think we are getting tired let them think that," he said.

United's victory over City meant the gap between O'Leary's men and leaders Manchester United, who had beaten Derby County the day before to go seven points clear, was back to four points. With other main rivals Arsenal losing to Middlesbrough and Chelsea and Liverpool both being held to draws, O'Leary's side had opened up a welcome little gap between themselves and their nearest challengers.

Such a situation can easily change but Old Trafford manager Sir Alex Ferguson was in no doubt at this stage that David O'Leary's young side presented the only serious threat to their title chances.

"To my mind, Leeds are the only ones who are contenders now," he reasoned, adding that Arsenal could win the UEFA Cup, so their attention would be concentrated on that, while he felt Chelsea, still in the Champions League, and Liverpool had a little too much catching up to do.

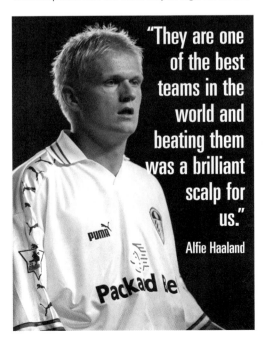

"They are one of the best teams in the world and beating them was a brilliant scalp for us."

Alfie Haaland

A police decision to charge Lee Bowyer and Jonathan Woodgate, among others, with causing grievous bodily harm and affray following their inquiries into an assault on a 19-year-old student hung over the club as they looked ahead to their UEFA Cup quarter-final first leg tie against Slavia Prague.

But manager David O'Leary, rightly, refused to suspend the players and stressed both would continue to be considered for games, pointing out again that in this country any individual remained innocent until proven otherwise.

Woodgate, however, missed the game because of an ankle injury but Bowyer turned out as usual – and played a starring role on what proved to be another remarkable European night at Elland Road. United fans showed how they felt about the little midfield terrier by cheering loudest and longest when his name was read out from the teamsheet.

If he felt in need of any encouragement there it was. In any event he was his usual energetic and tenacious self in what was a telling performance – his best for several games. A superb pass ripped

> # "I think after seeing us get past Roma the fans came thinking we could beat anybody."
>
> David O'Leary

open the Slavia defence in the 39th minute for Jason Wilcox to race through and open the scoring with a brilliant right foot finish and then Bowyer finished off the night in style by scoring United's third.

After getting through against AS Roma, expectations were high among another sell-out Elland Road crowd. "I think after seeing us get past Roma the fans came thinking we could beat anybody. We didn't look at it like that because football is not like that. We knew we had to respect Slavia and work hard," David O'Leary said.

"We had to make sure there was no

■ 'New boy' Jason Wilcox can celebrate with the best of them. Here he shows his joy after scoring in the home leg of the UEFA Cup clash with Slavia Prague.

complacency and that we knew we had to be professional about the job. And we were. It was a wonderful performance. We scored three good goals and could have had more. Yes, I'm a proud manager but the job is not done yet," David O'Leary said.

Slavia coach Frantisek Cipro, a former player with Slavia, said the tie was beyond redemption for his side but the United boss disagreed. "I don't think it is but having opened a 3-0 lead we have given ourselves a great chance of going through to the semi-finals," O'Leary said. "We could have scored more goals but it was a wonderful performance to get three. When you play in Europe you try not to concede a home goal and try to score as many goals as you can, so we have to be very satisfied with the scoreline."

But he warned: "I still think Slavia could be a threat if we let them play. I thought it was difficult at the start and it was down to us to get at them and try to bury them. I don't think we let them play at Elland Road. Our football was excellent and I don't think they could cope with the tempo we played at," he added.

"We want to get into the semi-finals and if we do, it will be a brilliant achievement for us," he added.

United could have opened up a second minute lead against Slavia had Harry Kewell, put through by a pass of great vision from Michael Bridges, come out on top in a one-on-one with goalkeeper Radek Cerny.

But when Bowyer surged to the forefront of the action, it was his superb through pass that allowed Wilcox to run through and blast in his third goal since his move from Blackburn. Eirik Bakke's great determination paved the way for United's second after 54 minutes, when his right wing cross gave Kewell the chance to fire in from close range.

Bowyer, who with Woodgate and others, was due to appear in court the following day, crowned a fine display almost on the hour mark when he took up a great pass from Bridges to beat the Slavia keeper. After several bad misses in recent weeks, this was just the tonic the midfield man needed.

That immediately set up the chants of 'Bowyer for England' from United fans. No one was more pleased for him than David O'Leary. "I was delighted he got a goal," said the United manager.

Referring to the decision to charge Woodgate and Bowyer with causing grievous bodily harm to a 19-year-old student, O'Leary remarked: "There was a lot in print the day before we went into this game and given what had been said earlier that was no shock to this club. But we'll bite the bullet," he added.

CHAPTER TEN

I WANT YOUR TITLE, NOT YOUR JOB!

MANCHESTER United manager Sir Alex Ferguson and Arsene Wenger, his counterpart at Arsenal, have been known to indulge in a spot of psychological warfare now and again. Sir Alex went into print on the day that Leeds United needed to beat Wimbledon to keep in the title hunt and suggested David O'Leary would be a top contender to succeed him at Old Trafford.

To some, that smacked of unsettling tactics. Was it an attempt to raise doubts among the young players at Elland Road? The News of the World quoted the Reds boss at length and among the quotes attributed to him was one that put O'Leary into the frame as his successor.

"If you were going to look around this country for a young manager capable of maintaining success here David would have to be one of the front runners. He has impressed me so much since taking over from George Graham and has learned a lot in a short space of time. He will certainly benefit from the experience they are picking up," Ferguson was quoted as saying.

"I want your title, not your job," was the essence of O'Leary's response. "Hopefully the chairman here at Leeds will be happy to put up with me for a long time to come," he said.

"But I can't honestly believe Alex would have said that about me. Who the hell would give me the Man United job on the basis of what I have done so far? I have seen a story that Barcelona coach Louis Van Gaal is a candidate for the job when Alex decides to call it a day. As far as I am concerned that would be closer to the mark because he is the sort of man they would go for," he added.

The Leeds boss had also been linked with a possible return to Highbury to succeed Arsene Wenger should the Frenchman leave to manage the French national side.

Talk, of course, can be cheap, but in the short space of time O'Leary has held the managerial reins at Elland Road he has made a major impact. He and his right hand man, Eddie Gray, could qualify as the brightest managerial partnership in the business.

United chairman Peter Ridsdale is as determined as anyone to see that United hold on to the man he was responsible for appointing to the manager's chair in the first place. "We are only just at the start of our journey...not the end of it," the chairman said.

"We have demonstrated to David that we have put money behind him to win things for this club and I know he is very, very happy at Leeds. I'm placing this on the record here and now - both he and I intend to be at this club in ten years' time.

> "Both he and I intend to be at this club in ten years' time"
>
> Peter Ridsdale

"In any case, why would he want to go anywhere else? Here at Leeds we have the best young side in the country who are emerging as a candidate to take over the mantle Manchester United have had for the last seven years. Why would you want to leave that and go somewhere where you have to start all over again?

"In my view both he and his family are well settled here and David is in an environment he enjoys. He has total freedom to act within clear parameters. I speak to him almost every day in the week and in my view he is very, very happy and will want to stay here as long as possible," he added.

Money should not really be an issue either. "His base is by no means meagre but his contract is geared to success. If we win things he will be the best paid manager in the country - bar none. David's contract has high incentives to perform with very lucrative bonuses aligned to performance. He and I agreed that was the best way to pay him," Ridsdale explained.

Speculation pieces in national newspapers are nothing new and United had more than their fair

> ## "David's contract has high incentives to perform with very lucrative bonuses aligned to performance."
>
> Peter Ridsdale

share of them this season. To name a couple, Harry Kewell was on his way to new pastures on the Continent as was Alan Smith... or so the newspapers would have you believe.

"This is what happens in football. There's nothing you can do about it," said the chairman.

"But we acted last year to get our players on long contracts because we intend holding on to them. People can come in with offers and remind us just how much our squad is worth, which would

be nice for our shareholders, and then we'll tell the bidders politely to go away," he added.

On the field United were striding on majestically, with another brilliant attacking display that brushed aside lowly placed Wimbledon, even though the Londoners had taken a shock second minute lead through Jason Euell. United's defence was caught cold when Marcus Gayle crossed from the left and Euell stole a march on his markers to power in a near post header off the underside of the bar.

Such is the fitness and confidence of O'Leary's talented side that you expected United to shrug off that disappointment without too much trouble – and that is just what they did.

The Dons had not won an away league game since their opening day victory at Watford and there was to be no Elland Road cure to their travel sickness.

Although they had to wait another 20 minutes to get back on level terms the signs were ominous for the Dons as United passed the ball around with ease and authority – none more so than Stephen McPhail. It was no real surprise when the equaliser came and was fashioned by the young Irishman.

Taking a pass from Harry Kewell, McPhail caught the Dons' defence flat-footed with a through pass to Eirik Bakke. The Norwegian midfield man, showing great ball control skills, swept between two defenders before knocking a great shot with the outside of his right foot beyond Wimbledon's Scottish international goalkeeper Neil Sullivan.

Five minutes later, Ian Harte's coolly taken penalty, awarded for a handling offence by Carl Cort, put United into a 2-1 lead before McPhail and Bakke menaced the Dons defence again to make it 3-1. David Hopkin, back in the side because of Lee Bowyer's knee injury, found McPhail and he knocked another crucial pass forward for Bakke to sweep the ball in.

United's response to the early set-back had been overpoweringly effective - three goals inside 16 minutes. With another game against Slavia Prague to think about United took their foot off the pedal a little in the second half, though Harry

■ On his knees. But it's Wimbledon who are down and out after Harry Kewell had scored in the 4-1 victory at Elland Road.

Kewell still found time to add a fourth – and take his personal tally for the season to 14.

Bakke had previously scored four goals for United but the two against Wimbledon were his first in the Premiership. "Of course it was nice to score two goals. I enjoyed them both but the first one was the best," he said. "We are playing very well as a team and it is important we go on picking up points to keep the pressure on Manchester United."

Although Bakke got the 'man-of-the-match' vote, the contributions of McPhail played a vital part in this emphatic victory. "As a midfield player, I get a real buzz out of creating a chance for a goal to be scored," McPhail said.

"We are doing very well as a team and I am very pleased with the way things are going for me personally."

Would tiredness take too much of a toll on United's youngsters as the finale was played out? In a bid to give his players the best chance, David O'Leary scaled down training to the absolute minimum and issued strict orders that his players should rest at all available times.

On his way out of Thorp Arch after a warm down session following the Wimbledon game – United's seventh energy-sapping game in 23 days - McPhail, the sun shining brightly, said: "I'm on my way home - to sit down, put my feet up and rest!

"That's what the boss has told us all to do. We've got nine league games left and we are chasing the UEFA Cup as well so it makes sense for us to get all the rest we can. With the end of the season not all that far away now, it's a small price to pay."

Skipper Lucas Radebe agreed that becoming

couch potatoes for a while was all in the line of duty. "If I didn't take it easy and rest up in a sensible way I wouldn't be doing myself justice," said the South African skipper.

"When we are at home we put our feet up, make sure we have the remote control beside us, drink plenty of water and eat our carbohydrates. Hopefully it will all seem worthwhile at the end of the season and we'll have something to celebrate."

Encouraged though he was by United's progress this season, the experienced central defender, refused to get carried away. "We want to win trophies, of course we do, and we'll try to win

every one of our remaining games. But it won't be a disaster if we don't win anything. It will still have been a great season for us.

"Qualifying for the Champions' League was the target for us when we set out on this season and if we manage that it will be a wonderful achievement. It will have shown just what an improvement we have made in a short time," Radebe added.

The United skipper and his teammates set off for the Czech Republic in buoyant mood. The high scoring victory against the Dons and the comfort of a 3-0 lead to take into the second leg of their UEFA Cup tie against Slavia Prague saw to that.

■ Happy chappies! Matthew Jones and Ian Harte haven't a care in the world as they grab Harry Kewell after he had scored in the away-leg of the UEFA Cup quarter final against Slavia Prague.

> "Qualifying for the Champions' League was the target for us when we set out on this season and if we manage that it will be a wonderful achievement. It will have shown just what an improvement we have made in a short time."
>
> Lucas Radebe

United were keen to guard against complacency against a Czech side smarting from the first leg embarrassment but determined to give their fans something to cheer in the return meeting. The banners that greeted United at the stadium emphasised the intensity of that support. "Slavia Hooligans," "Fans of Alcohol" "Slavia Fanatics" and "Fanatic Hooligan Boys' Club" they read.

An early goal for United would have virtually settled the tie in United's favour, leaving Slavia needing five goals to win. The early away strike United were hoping for didn't materialise but a couple of minutes into the second half Stephen McPhail slid an inch-perfect pass through the Slavia defence and Harry Kewell finished in style, drilling in his 15th goal of the season.

United eased off after that and were caught out on two occasions, as Slavia won the second leg 2-1 and at least appeased some of their followers in a crowd of only 13,500. But United were in the semi-final of a European competition – a wonderful achievement considering 25 years had elapsed since they last managed that.

SOMEONE once said that everyone has 15 minutes of fame in a lifetime and the visit to Prague provided Adam Pearson, United's commercial director, with his. Several Slavia fans approached him with determined requests for him to sign autograph books while others wanted a photograph taken with him.

Fame at last? Or simply a case of mistaken identity? Sadly it was the latter.

"I was suddenly approached by these supporters who asked for

my autograph and I couldn't understand why until it became known they thought I was Gary Lineker," United's commercial chief explained.

Asked if he thought there was a resemblance to Lineker, he quipped: "Only on the pitch!

"To be honest it's happened to me here at home. One or two friends have said that about me - along with a few other less complimentary things. Maybe it's the ears!"

With the serious business of reaching the semi-finals over, United discovered that Premiership rivals Arsenal, French club Lens and Galatasary of Turkey had also made it through and United manager David O'Leary clearly didn't fancy his old club in the semi-finals.

"A date with Arsenal in Copenhagen in a one-off in the final is something I would really relish," said the United boss. "They would be very difficult to beat over two legs and in my view they are the best team left in the competition. Far better to save the best until last."

O'Leary got his wish to steer clear of the Gunners. When the draw was made in Geneva, the two English teams avoided each other, but United were given what is always now regarded as "a trip to Hell" – namely Galatasary in Istanbul.

■ A case of mistaken identity. Football fans in Prague begged Adam Pearson for his autograph thinking he was Gary Lineker.

The reigning Turkish champions, who like Arsenal were in the UEFA Cup as Champions' League drop-outs, have truly fanatical support, the extent of which turns the Ali Sami Yen stadium into an intimidating place. Manchester United and Chelsea had already visited Istanbul to be greeted by screaming fans who displayed their "Welcome to Hell" banners.

Diplomatically, David O'Leary said all the right things prior to the trip. "We are looking forward to going there. I have been to Turkey several times as a player with Arsenal and as an international and enjoyed it. I always found the people to be friendly and in my view the hostility is over-hyped.

"Going there with my young team will be another step in our big European adventure. They won't be scared. In fact I'm sure they'll enjoy going there," he said.

Gary Kelly spoke for his teammates when he made it clear that "going to Hell" was not worrying the United team. "The boys are happy with the draw," he said.

"It was bound to be tough whoever we played at this late stage of the competition. But we've already played some great teams and beaten them. So we won't feel inferior."

Coming up before that trip was a visit to Leicester City where United needed a victory to restore the four point gap between themselves and Manchester United, who had thrashed Bradford City 4-0 the day before. But O'Leary's men were stepping into Filbert Street – a jinx ground for them if ever there was one. A 2-1 defeat did nothing to suggest otherwise.

Stan Collymore hit a cracker to put the Foxes ahead but Harry Kewell's individual brilliance conjured up the equaliser, and his 15th goal of the season, before Steve Guppy took advantage of United's slack defensive work to hammer in Stefan Oakes' right wing free kick.

"We're a better team than Leicester but talk means nothing. It's about doing the job on the pitch. We had just come back from playing in Europe but I am not using that as an excuse," O'Leary said.

The headlines in the papers the day after made miserable reading for O'Leary's side and United supporters. "All over bar the shouting" "Leeds hand it to Fergie" "Defeat paves way for Old Trafford glory" they screamed.

United themselves made encouraging noises about carrying on the fight for the title but

■ Jonathan Woodgate keeps hold of the ball under pressure from Chelsea's Chris Sutton.

realistically it was now down to a battle for a top three finish and Champions' League spot.

"Let's face it, the best team are winning the league and I think we are doing really well to be where we are. We've come a long way in a short time and even I didn't think we would be waiting, as we are now, to play in a UEFA Cup semi-final this season," said O'Leary.

United weren't to know it then, but that defeat kicked off what turned out to be a troubled week

O'Leary's side as young Jon Harley scored the only goal of the game to give the Blues a vital victory.

United had lost three games on the bounce – something not experienced before under O'Leary's management – and while United were losing out to Chelsea all their nearest challengers won. The warning signs were hoisted over Elland Road. Suggestions that United's young side could not last the pace were aired. The pressure was well and truly on.

> "We've come a long way in a short time and even I didn't think we would be waiting, as we are now, to play in a UEFA Cup semi-final this season."
>
> David O'Leary

for the club. Off the field matters reared their ugly head again.

Two more United players – Michael Duberry and Tony Hackworth – were both charged with offences connected to an alleged attack on a student in Leeds city centre. In addition the FA hit the club with a staggering £150,000 fine for an on-the-field skirmish involving Tottenham players during the game at Elland Road.

United had expected the FA, which had the power to deduct points, to impose a fine, but nothing above £50,000. Manchester United had escaped the wrath of the FA after several of their players had angrily harassed a referee the week before – and which also did not make for small screen family viewing. There was no such favour for Leeds and Spurs.

Chairman Peter Ridsdale, however, accepted the decision with good grace. What he might have thought privately may have been another matter. But he was delighted the FA found Ian Harte not guilty of deliberately treading on an opponent in the game against Spurs.

All this was hardly the ideal way in which to prepare for a tough home Premiership game against European qualifying rivals Chelsea. Predictably, matters went from bad to worse for

Liverpool had moved to within a point of O'Leary's side and Arsenal were hovering another place below but only two points adrift. "We needed points from the Chelsea game," O'Leary admitted. "I always felt the teams near us would win their games this weekend so it turned out to be a very disappointing day for us."

"It's been a long season, a tough one but an enjoyable one, though we looked tired in the second half against Chelsea when we didn't really play at all. It's easy to talk, and only time will tell whether we do it or not, but we have to regroup, go out and bounce back."

Quickly too, as United faced one of the toughest and most intense spells of the season – five top level games in the UEFA Cup and Premier League in 18 days. Two cup clashes against Galatasaray and away league games at Aston Villa and Newcastle with Arsenal visiting Elland Road in between. Make or break time for United?

■ Billy Bremner's statue adorned by scarves and flowers left by supporters as a tribute to the two fans murdered in Istanbul.

CHAPTER ELEVEN

TRAGEDY IN TURKEY

ONCE the draw had paired United with Galatasaray, the Elland Road club had received a steady stream of hate mail through their communications system. And as the first game approached United's e-mail system was choked when 8,000 messages were sent all at the same time.

It took half a day to put that right, but no sooner had that been done than 15,000 messages were despatched at the same time causing similar problems all over again. "I think it was done just to cause a nuisance to us," a United computer programmer said. "It was something we had never encountered before. We made some inquiries and we think they came from a university in Turkey."

Few in the United camp really had the stomach for it, including the players, who had seen some particularly gruesome pictures of the attacks screened on Turkish television. As matters unfolded it became apparent that UEFA wanted the game to go ahead.

Play it or withdraw from the competition. That, basically, was the stark choice United felt UEFA had left them. If it wasn't exactly an ultimatum it was at least a show of crass insensitivity on the part of Europe's soccer governing body.

After dashing to hospital to see what if anything could be done for United fans, chairman Peter Ridsdale, visibly shocked and saddened by the

> "The UEFA officials made it clear to me right away that they were the people with jurisdiction, therefore the decision relating to the game was in their hands and that they had decided the game would go ahead as scheduled."
>
> Peter Ridsdale

However, as we set out on the journey to Istanbul no one could have been prepared for the tragic turn of events that led to United supporters Kevin Speight and Christopher Loftus being knifed to death by Turkish thugs. The aftermath of this tragedy threw up some agonising choices, not least being the question of whether the first leg game should go ahead as scheduled.

horror of it all, was called to a meeting with UEFA representatives at an Istanbul police station.

"The UEFA officials made it clear to me right away that they were the people with jurisdiction, therefore the decision relating to the game was in their hands and that they had decided the game would go ahead as scheduled," the United chairman recalled. "If we did not concur with that then it was clearly up to us to withdraw from the competition.

"Had we done so my honest opinion was that Galatasaray, without actually having to play, would have gone straight into the final. That would not have been right," he added.

That in turn could have been interpreted as a victory for thuggery.

"Many people who have been to Galatasaray will tell you it is one of the most intimidating places in the world to go and play a game of football. But if UEFA have them in one of their competitions it is something we have to accept.

> ## "There was no way we should have had to play that night in Istanbul but we did because you cannot send out a message that by going out and murdering people one team can advance at the expense of the other."
>
> Peter Ridsdale

"There was no way we should have had to play that night in Istanbul but we did because you cannot send out a message that by going out and murdering people one team can advance at the expense of the other," he said.

United were an innocent party and had they pulled out of the game it would have handed Galatasaray a passport into the UEFA Cup final.

"However, given what else had happened I think that the problems were compounded and together with the time scale we were expected to play within I think it led to the first leg being unreasonably held.

"I think it would have been better had we not played but I don't know what would have

■ Leeds United chairman Peter Ridsdale shows the strain as he attends yet another Press conference after the tragedy in Turkey.

■ After learning there was not to be a minute's silence following the killing of two fans in Istanbul on the eve of the game, Leeds United fans turned their backs on the pitch at the Ali Sami Yen stadium to pay their own respects.

happened because no one was in a mind to go back there again. We did not want to withdraw because I felt that I didn't want hooliganism to overcome football.

"I did not make any suggestion as to what should happen because UEFA's representatives had made it absolutely clear that prior to us arriving at the hospital, they had consulted UEFA in Geneva and the only decision was to proceed with the game.

"That was the only decision they would tolerate because they were the people with jurisdiction so it was not even up for debate. Galatasaray were not at the meeting. I did not necessarily disagree with the decision to proceed because had the game been called off the sort of deliberations which caused such media interest would have been compounded by having to have another game there."

Flags at the Ali Sami Yen stadium flew at half-mast. Inside, however, the atmosphere was as intimidating as United had been led to expect it

would be and even a specially prepared message of condolence read out in English over the loud speaker system was treated with disrespect as Galatasaray fans greeted it with sustained whistling.

Given the terrible situation, a 2-0 first leg victory to the Turks did not seem too significant. For United's players and their fans, getting back home to loved ones was very much in the mind. It wasn't the end, of course, and there followed a fortnight of verbal sparring as both clubs made their feelings known and UEFA dithered over whether to ban the Galatasaray fans from the second leg at Elland Road.

"I didn't really have any problems with the Galatasaray club officials. But we all saw the photographs the morning after the game showing Turkish fans making gestures by drawing their fingers across their throats which I thought in the circumstances were not only inappropriate but offensive. Whatever people might say, that clearly added to the tension felt by Leeds fans," the chairman said.

■ Not the Berlin Wall but the Ali Sami Yen Stadium screen as Turkish riot police hold their shields high to protect Leeds United players before the game against Galatasaray.

The sight of riot police holding their shields high in the air to protect the United players from any missiles that may be hurled their way as they came out on to the field was a most depressing one. The whistling and jeering from Galatasaray fans when a message of condolence was read out over the loudspeaker system served only to demonstrate how insensitive and lacking in dignity some so-called supporters were.

Given the circumstances, hard though it was, the United players had to try to remain professional in their approach. An impossible task, especially with so many younger players in their ranks. It quickly became apparent that the situation had affected them. Uncharacteristically slow to get to grips with the game, they found themselves two goals down by half time.

Thirteen minutes into the game, Hakan Suker caught the United defence napping when he

nipped in to head home a well struck centre from Arif Erdem and the Turks were two goals up just before half time when Oliveira Capone forced the ball home from another cross.

United were not without chances of their own but they were left again to count the cost of missed opportunities, Michael Bridges being the chief culprit. The strain had told but once the final whistle had blown, the only thing on the minds of players, officials, media and fans alike was to get back home safely.

The horribly intimidating atmosphere of the Ali Sami Yen stadium, with its baying fans, some making cut throat signs, riot police holding their shields high to afford protection to players and the deafening noise of the pre-match music, made the entire experience one to forget.

In no time at all we were all on our way to the

airport, escorted by police. We drew the curtains across the coach windows to give some protection against any missiles that might be hurled at us.

Thankfully that turned out to be unnecessary. Once at the airport we were marched through two lines of police to our aircraft. Four hours later we were back in Leeds.

Whether the game should have gone ahead or not inevitably divided opinion. "One newspaper in particular criticised me but others were very supportive," the chairman recalled. "The one that criticised was ill-informed, particularly given that their journalist who was at the game wrote a very balanced piece in another part of the newspaper," he added.

The Daily Mail was scathing in its condemnation of the decision to go ahead with the game. They filled their entire front page under the banner headline "Grotesque" with a comment piece that claimed greed was at the core of the play-on decision.

A day later the paper repeated itself when one of its columnists, billed as 'irrepressible, irascible and irreverent' wrote that the match went ahead because cancellation would have been costly to both clubs.

He further pronounced that the public should interpret the decision to play the game as final proof that they were taken for mugs by people who shared little of their regard for the game as a sport. It's clear he didn't know the United chairman and that he had written from afar!

"We didn't get a penny out of the game in Istanbul," explained the chairman. "We don't get anything from the away leg of our ties and neither do we receive television fees. The money goes to the home club."

And United, in their desire to guard against further trouble when the second leg was played at Elland Road, spent £125,000 on full page advertisements in national newspapers appealing for calm, a sizeable share of that going to the Daily Mail.

There had been, however, almost a universal groundswell of sympathy for the two fans and the Elland Road club from a disbelieving public. United's chairman was particularly affected by it all

yet despite looking gaunt and tired, the result of losing many hours of sleep, he battled against both mental and physical fatigue to carry on doing the best for his club and its fans.

I don't think anyone connected with the club, or for that matter much further afield, could have any doubts that Ridsdale handled the entire situation surrounding the sickening events in Turkey with anything other than the utmost decency and understanding. I doubt any other Premier League chairman would – or indeed could - have done as much in such dire circumstances.

> ## "In situations like the one we faced you don't have time to stand around and think. The events unfolded so quickly. I don't think there was a day when I had time to sit and think. It was almost day and night."
>
> **Peter Ridsdale**

As a supporter who once queued all night for tickets for United's 1965 FA Cup final, Ridsdale, one of the most go-ahead chairmen in the league, has a genuine 'feel' for the club and its followers.

"I associate with supporters because I am one whenever we play a game. I do my job to the best of my ability. How others do theirs is up to them. I respond as I believe it right to respond.

"I am a businessman the rest of the time. That does not change and I like to feel that the balance means I can do my job as well as possible. You don't run away the first time that you have a problem. You try to say to supporters: 'I am doing this job because I feel I can contribute' and I like to feel that was the situation in the aftermath of the terrible events in Turkey," he said.

Ridsdale's reaction to the troubles was both instant and natural. A genuine willingness to associate with people in the darkest hour has endeared him to many.

"In situations like the one we faced you don't have time to stand around and think. The events unfolded so quickly. I don't think there was a day when I had time to sit and think. It was almost day and night.

"But when someone tells you one of your supporters is either critically injured or dead I don't see there is any other decision but to go to the hospital and see what you can do.

"Faced with the things that followed on from there, what I did was what I have believed to be right. It is only the benefit of hindsight that judges whether you have or not. You are living in a goldfish bowl with the world's press watching your every move and hanging on your every word and it is sometimes difficult to make sure you say things that don't result in headlines you would not want.

"Over the three days after it happened I probably had maybe five or six hours sleep, no more. I was knackered at the end of it all," he admitted.

Did the tragedy of Turkey ever make him think twice about carrying on in the job? As soon as I posed the question I knew it was a ridiculous one. "Charged with the responsibility of being chairman, a job I love and at the club I love, you cannot suddenly throw in the towel in times of adversity," he answered.

"The good times are easy. When adversity comes you then attempt to demonstrate why you were given the responsibilities of being chairman in the first place. And if I come out of all this with people still feeling I am capable of doing the job then I am delighted. From my personal perspective I think that is part of the job."

Two piles of mail were stacked high on his desk at Elland Road, including some from as far afield as the States, Africa and the Far East – all letters of sympathy. "I'll answer all of them individually but it's going to take time – and that is something I seem to have had very little of lately," he said.

The rapid way in which supporters responded

with floral tributes at Elland Road amazed the chairman. "The speed was surprising because it was not a co-ordinated response. So many people had the same idea but the thing that stunned me was from how far away people have wanted to write or bring things to the ground," he recalled.

"One other thing I found quite remarkable was the peaceful way in which people paid their respects at Elland Road. On the Friday night when I was present just about every adult who was there had a child with them and even the children were quiet and sombre. No one, I am sure, told them to be quiet. It was almost as if in situations like that it comes naturally to everyone - including the very young," he added.

For all their splendid exploits in the UEFA Cup, highlighted by the admirable victories over crack Italian side AS Roma and Russian champions Spartak Moscow, United's efforts in this European competition were inevitably totally overshadowed by the two killings.

> "When I first heard that Kevin had two young children, one of the first things I wanted to do was get home and hold my two young children."
>
> Peter Ridsdale

The horror of that night in Istanbul is something that will forever be etched on the mind of the United chairman. "I saw the stab wounds and I never want to see anything like that again," said the chairman, whose attitude and actions throughout the saddest chapter in United's history have been dignified and exemplary.

"When I first heard that Kevin had two young children, one of the first things I wanted to do was get home and hold my two young children. You have left them behind but it was one of those occasions where you almost needed the security of knowing they were all right, even though you knew they were," he said.

He and his fellow directors were having the customary eve-of-match dinner with Galatasaray officials on an island at a restaurant owned by the club when they first heard news of the troubles.

"We were informed there had been an incident and one of our supporters had been very badly injured and potentially fatally injured. We immediately left the island and went to the hospital," Ridsdale recalled.

Once there, the United officials faced a quite horrifying scene. "On the one hand there were the injuries and on the other a complete lack of organisation," the chairman recalled.

"Leeds fans were obviously very emotional. Christopher's brother was distraught and we had to try to get blood for Kevin so we had to attempt to calm things down a bit. It was a terrible situation all round and when you look back on it you realise just what a shambles it was.

"The British ambassador came along and we tried to find out what the situation with Kevin was. There was no one obviously in charge when we got there. I saw one lad who was on an intravenous drip who turned out to be the brother of one of the dead. There was also a media scrum and a number of fans were in an emotional state.

"We were told one person had died and after having him identified we went back upstairs and a nurse ran out with some purchasing orders saying another fan needed some blood and could we go out and buy some because there wasn't any in what they called the operating theatre.

"We had to find some form of paying for the blood ourselves and David (Spencer) provided his credit card for use. We were told where the blood bank was and we sent the driver to try to get some blood.

"Another of our fans we were told had a suspected fractured skull but that there was no means of being able to treat him because there was no X-ray machine. He had to be taken to the German hospital but they would not take him unless we paid for the ambulance.

"It would appear that the first hospital was not equipped to cope with the severity of the wounds but, frankly, I doubt it would have made any difference if it had been such was the nature of the wounds."

The United officials were then summoned to the police station where UEFA officials were waiting to tell them that the game would still go ahead. On the morning of the match the usual UEFA meeting took place and while Ridsdale made sure everything was being looked after as it should be and attempted to satisfy the insatiable appetite of the media, David Spencer represented the club at the meeting.

UEFA's insensitivity amazed United. "I was told the UEFA official had said that for reasons he felt might antagonise the situation they believed it was right not to have a minute's silence. And that neither team should wear black armbands. I really couldn't believe that – and I could not accept it.

"When I heard that I said that whether UEFA liked it or not our players would be wearing black armbands. David Spencer informed the UEFA official that it was a club decision to wear the armbands and the official replied that he had not insisted on a ban on armbands and that it was up to each club to decide for themselves.

"Had the roles of the two clubs been reversed we would certainly have worn black armbands as a mark of respect for the dead," Ridsdale added.

No words, of course, can ever adequately express the revulsion all right-minded people felt about the killings. Having travelled all over Europe and ventured as far as Japan to chronicle the fortunes of the Elland Road club in the past 30-plus years, I have experienced many highs and lows. Never, however, I have ever felt as sick and saddened as I did in Istanbul.

How the greatest gift of all – that of human life – can be so savagely and totally disregarded is beyond belief. What kind of minds can the brutal perpetrators of such foul deeds have? I shudder to think.

Football is, after all, a game and for two fans to pay with their lives for following their team is incomprehensible. By the very nature of their job, journalists become hardened professionals yet those of us who were in Istanbul were left feeling numb with shock when news of the killings filtered through.

Most of us had a job to do and did it as professionally as possible under trying circumstances. The safety advice phoned through to our hotel on the morning of the game had warned us not to venture onto the streets. That added to the tension and made us feel more vulnerable. And when evening finally came we made our way under escort to the stadium for a game none of us had the heart for before returning home.

After two nights without any sleep, Ridsdale went to a hotel when he returned to Leeds just to get a wash and a change of clothes before going to Elland Road. "We felt that if we invited Turkish supporters to the second leg there was a real risk of further violence," he recalled.

"Therefore we felt the only considered decision was to ask UEFA to support us in our intention to keep their fans away. Before I said anything to the media I consulted with both UEFA and the FA who concurred at that time that it seemed a sensible suggestion.

"The thing I felt led to it getting out of hand was when people then started saying if you cannot guarantee our safety the game should be played on neutral territory or behind closed doors, which frankly was unfair on two counts.

"Firstly we had played in Galatasaray under extreme provocation and it was supposed to be a home and away tie. We weren't trying to inflame the situation but trying to suggest that the safety and well being of individuals, which is our responsibility, would be better if the Turkish fans did not come. That was why we cancelled the day flight of our supporters to Istanbul.

"So it seemed to me to be a perfectly reasonable request but obviously from the comments coming from Turkey it was not accepted

"They did not think it a reasonable request and appeared to want to play elsewhere which I thought would penalise the innocent party twice. We had not been in a fit state to play in the first leg in Galatasaray and frankly not to have played at Elland Road would have been unreasonable."

Peter Ridsdale

by Galatasaray. They did not think it a reasonable request and appeared to want to play elsewhere which I thought would penalise the innocent party twice. We had not been in a fit state to play in the first leg in Galatasaray and frankly not to have played at Elland Road would have been unreasonable.

"I was criticised in some quarters for arguing that I thought Galatasaray's request was opportunistic. I was arguably emotionally involved but I think anyone who took a step back would recognise that it was not something that we would have done.

"Given what happened and that I said football had become secondary, I would have liked both parties to have acknowledged that. Our view was

that life was more important but one could interpret Galatasaray's response was arguing that winning the tie was far more important than safety.

"I would hope that that was an unfair interpretation but were it to be fair I think it very disappointing," Ridsdale added.

Having failed in their attempts to persuade UEFA to either allow their fans to attend the second leg or play the game at a neutral venue, Galatasaray remained abrasive to the end. Over-reaction on their part led to them bringing over their own protection force and the refusal to accept United's hospitality and attend the customary eve-of-match directors' dinner on safety grounds served only to further damage the poor image they had with football supporters in general.

■ As a mark of respect for the two fans who were killed in Istanbul, a minute's silence is observed before the second leg of the UEFA Cup semi final against Galatasaray.

The chairman stressed it was important that Leeds United, as a club, were seen to have taken every precaution to make sure that people could come in safety to watch a football match. "If we had reached the final and then brought the trophy back to Elland Road it would have been particularly fitting to have used that in some way or other as a catalyst for a lasting tribute to the two fans who lost their lives in Istanbul," he added.

That was not to be, however, as United were held to a 2-2 draw in the second leg. A number of arrests were made at the game and a window was smashed on the Turks' team coach but, by and large, supporters adhered to United's pleas to stay calm and avoid trouble.

Words of condemnation, apology or comfort from the Galatasaray club were, largely, conspicuous by their absence throughout the traumatic two-week period of the tie, though coach Fatih Terim did show his emotions when he rightly said winning the tie was not worth two lives. "No result can forgive what happened two weeks ago. Human life cannot be measured in football. But Turks are emotional and hospitable people and we wish Leeds good luck," he said after the Elland Road game.

For their part, United were just relieved that the tie was over. "The two weeks felt like one long day and the sense of having been beaten never really struck home against the tragedy of what happened in Istanbul. It seems it over shadowed the whole of the UEFA Cup run," added the United chairman.

The curtain had come down on the saddest chapter in United's 80-year history. It is a chapter that can never be forgotten.

■ Eirik Bakke, who scored twice in the 2-2 second leg UEFA Cup tie against Galatasaray, beats goalkeeper Claudio Taffarel.

CHAPTER TWELVE

CHAMPIONS' LEAGUE RUN-IN

AFTER their 2-0 defeat in Istanbul, United had to prepare for a Premier League fixture at Aston Villa where, courtesy of the Midlands club, due respect was paid to the two dead United fans. A minute's silence was held and impeccably observed and both teams wore black armbands as a further mark of respect.

On the field, however, it was becoming a familiar story for United as they lost for the fifth time in succession. Gary Kelly's slip, under a close challenge from Julian Joachim and referee Barry Knight's refusal to see anything amiss, allowed the Villa striker to charge forward and score the only goal of the game.

United had the chance to get something out of the game when Harry Kewell set Michael Bridges up with a great opportunity from six yards but United's top marksman fired over.

This latest reverse pushed David O'Leary's side out of the Premiership's top two places for the first time in seven months – and gave rise to the belief that his promising young side were suffering burn-out as the climax of the campaign loomed large.

While the repercussions of the sad events in Turkey were being debated publicly, and in United's view, not always with the best of taste, O'Leary and his players had a week to rest and sort themselves and their on-the-field problems out before the visit to Elland Road of Arsenal.

This being United's first home appearance since the deaths of Kevin Speight and Christopher Loftus, Elland Road was an emotional place as the Arsenal players presented bouquets of flowers to

their United counterparts. They, in turn, gave the flowers to fans in the crowd to add to the many tributes already on display outside the stadium.

You could hear a pin drop in the minute set aside for silent remembrance, as fans of both clubs stood with heads bowed.

Once the game got under way, however, it became an uncompromising affair with some heavy challenges. Ian Harte was shown the red card when, although grounded by Dennis Bergkamp's challenge, he kicked out at the Dutchman just before the break. But Lee Dixon escaped punishment for an off-the-ball incident in which he appeared to brush a fist against Harry Kewell's face.

In the final count referee Steve Dunn added to his red card showing by producing his yellow card on five other occasions – four of those yellow cards being brandished at Arsenal players. Goals from Thierry Henry, Martin Keown, Kanu and Marc Overmars dealt United a 4-0 defeat – their biggest of the season.

Sadly United's overall performance against the Gunners served only to provide ammunition to those pundits who were predicting Manchester United, Arsenal and Liverpool would grasp the Premiership's top three places. The defeat dropped them to fourth place and with Chelsea only two points adrift in fifth place, there were some who felt O'Leary's boys might miss out on Europe altogether.

The headlines continued to centre on United's second leg meeting with Galatasaray at Elland

■ Off you go! Harry Kewell is given his marching orders by referee Lubos Michel following a challenge on Galatasaray's Gheorghe Popescu. A harsh decision and UEFA later decreed the young striker should not serve any suspension.

Road. UEFA had taken longer than anticipated to back Peter Ridsdale's request for Turkish fans to be banned from the game purely on a safety point of view.

Four days after losing to Arsenal – their sixth successive defeat – David O'Leary's talented but tiring young side were faced with attempting to pull back a two goal deficit against the Turkish champions. United fans were in good voice but sadly for United the tie was as good as over after just five minutes when Gheorghe Hagi scored a penalty awarded for Jonathan Woodgate's ill-judged challenge on Hakan Suker.

That left United needing to score four times to go through to the final. That really was mission impossible. The admirable Eirik Bakke scored twice from close range headers but Hakan Suker's excellent strike after 47 minutes kept the Turks in the comfort zone.

United's great European adventure was over, beaten 4-2 on aggregate at the semi-final stage,

and as O'Leary pointed out, UEFA had got their wish of having the final contested by two teams from the Champions' League, Arsenal having disposed of Lens to face Galatasaray in the final. "It was set up for this right from the start," O'Leary said.

But United's exit at the semi-final stage was not without its drama, the young Slovakian referee dismissing Harry Kewell for a challenge which left former Spurs player Gheorghe Popescu writhing about clutching his face. However, video playbacks showed the United striker had not touched Popescu's face.

Galatasaray's Emre Belozoglu's dismissal for a foul on Lee Bowyer a minute later also seemed harsh but with United having to chase goals, Kewell's dismissal was a disaster for United.

O'Leary knew it as well as anyone and he could not resist afterwards labelling Popescu a cheat for having got Kewell sent off. "The dismissals were a joke, particularly Harry's," said the United boss.

"Harry made a deliberate attempt not to touch him and jumped over him. Popescu knows himself what he did. There wasn't a scratch on him and he should be ashamed of himself. He cheated to get a player sent off."

Although Kewell's sending-off was such a major blow to United and clearly angered O'Leary, the United manager had no other complaints. "The Turks got the goals and took them well. I am not making excuses about tired minds or tired legs. We gave away silly goals and missed a chance to get an away goal. We made it hard for ourselves," he said.

He went on: "Our European adventure is over. It's been good while it lasted – and frankly it went on longer than I thought it would.

"Naturally I am disappointed that having reached the semi-finals we have not made it to the final but if anyone had told me at the beginning of the season that we would get to the semi-finals of the UEFA Cup I would have said they were crazy."

Galatasaray coach Fatih Terim was delighted with the victory. "I feel like a father who has just had his first child. I am emotional and happy," he said

A handsome enough return for a player in his first season of Premiership action.

It was not that he hadn't had any chances. They had come his way - and been missed. "There had been a lot at stake for us and I have been snatching at my chances. But I would have been more upset with myself if I had not been getting into the right places at the right time. My luck has got to change," he said.

Prophetic words they turned out to be, for Bridges was back on the scoresheet when United played at St James' Park. The 13th minute proved to be lucky for the Elland Road side as Bridges thumped a fierce right foot shot past Newcastle goalkeeper Shay Given following a cross from Jason Wilcox.

Four minutes later and O'Leary's side went further ahead when Wilcox's curling free kick, which Bridges challenged for, went in. United looked to be coasting, but it all went pear-shaped when Alan Shearer, who has amassed a bagful of goals against Leeds over the years, scored twice to level matters. On top of that the usually reliable Ian Harte missed a penalty.

"It was a case of two points lost rather than one

> "You cannot legislate for the sort of stupid mistakes we made at the back which allowed Newcastle to score twice. But that sums us up over the last few weeks."
>
> David O'Leary

United's exit from Europe overshadowed the two goal display of the ever-improving Bakke. His latest "double" took his tally for the season to eight and ended a barren spell for the United side, who had failed to score in their four previous games.

Seventeen-goal leading marksman Michael Bridges had failed to score in his previous eight outings and the £5million former Sunderland man travelled to Newcastle having set himself a target of three goals in United's last five matches that would take him to the 20 goal mark for the season.

gained – and that's what I've told the players in the dressing room," O'Leary said. As Liverpool had taken only a point from the "derby" clash with Everton and Chelsea had gone down at Old Trafford, O'Leary's men had missed out on a chance to make up some lost ground.

"You cannot legislate for the sort of stupid mistakes we made at the back which allowed Newcastle to score twice. But that sums us up over the last few weeks," O'Leary added.

Bobby Robson, a gentleman among managers,

was delighted with his team's fight-back but had words of sympathy for the Elland Roaders. "Leeds have had a long, long season and football can be a cruel game, I feel sorry for Leeds because I admire the way they play," he said.

"Who would have said at any time between September and April that Leeds United would lose six games on the bounce? You would put your house on that not happening and so would I. It just shows how little we know about it.

"In the first 20 minutes of this game, Leeds' display was as good as I have seen from any team who have played against us here since I came – and that includes Manchester United," Robson added.

■ David Hopkin - first goal of the season.

DAVID HOPKIN'S first goal of what for him had been a limited first team campaign set United on the way to victory against struggling neighbours Sheffield Wednesday at Hillsborough. The Scottish international, who had had to settle for a place on the substitutes' bench for much of the season, struck within 40 seconds of the game when he fired in from 14 yards after taking a pass from the grounded Michael Bridges.

Welcome though that early strike was for Hopkin and United, who had set themselves a target of 12 points from their final four matches of the season, it was later to be overshadowed, in brilliance more than importance, by one from Harry Kewell.

United had increased their advantage to 2-0 when Bridges curled in a right foot shot in the 53rd minute before Kewell treated United's 5,500 following with a piece of individual brilliance and inventiveness.

From a position near the edge of the penalty area, he suddenly hit a curling shot with the outside of his left foot that mesmerised Wednesday goalkeeper Kevin Pressman. "I do practice that kind of thing in training, we all do. So why not use it in a match," Kewell remarked.

"When I got possession I looked up and saw Pressman was off his line and I thought 'why not go for it' and that is what I did."

It helped to earn the young striker the man-of-the-match award from Sky television viewers and while manager David O'Leary raised an inquiring eyebrow to that, the United boss was high in praise of Kewell's talents.

Asked if he thought Kewell had played well, O'Leary replied: "I thought he scored a very good goal." Speaking generally, the United boss went on: "He's the best young player in the country by far and he's not far away from being one of the best senior players in the country as well. There are some outstanding young players in the country but Kewell is a very special player."

O'Leary had taken the decision to drop Jonathan Woodgate in favour of Michael Duberry. "I left Woodgate out because he had not been playing anywhere near the form he can play," he said.

Three points at the expense of the Owls took United, striving to clinch a European place, from fifth back into fourth place. "Our goal all season has been to get into the Champions' League and at least to qualify for Europe through the UEFA Cup," he said. "We'll keep plugging away and if we get maximum points from our last three games we'll see where that takes us."

To gain a Champions' League spot United were dependant on Arsenal or Liverpool dropping points while Chelsea were challenging United strongly for the fourth place which would gain entry into the UEFA Cup.

"We have got to get into the UEFA Cup, at least," O'Leary said. "I think we deserve that. No one has anything given but it would be a crying

Kewell also rated highly among the voters for the Football Writers' Association award, where he also came third. He was the winner of the United Supporters' Club Player of the Year award and also of the Packard Bell yearly award.

On the league front, the return to winning ways at Hillsborough sent David O'Leary's side into Elland Road action against an already relegated Watford with high hopes of adding three more precious points to their tally.

Their 3-1 win was notable not merely for the three points but also for Michael Duberry's first goal for United – in fact his first Premier League strike for more than three years – and Michael Bridges' 20th goal of the season.

> "We have got to get into the UEFA Cup, at least. I think we deserve that. No one has anything given but it would be a crying shame if we didn't even make the UEFA Cup."
>
> David O'Leary

shame if we didn't even make the UEFA Cup. I think we would do well in that competition next season. Hopefully we would have a stronger squad by then and we would have the benefit of the experience gained in this season's competition to draw on," he reasoned.

O'Leary's overall opinion of Kewell's talents was matched by members of the Professional Footballers' Association who voted the striker their Young Player of the Year and also placed him third in the senior award behind, Roy Keane and runner-up Kevin Phillips.

The PFA'S annual awards also reflected the strength of the United side in general as four of their players – Nigel Martyn, Gary Kelly, Ian Harte and Kewell - made it into the Premiership team of the year.

For the record the full Premier League team of the season was: Martyn; Kelly, Stam (Man Utd), Hyypia (Liverpool), Harte, Keane (Man Utd) Beckham (Man Utd), Kewell, Viera (Arsenal), Phillips (Sunderland), Cole (Man Utd).

Having achieved the 20-goal target, Bridges duly won his £20 bet with United chief scout Ian Broomfield. But his 21st minute strike against Watford was cancelled out when Dominic Foley scored five minutes later.

Duberry's goal just before half-time restored United's lead and Darren Huckerby set the seal on victory with a fine individual effort in which his speed played a part as he weaved around the Watford defence to hit the sweetest of angled shots.

Huckerby's speed is well enough known in the Premiership, so there is no prize for guessing which of United's players is the fastest. That distinction does, indeed, belong to the ex-Coventry and Newcastle player – but only just. United's fitness coach Ed Baranowski takes up the story.

"If I had to put my money on a race over 60 metres, I would say that Huckerby is the quickest," said the coach.

■ He went that way!
Speed coach Ed
Baranowski points
the way as a player
whizzes by.

Yet it wouldn't be quite the sure-fire thing many of us would have thought. "To be honest it would be pretty close between Huckerby, Jason Wilcox and Gary Kelly. They are the three quickest players at the club.

"Having said that, we have a lot of others, like for example Harry Kewell and Danny Mills who are not going to be far short of the pace. Over 60 meters it would be a very tight race but I think Huckerby would probably pip it," Baranowski added.

Central defenders are not usually renowned for their speed but Baranowski says of those at United: "None of them are slouches. I know Robert Molenaar has been out all season with an injury but he was very quick. When you look at the size of him you would have been quite shocked to see how fast he covered the ground. Jonathan Woodgate is quick too. He is another one who you would maybe think does not look all that quick. But if you run alongside him you realise just how quick he is.

"Lucas is not overly quick but he has the experience and is clever enough to make up the bit

of speed he may lack. He is what I call 'football aware' and he uses that to good effect."

Midfielder Lee Bowyer is talked of as "Mr Perpetual Motion" and the coach would not argue with that description. "He has great endurance and that suits the position he plays where he is required to get from one penalty area to another, back again and so on without becoming fatigued. The same goes for Alfie Haaland.

"These two in particular are very fit endurance-wise, though having said that a lot of the Leeds players have good levels of endurance. Logic says the midfield players are there because they are best able to do that sort of continuous work. But I would say that 'Bows' is the fittest on endurance," he added.

Before he left the club, Hasselbaink always looked to be up there with the quickest of the United players. So just where did he figure in the Baranowski ratings? "Jimmy was very quick, but over a short distance. Over 10 to 20 metres he was fast but probably not so good when you get to the 40 or 60 metres distance.

"But for the shorter distance I would say he was

the quickest we had at the club then. He is built for that short power-explosive speed. But he would start to fatigue once you increased the distance. He was that type of short, sharp runner," he added.

United used Baranowski's services for two sessions a week for the senior professionals when George Graham managed the club but after O'Leary took over he increased that to four sessions a week. "He had seen the benefits and he introduced it all the way through the club, down to the YTS lads," said the coach.

How does it all work? "First you assess all the players to find their level of ability on endurance and speed, strength, power and flexibility and then you prepare individual and group programmes. The idea is to collectively improve them as a unit and individually to work on their weaknesses or their strengths.

"I would say there was probably only Manchester United who were the equivalent of, if not slightly fitter than, Leeds. We are definitely one of the top two or three Premier League teams. On a scale of one to ten we would probably come out at 9.5. They are very fit athletic lads who work very hard on their conditioning," he explained.

You could be excused for thinking United's final home fixture of the season was more a game of cards than a football match as referee Andy D'Urso brandished yellow and red cards as though they were going out of fashion.

The Essex official had his yellow card out nine times and produced the red one on three occasions as Everton, with little at stake other than pride, made life tough for United in their final home game of the campaign.

Everton's Richard Dunne was the first to leave for an early bath when he was red carded for a jarring tackle on Michael Bridges and he was

quickly followed by Michael Duberry for the second of two bookable offences. Don Hutchison went a couple of minutes from the end, also for a second yellow card offence.

In addition Michael Ball, Mark Hughes, Dave Unsworth, Nick Barmby and Stephen Hughes also saw yellow. But this was not quite the video nasty such statistics might suggest. Sure, it was tough and keenly contested, but no more so than most games.

A draw at Newcastle and successive victories against Sheffield Wednesday and Watford left David O'Leary's side looking for a victory that would have meant them needing only to draw their remaining game, at West Ham, to make sure of a Champions' League place ahead of Liverpool.

But they had to settle for a draw, Nick Barmby taking full advantage of a misjudgement by Nigel Martyn to score Everton's equaliser. That took some – though not all - of the shine off Michael Bridges' 21st goal of the season, scored in fine style after a superb long pass from Lee Bowyer.

The season – his first in the Premier League – has been a personal triumph for the young striker – and vindication of manager David O'Leary's decision to pay £5.25m for the youngster. "I made the right decision to come to Leeds. I have no doubts at all about that. The experience this season has been great," Bridges said.

"I didn't really set myself any goal target but taking £20 off our chief scout Ian Broomfield for reaching the 20 goal mark delighted me. I think he was happy to pay up."

But little changed for Lucas Radebe. The United skipper, as usual, lost out to physiotherapist David Swift, who bet the United skipper that he couldn't score three goals during the season. Radebe finished with two to his name, though he did score an own goal that he tried to claim should count in

> "I didn't really set myself any goal target but taking £20 off our chief scout Ian Broomfield for reaching the 20 goal mark delighted me."
>
> Michael Bridges

the bet. But Swift was having none of that. "Only the goals for us, not against, are valid," he said. Lucas paid up in the dressing room after the game at West Ham.

The sounds emanating from the telephone earpiece were hardly the most melodious as David Wetherall answered his phone on Sunday night after the Premier League campaign had been successfully completed. But they were certainly well intentioned.

"There's only one David Wetherall," the raucous chants blared out as the United players left little doubt that they are much better footballers than they are singers. It was a well meant gesture all the same as David O'Leary's players sang the praises of their ex-teammate, whose goal for Bradford City had defeated Liverpool and assured his former club of Champions' League football.

United went into the final game of the season in control of their own destiny. A victory at West Ham would have done the trick. But they were held to a goalless draw by Harry Redknapp's side, who lacked nothing in the way of commitment. Had Liverpool won or drawn at Valley Parade they, not United would have finished third.

But all's well that ends well...and few could argue that David O'Leary's young musketeers hadn't done enough to deserve a crack at the Champions' League.

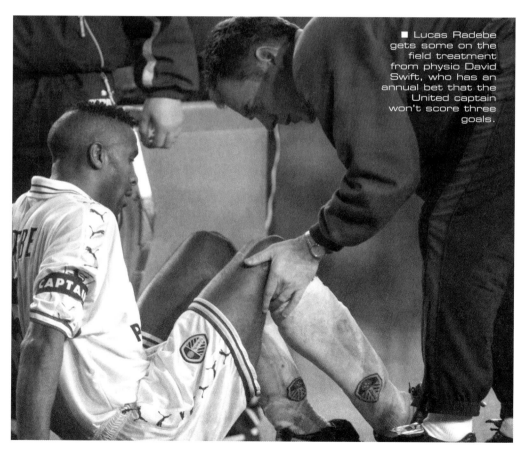

■ Lucas Radebe gets some on the field treatment from physio David Swift, who has an annual bet that the United captain won't score three goals.

CHAPTER THIRTEEN

REVIE COULD HAVE BEEN WRONG!

WHEN Leeds United were flying high at the forefront of English and European football in the early 1970s Don Revie told my wife Margaret, and myself, in all seriousness, to make the most of the era. We were at a celebration dinner to mark one of the successes his team had in that never to be forgotten period of the Elland Road club's history.

"Mark my words, a team as good as this and the successful times it brings come along only once in a lifetime. So make the most of it while it is here," he told us.

Having done so much in football, both as a player and manager, Revie's views were, quite naturally, respected. His comments have stayed with me and my wife down the years and his words kept flooding back as United's fortunes went into serious decline not all that long after he left to become England manager.

An inevitable lowering of playing standards eventually brought about the dreaded drop from the First Division where United had been such a force for the vast majority of their occupancy that covered 18 seasons. The good times were over.

Eight seasons in the Second Division wilderness followed and served to underlined Revie's beliefs, before United's fortunes took a much-awaited upturn shortly after the surprise appointment of Howard Wilkinson as manager. Safety from relegation to the Third Division was achieved in his first season and promotion to the First Division - as champions of the Division Two - was the coveted prize in his second.

United quickly established themselves in the top flight by finishing in fourth place in their first season back and though Wilkinson brought the top domestic honour to Elland Road when his side won the First Division championship next term, the success, sadly, proved to be a false dawn. Revie's words of warning came to the forefront of my mind once again.

> "Mark my words, a team as good as this and the successful times it brings come along only once in a lifetime. So make the most of it while it is here."
>
> Don Revie

However, after a successful Millennium season and as we look ahead to the 2000-2001 campaign I have a sneaking feeling that Revie might just be proved wrong. United, I believe, might just be standing on the threshold of another of those highly successful and enjoyable eras. My feeling is based on the improvement United have shown over the season just ended and the one before it.

Making predictions in the highly unpredictable world of professional soccer has left many who were far better qualified than me with egg on their faces. But having had the opportunity to work behind the scenes at Leeds United over the past 12 months, I have to say that, judged on what I have seen and heard, the future of the club looks to be rosier now than it has for many years.

With arguably Leeds United's most accomplished chairman in Peter Ridsdale at the helm - backed by a determined board - and David O'Leary in the managerial chair, United could well be at the start of something great.

After George Graham had steadied the United ship, O'Leary has carried on at a pace, giving youth its fling and being rewarded for it. I wouldn't say his style of management is carefree. United don't throw caution to the wind all the time but the O'Leary brand of football is exciting and entertaining.

Watching Leeds United in a professional capacity, I have cast a critical eye over proceedings for more than 30 years. I now find myself pointing

out to people that the current United side possesses welcome similarities to that which became one of the finest English club sides of all time back in the late 1960s and early 1970s.

As far as United's on-the-field activities were concerned, last season proved to be one of achievement and considerable satisfaction. At the outset, O'Leary had set a target of qualifying for the Champions' League and having a good run in one of the cup competitions. As far as that went it was mission accomplished.

Nigel Martyn again confirmed himself a top class goalkeeper, Gary Kelly made a highly successful comeback after a year out of action with shin problems and fellow full-back Ian Harte improved his standing still further as did central defenders Lucas Radebe and Jonathan Woodgate.

Young Norwegian midfielder Eirik Bakke settled in to Premiership football at a rapid pace, showing skill, strength and vision, while Stephen McPhail

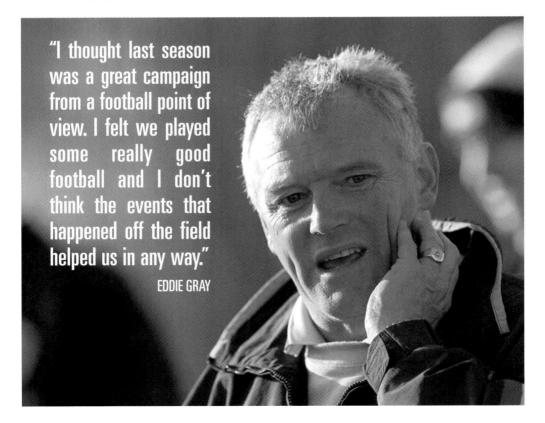

"I thought last season was a great campaign from a football point of view. I felt we played some really good football and I don't think the events that happened off the field helped us in any way."

EDDIE GRAY

displayed his creative skills to good effect as Lee Bowyer again showed why he was considered such an outstanding prospect as a teenager.

Harry Kewell proved to be one of the country's best players and also increased his standing in Europe and Michael Bridges quickly established himself as a favourite with United fans, lacing some skilful displays with goals, some 21 in all, and in his first season of Premiership football too.

These were undoubted plus signs for United. But while the targets set at the start of the season were duly achieved, it is a measure of the confidence and ambition that exists among players and staff that there remained a feeling of some disappointment within the camp.

Left on their own as serious challengers to champions Manchester United as the final stage of the campaign was being fought out, United were disappointed to fall away and leave the Reds with a comfortable run-in, as O'Leary's capable and experienced assistant and ex-Revie 'old boy' Eddie Gray pointed out.

"At the outset of the season we would have been delighted to have finished third and qualify for the Champions' League," he said. "We did well to get that but as a professional player you approach every season thinking you can win the league. As a winner, I always did and I think David would do the same.

"But before the start of last season David and I looked back to the term before when we finished fourth and the aim was to improve on that which by finishing third we did. We'll look to improve further on that in the new season but the objective at the end of the day is to have a photograph at the start of a new season with a bit of silverware on it.

"That, really, should be the aim of all clubs but I think we are in the fortunate position of being one of the clubs for whom that is a realistic ambition. I think we have a chance of winning something.

"I thought last season was a great campaign from a football point of view. I felt we played some really good football and I don't think the events that happened off the field helped us in any way.

"You only have to look at the number of goals

Lee Bowyer scored before he had that off-the-field problem. He didn't score a goal after that. I am sure it affected him and, in a way, it affected the club too. But when you are as young as he is you just have to keep battling away.

> # "Realistically we were the only team that challenged Manchester United towards at the end of the season. We hung on in there as serious challengers for a long period and once we fell off there was no one else."
>
> Eddie Gray

"Realistically we were the only team that challenged Manchester United towards at the end of the season. We hung on in there as serious challengers for a long period and once we fell off there was no one else. For me the turning point in the championship race was the game at Elland Road in late February when Manchester United beat us 1-0.

"Had we managed to win that match who knows what might have happened? We were as good as they were that day but we missed a few chances and the only difference was that Andy Cole took his goal exceptionally well. The win that day really handed them the title," Gray added.

IT MAY still have been the summer but Old Trafford boss Sir Alex Ferguson lit the fuse early for the new season when he claimed that his side was virtually uncatchable or that if any club was to do so they would have to spend £100million.

"Alex knows his players but we don't think it will need £100million because we have players here at Leeds who are as good as theirs," said Gray. "You know that Manchester United are very, very strong all round but we are getting there. Our summer signings will make us all that much stronger and we know that our young players are learning and improving all the time and will get stronger and stronger."

Chairman Peter Ridsdale would love to see the Elland Road club make Sir Alex eat his words. "I saw his remark about the rest of us not being able to catch them," he said. "We were above them for a lot of last season and then kept on their heels longer than any other side and I am convinced that we will be well equipped to give Manchester United a fright in the coming season," he added.

The difference between the two Uniteds last season as Gray pointed out, was that the Reds had a bigger and stronger squad. "They had top class players all over the park. Players in every position and on the substitutes' bench are all top class. All clubs have got to try to achieve that and it is our aim too," he said.

United's progress to the semi-final of the UEFA Cup was also a fine achievement. "It was very satisfying to have gone so far in a European competition but having played so well to get that far I was disappointed we did not make the final," Gray added.

There were, of course, extenuating circumstances following the killings of two fans in Turkey on the eve of the first leg of the semi-final clash with Galatasaray in Istanbul. United came away from the cauldron of hate that is the Ali Sami Yen stadium with a two goal deficit and without an away goal to their credit.

Yet Gray was far from downhearted at the situation. "To be honest I thought that from an all-round point of view Galatasaray were one of the poorer teams that came up against in Europe," Gray recalled.

> "Arsenal have a top class squad and so, too, have Chelsea and for us to have finished above Chelsea was quite an achievement in my view. It was a great season and an exciting one for us."
>
> Eddie Gray

"Arsenal have a top class squad and so, too, have Chelsea and for us to have finished above Chelsea was quite an achievement in my view. It was a great season and an exciting one for us. It was also good to hear from Bradford on the last day of the season that we had got into the Champions' League and that Bradford had stayed in the Premiership after beating our rivals, Liverpool.

"The season overall delighted David and myself. It was alive right from the first game of the season to the very last one. There was always something there and after doing so well we know that expectations will now be even higher. That is only to be expected and I don't mind it at all. I'd much rather have fans expecting a great deal from the team than have them think the other way," he added.

"Actually, I was more confident of us being able to pull back that two-goal deficit and beat Galatasaray than I about us beating Roma when we came back to Elland Road at 0-0 in an earlier round. Unfortunately, though, we gave away a stupid penalty in the opening minutes and missed a chance or two ourselves against Galatasaray," he added.

That disappointment apart, United could look back on another season of progress and promise. "As a club we are at an exciting and interesting stage of development. Leeds is a great place to play and a great place to be. It should be a great attraction to young players and those who are already here have shown how much they like being here by signing long term contracts," he added.

United's continued all-round improvement was underlined twice in the summer. First UEFA

The tragic deaths of Leeds United fans Kevin Speight and Christopher Loftus are remembered.

■ Leeds United's young stars Danny Mills, Lee Bowyer, Alan Smith, Phil Robinson and Michael Bridges made up almost half of England's team for the Under 21 international with Luxembourg at Reading in September 1999.

■ Not quite Sydney, but
Aussie Harry Kewell turns
on the style in Rome's
Olympic Stadium.

■ Michael Bridges keeps possession in Rome.

■ The preformance in the Olympic Stadium saw many heroes, but the gold medal surely went to Nigel Martyn.

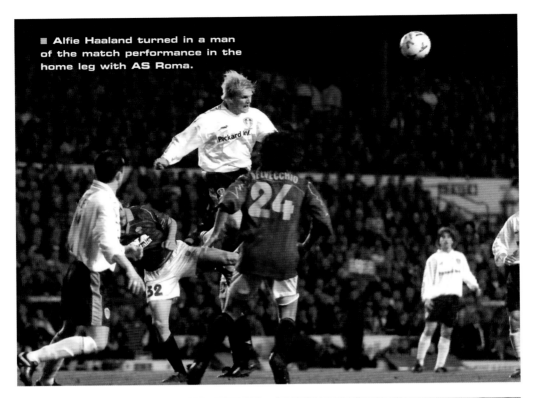

■ Alfie Haaland turned in a man of the match performance in the home leg with AS Roma.

■ A chance goes begging for David Hopkin.

■ Lucas Radebe proves too strong for Sunderland's Kevin Phillips.

■ **Happiness... is a goal.** Michael Bridges (left) has no doubt about that. Ian Harte (above) strains the sinews after scoring.

■ Below: Lee Bowyer shakes off a challenge from Sheffield Wednesday's Danny Sonner.

■ **UEFA Cup semi-final action as Ian Harte, Harry Kewell, Michael Bridges and Stephen McPhail do their best to overturn Galatasaray's first leg lead.**

■ For most of the season it was Leeds v Manchester in the race for the Premiership title and in January it was Leeds v Manchester for a place in the fifth round of the FA Cup. Pictured on this page are Harry Kewell, Alan Smith and Lee Bowyer, who all scored at Maine Road in the Cup. On the facing page it's Kewell again, in action against the eventual champions at Elland Road.

■ Michael Bridges and Harry Kewell probe at the Arsenal defence, but the Gunners kept their rearguard in order and ended Leeds' title hopes with a 4-0 win at Elland Road.

■ Gary Kelly and Stephen McPhail (below) in action against Everton.

■ Michael Bridges scores the final home goal of the season in a 1-1 draw with Everton.

■ Eirik Bakke keeps his eyes on the ball whilst being challenged by Everton's Ball.

158

■ Nigel Martyn and Danny Mills acknowledge the applause of the fans after Leeds United had rung down the curtain on their home programme.

■ Michael Duberry joins Lee Bowyer and Jon Woodgate on the end of season lap of honour.

■ Not 72 but £7.2 million.
That's what the numbers
on the back of record
signing Olivier Dacourt
represent. The Frenchman
is pictured, along with
chairman Peter Ridsdale,
after his transfer from
RC Lens.

upgraded David O'Leary's side to a seeding for the Champions' League third qualifying round - which meant they would miss teams such as AC Milan, Inter, Dynamo Kiev last year's runners-up Valencia and Galatasaray who, of course, won the UEFA Cup.

Secondly the bookmakers rated the Elland Road boss - along with Sir Alex Ferguson at Old Trafford - as the Premiership managers least likely to be sacked in the new season!

As a matter of interest the full betting was: 8/11 Chris Hutchings; 6/4 John Gregory; 15/8 Bryan Robson, Glenn Hoddle; 2/1 Jim Smith, Gianluca Vialli; 9/4 Peter Taylor; 5/2 George Burley, Alan Curbishley, George Graham, Walter Smith; 11/4 Gordon Strachan; 3/1 Joe Royle; 4/1 Gerard Houllier; 5/1 Harry Redknapp, Bobby Robson; 6/1 Peter Reid, Arsene Wenger; 10/1 Sir Alex Ferguson, David O'Leary.

There is little doubt that O'Leary's side won many new friends and influenced people with their exciting brand of football last season but there was the odd blip out on the pitch. The FA's decision to charge United with failing to control their players during the home game against Tottenham was a blow to the club's image and then there was the decision to charge four players following an alleged attack in Leeds.

United are keen to improve their general image and the chairman said: "The club need to instil the correct attitude into players while the players have to understand the responsibilities they have. They are part of the community and they have a clear responsibility to that community. Most of the time, though, it works."

The departure of Alfie Haaland and David Hopkin, to Manchester City and Bradford City respectively, saw United lose two popular players - though both left with the best wishes of the Elland Road club.

A lack of first team football last season for both men and the possibility of that situation continuing in the new season led to the transfers. "I'm hoping my move will give me more first team opportunities," explained Hopkin, who became the fourth United player in just over 12 months to leave Elland Road for Bradford City.

> "I have always thought that top sides are judged by the quality of the players they have on the substitutes' bench who are capable of coming on in any situation and possibly turn it round."
>
> David O'Leary

"There had been rumours for a while concerning me leaving Leeds and having sorted out my future I'm pleased that the speculation is now at an end. I think I went as far as I could at Leeds, particularly as the club are now going into a new era.

"David O'Leary told me it was down to me whether I wanted to go or stay but I had been frustrated at not being in the first team and I didn't want another season where I just played the odd game or two," he added.

As the United manager was keen to increase the size and ability of his first team squad for a determined assault on honours, the arrival of Olivier Dacourt and Mark Viduka offset the departures of Haaland and Hopkin. But O'Leary was still seeking to make more signings.

"When you take stock of our players we have a 19 strong first team squad but I would like to increase that to 22 which would put us in a similar position to the current top clubs such as Manchester United, Arsenal and Chelsea enjoy," the United boss said.

"I have always thought that top sides are judged by the quality of the players they have on the substitutes' bench who are capable of coming on in any situation and possibly turn it round," he added.

With such a lot at stake these days, few United fans, I suspect, will disagree with the manager's views.

CHAPTER FOURTEEN

DAVID O'LEARY - MY FUTURE

DAVID O'LEARY looked back over an exciting and enjoyable action-packed season as manager of Leeds United and then pledged his long-term future to the club.

"I'm not going anywhere – I'm here for as long as I'm wanted," he said.

The popular United boss, who had watched his team clinch a place in the Champions' League, knocked down speculation that had linked him with Glasgow Celtic and also put him in the frame for a move back to Arsenal should Arsene Wenger leave.

"The only way I would take the Arsenal job or any other, is if I got the sack from Leeds. As long as I have this job and the chairman wants me to stay I will not be going anywhere else. It's as simple as that," he said.

"I cannot stop rumours. Some people are always going to speculate. But my hope is that ten years down the line from now I am still here at Leeds. The proudest thing I could do would be to stay in Yorkshire for that length of time and succeed in making this club a truly great one.

"Time will tell what I do achieve but I would be a very, very happy man if I could make it all happen

for this club. That is my hope and my aim," he added.

O'Leary had nearly 20 years as player with the Gunners and reached the pinnacle of his profession at both club and international level. But he hopes to be best remembered as a manager – a job he says he always fancied doing.

George Graham told O'Leary a few years before his playing career came to an end that he had all the makings of becoming a good manager. "Yes, George told me that and it was obviously very encouraging to hear it because I had intentions of going into management when my playing days were over," said the Irishman.

"I would like to be remembered as having been a great manager rather than a great player. I get more joy out of winning as a manager than I did as a player."

Management brings greater pressures but O'Leary squares up to it. "It would be easy to say, yes, I love pressure. That is being macho, but I prefer to say I enjoy the buzz of management. I had 20 years as a player and while the pressure you feel as a player may be different to that as manager, I seemed to be able to handle it without a problem. It is the same now," he said.

> "Time will tell what I do achieve but I would be a very, very happy man if I could make it all happen for this club. That is my hope and my aim."
>
> David O'Leary

"I am not afraid of the sack, though I don't want to be sacked. But I am managing the way I want to manage and if I fail then at least I will have failed doing it the way I wanted to do it."

O'Leary admits that his first full season in charge has, as he puts it, "been a hell of an experience" and that he has learned a great deal. "I am pleased to say that I did not have too much difficulty in coping with the job. I didn't feel the need to seek any advice from anyone," he revealed.

"Some people seem to be born into jobs and I think it is the same with management. I really don't know how I became a footballer. My dad could not kick a ball to save his life so why should I be able to kick a football?

"As far as management goes it doesn't necessarily follow that if you have been a top class player you will be a top class manager. Having been a high class player will probably get you your first job in management but once you get the job that's it. Your name will mean nothing unless you prove yourself up to the challenge."

O'Leary has done very nicely, thank you, since taking over at Elland Road. So what was it really like heading up United's big push for the Champions' League? "It has not been any harder than I thought it would be. But it has been constantly hard and I admit that I am mentally tired from it and looking forward to a summer break," said O'Leary as the season ended.

"Lots of people have told me that I will need a month-long break and I am going to make sure I get it because I don't want to run the risk of becoming stale.

"Having had so few Saturday matches – I think 12 in all throughout the season – has meant that I have gone elsewhere on a Saturday to see matches and then prepared for our games either on the Sunday or Monday. It got to the stage where I could not remember when I had a day off.

"I am a hands-on type of manager. I am not one who sits back and lets the coaches do all the work. Eddie Gray is a great help – and very experienced. But I also like to get out on the training pitch with the players."

"We became victims of our own success. Playing 12 matches in Europe and four of them in the month of March was a big problem for us."

O'Leary rightly takes pride in what has gone on since he took over the managerial reins. "At the end of the previous season we were all overjoyed at finishing fourth in the Premier League. We asked ourselves if we could improve on that and, with only a small deficit on transfers, something like £6million, we have come quite some way forward," he said.

"People have said we are not fully equipped for the Champions' League and maybe we aren't but we're in there and we're delighted. We won't win it, that's for sure. But, believe me, we won't be afraid of anyone. We'll hold our heads high, give it our best shot and pick up some valuable experience along the way."

> "We have improved our reputation greatly and come a long way. We now have to look to go further. I have a great chairman and speaking as a young manager, he is fantastic to work for and I have the highest respect for him. Nothing would give me greater joy than, in addition for myself, winning something for him and to see how happy he would be for Leeds United."
>
> David O'Leary

"We were in the top one or two of the league for about five months of the season, we have broken attendance records at Elland Road and set up a new winning sequence. We also reached the semi-finals of a European competition for the first time in 25 years and improved our popularity with the type of football we strive to play.

"But we became victims of our own success. Playing 12 matches in Europe and four of them in the month of March was a big problem for us. It hurt us. Where we have got to improve – and where Manchester United don't need to – is in the strength of the squad. They could change their side to give players a break when it was needed but I didn't have that luxury and this is something we have to look to change.

"Arsenal have a far superior team than we have. Their players are older, more experienced and are part of a world class squad yet they were dumped out of the Champions' League in the last couple of seasons. If we hadn't have got into it, it wouldn't have done us any harm to have had another year's experience in the UEFA Cup and try for the big league next season.

The United boss knows as well as anyone that he needs to increased the strength of his first team squad. He began that task by signing French midfielder Olivier Dacourt for £7.2million. but revealed that he had already had set-backs in his bid to tempt other big name players to Leeds.

"Some of the players I want to bring to this club don't want to come to Leeds. The reason is they rate Manchester United and Arsenal as bigger and better than we are. But at least they didn't dismiss our club out of hand. They gave it quite a bit of thought before turning us down," he said.

"This is a big problem and one that we must seek to overcome. We have made great strides in the last year or so and we are moving in the right direction. But we have to take another step forward and being in the Champions' League is a definite boost to our image.

"Another problem is that at the moment we do not have the wage structure to pay the top world class players. That is not a criticism of the club. If we do well in the Champions' League then we might have next year.

"We have improved our reputation greatly and come a long way. We now have to look to go further. I have a great chairman and speaking as a young manager, he is fantastic to work for and I have the highest respect for him. Nothing would give me greater joy than, in addition for myself, winning something for him and to see how happy he would be for Leeds United."

Casting his mind back to the tragic events in Istanbul, the United manager agreed it was difficult for his team to concentrate. "No one seemed to have their mind fully on the game. I couldn't blame them for that because it affected me too. It was a European semi-final but the game was irrelevant because of the tragedy. Had we been able to pull the tie round in the second leg it would have been too cheap to say we did it for those two people who lost their lives.

"Leeds had not been in a European semi-final for 25 years, yet the second leg at Elland Road never felt like a semi-final. There was too much surrounding the game.

"There had been a lack of respect shown over in Turkey. And it makes me laugh what they get away with over there. UEFA seem to clamp down on anything over here yet things can be thrown over there and it just seems to be accepted," he said.

United's aim right from the start of the season had been to break into the top three of the Premier League and qualify for the Champions' League. "It's just reward for what my side have put into the season," O'Leary said. "I set them the target but I didn't think they would achieve it.

"We were a ship that did brilliantly in sailing across three-quarters of the ocean. Then the engines stalled and we limped into port. But we got what we wanted and I think we earned it, too. It's a wonderful feeling."

■ United's winning team; chairman Peter Risdale with manager David O'Leary.

CHAPTER FIFTEEN

AND FINALLY... CHAIRMAN SUMS UP AND LOOKS AHEAD

PETER Risdale has no doubt that the Millennium season was a very successful one for Leeds United.

"The risk is, I think, that people will remember some of the off-the-field incidents as overshadowing the on-field efforts. If that were the case it would be a pity because at the start of the season, had we known we would finish third in the Premier League we would have been delighted.

"Given the distractions, the performances were even more outstanding and I think every one of our supporters should be proud of the way in which we achieve that third place. We also reached our first European semi-final for 25 years.

"People talked about Leeds United as an exciting new football team and the majority of the Press supported us so well, particularly in the distressful times. We appear to be a team people want to watch either at Elland Road or on television. We topped the one million attendance mark at our home games and experienced our highest ever attendance average. So in a general sense I believe it has been a season we should all look back on with great satisfaction.

"Clearly there were some things that should not be forgotten - an incident in January where a young man was badly hurt and the tragic incidents in Istanbul. In saying how well the season went I am not trying to dismiss those. Those incidents will never go away from our thoughts. But if we do concentrate on football then it was a most satisfying season.

"We went on record at the start of the campaign saying our objective was to qualify for the

Champions' League and in that respect it was a case of mission accomplished. While we were at the top of the league for quite a time there is no doubt at all that Manchester United always looked the strongest team in the league.

"However we at Leeds can look forward to the future with much confidence. Having progressed again, we now have to add to our squad and make sure that we are in a position to take a further step forward. The last three seasons have seen us finish

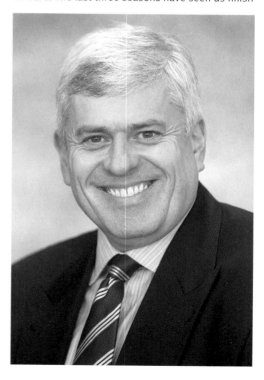

> ## "We appear to be a team people want to watch either at Elland Road or on television. We topped the one million attendance mark at our home games and experienced our highest ever attendance average."
>
> Peter Ridsdale

fifth, fourth and third. Now let's see what we can achieve in the next campaign.

"We are not yet as good as Manchester United but we are not that far away. Our talented young squad is maturing all the time and with the addition of two or three quality new signings – which we are looking to bring about - I think we would be able to give Manchester United a fair old game.

"Funnily enough, while our record against the top teams was not all that good I thought two of our best and closest performances were against Manchester United home and away. They were very lucky to win at our place and we played some wonderful football at Old Trafford."

United started their summer recruiting with the signing of tough tackling midfielder Olivier Dacourt for £7.2million from RC Lens. The 25-year-old was the first of a number of quality signings the chairman said United had planned.

Twenty-four-year-old Australian international striker Mark Viduka was the next star to arrive at Elland Road for a fee in the region of £6million as United further strengthened their talented squad. The powerfully built former Croatia Zagreb marksman was top scorer for Glasgow Celtic last season with a 27-goal tally that earned him the Scottish Premier League player of the year award.

"We are building for the future but, as I say, last season was an outstanding one on the field and while people may think of David O'Leary as having been around a long time we should not forget that it was his first full season as a manager. I have every confidence that we shall go on improving.

"Our aim is to be the best and it was with this in mind that we signed Brian Kidd to oversee all our youth recruitment and development. Brian has a great amount of experience, having had a leading part in football for many years and we see him as being very important to the future success of our club. He will be working very closely with David O'Leary," added the chairman.

The 51-year-old Kidd has known O'Leary since the United manager was a teenager seeking to make the grade as a player at Arsenal.

When he was assistant to Sir Alex Ferguson at Old Trafford, Kidd played a key part in the development of many of the young players who came through the ranks to be hugely successful and influential at the top level of the game. The Elland Road club are now looking to him to carry on the good work.

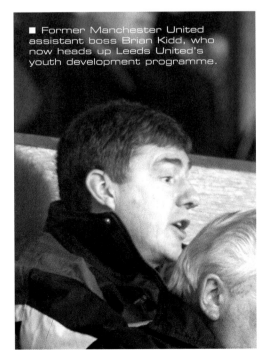

■ Former Manchester United assistant boss Brian Kidd, who now heads up Leeds United's youth development programme.

Developing their own talent can of course be vital to clubs in the current climate of multi-million pound transfers and United's recent record in bringing young players through the ranks was a key factor in the ex-Manchester United man moving across the Pennines to Yorkshire – and Leeds United.

"We were delighted to get someone of his calibre. I think his appointment underlines our desire to become the best and with this in mind I want to assure all our supporters that the board will continue to give David O'Leary and the team our total support.

"Finally I want to place on record my sincere thanks to everyone who supported the club during the Millennium season. The fact that Elland Road attendances went through the million mark for the first time in our history is testimony to the great support we have received and also to the type of football the team plays," the chairman added.

APPENDIX ONE

MILLENNIUM SEASON FACTS & FIGURES

THE popularity of David O'Leary's talented side was underlined forcibly as attendances at Elland Road soared past the one million mark for the first time in the club's 80-year history. The total, for League and cup games, was 1,014,633.

Aggregate attendance for Premier League matches at Elland Road reached 743,942, giving a record-breaking home league average of 39,155 – compared to the previous best of 38,702 set by Don Revie's 1973-74 Championship winning side.

The six UEFA Cup home ties attracted 234,426 spectators (average 39,071) while 11,912 watched United's one home tie in the FA Cup, against Port Vale. The Worthington League Cup- tie against Blackburn Rovers at Elland Road was seen by 24,353 fans.

AWARDS

Packard Bell Player of the Season: Harry Kewell
Young Player of the Season: Eirik Bakke
Goal of the Season: Harry Kewell v Sheffield Wednesday (a)
Goal celebration of the Season: Gary Kelly and Stephen McPhail v Chelsea (a)
Most memorable moments: Nigel Martyn v AS Roma
United Supporters Club Player-of-the-Season: Harry Kewell.

■ He's the tops. Leeds United's young Australian striker Harry Kewell won the Packard Bell Player of the Year award as well as the PFA Young Player of the Year award.

APPEARANCES
(including substitute outings)

	Lge	UEFA	FAC	LC	Ttl
Nigel Martyn	38	12	3	2	55
Harry Kewell	36	12	3	2	53
Michael Bridges	34	12	2	2	50
Ian Harte	33	12	3	1	49
Jonathan Woodgate	34	10	3	2	49
Lee Bowyer	33	11	3	1	48
Gary Kelly	31	11	3	2	47
Darren Huckerby	33	9	3	1	46
Lucas Radebe	31	11	2	2	46
Eirik Bakke	29	10	3	2	44
Stephen McPhail	24	9	3	2	38
Alan Smith	26	8	3	1	38
Jason Wilcox	20	4	2	0	26
David Batty	16	4	0	2	22
Danny Mills	16	2	1	1	20
Alfie Haaland	13	6	0	0	19
David Hopkin	14	3	0	1	18
Matthew Jones	11	5	1	1	18
Michael Duberry	13	1	1	1	16
Martin Hiden	1	0	0	0	1

GOALSCORERS

	Lge	UEFA	FAC	LC	Ttl
Michael Bridges	19	2	0	0	21
Harry Kewell	10	5	2	0	17
Lee Bowyer	5	5	1	0	11
Eirik Bakke	2	2	4	0	8
Ian Harte	6	1	1	0	8
Alan Smith	4	1	1	0	6
Jason Wilcox	3	1	0	0	4
Darren Huckerby	2	1	0	0	3
Stephen McPhail	2	0	0	0	2
Danny Mills	1	0	0	1	2
Lucas Radebe	0	2	0	0	2
Jonathan Woodgate	1	0	0	0	1
Michael Duberry	1	0	0	0	1
David Hopkin	1	0	0	0	1
OG: Song (Liverpool)	1	-	-	-	1
Totals	58	20	9	1	88

MATCH DETAILS

■ **Aug 7 v Derby County (H) Draw 0-0**
Att 40,118. Ref: Graham Barber
Leeds United: Martyn, Mills, Radebe, Woodgate, Harte; Batty, Hopkin, Kewell, Bowyer; Bridges, Smith (McPhail 52min). Subs not used: Haaland, Hiden, Duberry, Robinson.
Derby County: Poom; Carbonari, Prior, Laursen, Eranio (Borbokis 76min), Powell, Johnson, Delap, Dorigo, Baiano (Beck 67min), Sturridge (Burton 46min). Subs not used: Schnoor, Hoult.

■ **Aug 11 v Southampton (A) Won 3-0** (Bridges 3)
Att: 15,206. Ref: Alan Wiley Position: 4th.
Southampton: Jones, Dodd, Richards, Lundekvam, Benali, Le Tissier, Hughes, Marsden (Oakley 46min), Kachloul (Ripley 65min), Pahars, Ostenstad. Subs not used: Beresford, Almeida, Moss.
Leeds United: Martyn, Duberry, Radebe, Woodgate, Mills, Hopkin (Jones 85min), Batty, Bowyer, Harte, Kewell, Bridges (Bakke 82min). Subs not used: Haaland, Hiden, Robinson.

■ **Aug 14 v Manchester United (A): Lost 2-0**
Att: 55,187 Ref: Neale Barry Position: 7th
Manchester United: Bosnich (Van der Gouw 21min), P Neville, Berg, Stam, Irwin, Beckham, Scholes (Butt 73min), Keane, Giggs, Yorke (Sheringham 81min), Cole. Subs not used: Solskjaer, Curtis. Scorer: Yorke 2.
Leeds United: Martyn, Radebe, Duberry, Woodgate, Mills, Bowyer, Batty, Harte, (Hiden 78min), Huckerby, Bridges (Hopkin 18min), Kewell (Bakke 83min). Subs not used: Haaland, Robinson.

■ **Aug 21 v Sunderland (H) Won 2-1** (Bowyer, Mills) Att: 39,064 Ref: Paul Alcock Position: 6th.
Leeds United: Martyn, Mills, Woodgate, Radebe, Harte, Bowyer, Batty, Hopkin, Kewell, Huckerby, Bridges (Smith 58min). Subs not used: Kelly, McPhail, Duberry, Robinson.
Sunderland: Sorensen, Makin, Butler (Quinn 72min), Helmer, Gray (Holloway 63min) Summerbee, Rae, Ball (Dichio 90min) Schwarz, McCann, Phillips. Subs not used: Oster, Marriott. Scorer: Phillips pen.

■ **Aug 23 v Liverpool (H) Lost 2-1** (Song og)
Att: 39,703 Ref: David Elleray Position: 7th.
Leeds United: Martyn, Mills, Radebe, Woodgate,
Harte, Batty, Bowyer, Hopkin (Bakke 68min),
Huckerby, Bridges (Smith 56min), Kewell.
Subs not used: Kelly, Duberry, Robinson.
Liverpool: Westerveld, Matteo, Hyppia, Carragher,
Song, Redknapp, Gerrard, Thompson, Berger,
Fowler, Camara. Subs not used: Staunton, Meijer,
Murphy, Traore, Friedel.
Scorers: Camara, Radebe og

■ **Aug 28 v Tottenham (A) Won 2-1** (Smith, Harte)
Att: 36,012 Ref: Mike Reed Position: 5th.
Tottenham Hotspur: Walker, Carr, Perry, Young,
Taricco, Freund, Sherwood, Leonhardsen, Ginola,
Ferdinand (Dominguez 46min), Iversen (Nielsen
85min). Subs not used: Fox, King, Baardsen.
Scorer: Sherwood.
Leeds United: Martyn, Duberry, Radebe, Woodgate
(Hopkin 46min), Mills (Kelly 66min), Bowyer, Batty,
Harte, Kewell, Smith, Bridges (Huckerby 46min).
Subs not used: Haaland, Robinson.

■ **Sept 11 v Coventry City (A) Won 4-3** (Bowyer,
Huckerby, Harte pen, Bridges) Att 23,532
Ref: Steve Dunn Position: 4th
Coventry City: Hedman, Quinn (McSheffrey 76min),
Shaw, Williams, Edworth. Chippo, McAllister, Hadji,
Froggatt (Strachan 76min), Aloisi (Hall 45min),
Keane. Subs not used: Nuzzo, Konjic.
Scorers: McAllister pen, Aloisi, Chippo.
Leeds United: Martyn, Mills, Duberry (Woodgate
64min), Radebe, Harte (Kelly 60min), Bowyer,
Batty, Hopkin, Kewell, Bridges, Huckerby.
Subs not used: Robinson, Haaland, Jones.

■ **Sep 14 v Partizan Belgrade (UEFA Cup 1st rd
1st leg) (A) Won 3-1** (Bowyer 2, Radebe)
Att 4,000 Ref: Herbert Fandel (Germany).
Partizan Belgrade: Damjanac, Savic, Stanojevic,
Rasovic, Krstajic, Ivic (Stojakovic 88min), Ilic
(Gerasimovski 82min), Trobok, Tomic, Kezman, Iliev
(Pekovic 70min). Subs not used: Duljaj, Vukovic,
Pantic, Miskovic. Scorer: Tomic.
Leeds United: Martyn, Mills, Woodgate, Radebe,
Harte, Kelly, Batty, Bowyer, Hopkin, Kewell, Bridges
(Smith 70min). Subs not used: Haaland, Huckerby,
Robinson, Bakke, Hiden, Hay.

■ **Sep 19 v Middlesbrough (H) Won 2-0** (Bridges,
Kewell) Att 34,122. Ref: Dermot Gallagher
Position: 2nd.
Leeds United: Martyn, Mills, Radebe, Woodgate,
Harte, Hopkin (Kelly 45min), Batty, Bowyer, Smith,
Bridges (Huckerby 52min), Kewell.
Subs not used: Haaland, Bakke, Robinson.
Middlesbrough: Schwarzer, Ziege, Cooper,
Pallister, Vickers, Festa, Mustoe, Ince, O,Neill,
Armstrong (Ricard 72min), Deane. Subs not used:
Fleming, Maddison, Gavin, Beresford.

■ **Sep 26 v Newcastle Utd (H) Won 3-2** (Bowyer,
Kewell, Bridges) Att 40,192 Ref: Barry Knight
Position: 2nd
Leeds United: Martyn, Kelly, Woodgate, Radebe,
Harte, Bakke (Haaland 78min), Batty, Bowyer,
Kewell, Smith (Huckerby 72min), Bridges.
Subs not used: Robinson, Mills, Jones.
Newcastle United: Harper, Barton, Marcelino,
Goma, Domi, Solano, Dyer, McClen (Charvet
72min), Speed, Shearer, Ketsbaia (Robinson
43min). Subs not used: Glass, Hughes, Wright.
Scorer: Shearer 2.

■ **Sept 30 v Partizan Belgrade (UEFA Cup 1st rd
2nd leg) (H) Won 1-0** (aggregate 4-1) (Huckerby)
Att 39,806 Ref: Fritz Stuchlik (Austria).
Leeds United: Martyn, Kelly, Woodgate, Radebe,
Harte, Hopkin (Bakke 80min), Batty, Bowyer,
Huckerby, Bridges (Smith 68min), Kewell (Jones
85min). Subs not used: Haaland, Robinson, Mills,
Hay.
Partizan Belgrade: Damjanac, Savic, Gerasimovski,
Stanojevic, Sabo, Stojisavlevic, Ivic (Stojakovic
87min), Tomic, Trobok, (Duljaj 67min), Pekovic,
Obradovic (Baljak 63min). Subs not used: Ilic,
Arnaut, Vukovic, Miskovic.

■ **Oct 3 v Watford (A) Won 2-1** (Bridges, Kewell)
Att: 19,677. Ref: Paul D'Urso Position: 1st
Watford: Chamberlain, Robinson, Page, Williams,
Lyttle (Gibbs 46min), Kennedy (Easton 80min)
Palmer, Hyde, Wooter, Foley (Miller 69min),
Ngonge. Subs not used: Wright, Day. Scorer:
Williams.
Leeds United: Martyn, Kelly, Radebe (Mills 42min),
Woodgate, Harte, Bakke, Batty, Hopkin (Haaland
89min), Kewell, Bridges (Huckerby 70min), Smith.
Subs not used: Robinson, Jones.

■ **Oct 13 v Blackburn Rovers (Worthington Cup rd 3) (H) Won 1-0** (Mills)
Att 24,353 Ref: Jeff Winter.
Leeds United: Martyn, Kelly, Radebe, Woodgate, Mills, Bakke, Hopkin (McPhail 46min), Batty, Kewell, Smith, Bridges (Huckerby 46min). Subs not used: Robinson, Haaland, Jones.
Blackburn Rovers: Filan, Kenna, Short, Johnson, Dunn, Jansen, Taylor, Gill, Duff, Ward, Richardson. Subs not used: Ostenstad, Kelly, Corbett, Grayson, Brown.

■ **Oct 16 v Sheffield Wednesday (H) Won 2-0**
(Smith 2) Att 39,437 Ref: Graham Barber
Position: 1st
Leeds United: Martyn, Kelly, Radebe, Woodgate, Mills, McPhail, Bowyer, Batty, Kewell, Smith, Bridges (Huckerby 62min). Subs not used: Robinson, Haaland, Hopkin, Bakke.
Sheffield Wednesday: Srnicek, Atherton, Thome, Walker, Hinchcliffe, Alexandersson, Jonk, Sonner, Rudi, De Bilde, Booth. Subs not used: Pressman, Sibon, Cresswell, Nolan, Briscoe.

■ **Oct 21 (UEFA Cup 2nd rd 1st leg) v Lokomotiv Moscow (H) Won 4-1** (Bowyer 2, Smith, Kewell)
Att 37,814 Ref: Wolfgang Stark (Germany)
Leeds United: Martyn, Kelly, Radebe, Woodgate, Harte, Bowyer, Batty, McPhail, Kewell, Smith, Bridges (Huckerby 62mins). Subs not used: Robinson, Haaland, Hopkin, Mills, Bakke, Jones.
Lokomotiv Moscow: Nigmatullin, Arifullin, Chugainov, Pashinin (Hovannisyan 61mins), Lavrik, Drozdov, Smertin. Loskov, Kharlachev, Dzanashia (Bulikin 38mins), Sarkisyan (Maminov 76mins). Subs not used: Poliakov, Solomatine, Semenenko, Neretine. Scorer: Loskov.

■ **Oct 24 v Everton (A) Draw 4-4** (Bridges 2, Kewell, Woodgate) Att 37,355.
Ref: Dermot Gallagher Position: 1st
Everton: Gerrard, Weir, Watson, Gough, Ball (Johnson 78min), Barmby, Collins, Gemmill (Pembridge 28min), Unsworth, Hutchison, Campbell. Subs not used: Cadamarteri, Ward, Simonsen. Scorers: Campbell 2, Hutchison, Weir.
Leeds United: Martyn, Kelly, Radebe, Woodgate, Harte, Bowyer, Batty, McPhail, Kewell, Smith (Huckerby 68min), Bridges. Subs not used: Robinson, Hopkin, Haaland, Mills.

■ **Oct 30 v West Ham (H) Won 1-0** (Harte)
Att 40,190 Ref: Graham Poll Position: 1st
Leeds United: Martyn, Kelly, Radebe, Woodgate, Harte, Bowyer, Batty, McPhail, Kewell, Smith (Huckerby 58min), Bridges. Subs not used: Robinson, Hopkin, Mills, Bakke.
West Ham United: Hislop, Margas, Ferdinand, Ruddock, Lomas, Foe (Cole 70min), Lampard, Moncur, Keller, Kitson, Wanchope. Subs not used: Potts, Carrick, Forrest, Newton.

■ **Nov 4 v Lokomotiv Mosow (UEFA Cup 2nd rd, 2nd leg) (A) Won 3-0** (Harte pen, Bridges 2)
Att: 8,000 Ref: Alain Sars (France).
Lokomotiv Moscow: Nigmatullin, Arifullin, Chugainov, Pashinin (Kharlachev 45min), Lavrik, Loskov, Smertin, Solomatin, Hovannisyan (Semenenko 86min), Sarkisyan, Bulyikin (Pimenov 75min). Subs not used: Maminov, Neretine, Poliakov.
Leeds United: Martyn, Kelly, Radebe, Woodgate, Harte, Bakke, Batty, Bowyer (Haaland 45min), McPhail (Hopkin 80min), Kewell (Huckerby 65min), Bridges. Subs not used: Robinson, Smith, Mills, Duberry.

■ **Nov 7 v Wimbledon (A) Lost 2-0** Att: 18,747.
Ref: Peter Jones Position: 2nd
Wimbledon: Sullivan, Cunningham, Hreidarsson, Thatcher, Kimble, Cort (Andresen 90min), Earle, Euell, Anderson, Hartson (Leaburn 88min), Gayle (Badir 80min). S,ubs not used: Blackwell, Davis. Scorers: Hartson, Gayle.
Leeds United: Martyn, Kelly, Radebe, Woodgate (Duberry 46min), Harte, Bowyer (Bakke 62min), Batty, McPhail, Kewell, Huckerby, Smith (Hopkin 78min). Subs not used: Robinson, Mills.

■ **Nov 20 v Bradford City (H) Won 2-1** (Smith, Harte) Att: 39,937 Ref: Paul Durkin Position: 2nd
Leeds United: Martyn, Kelly, Radebe, Woodgate, Harte, Bakke, Batty, Bowyer, McPhail, Smith (Huckerby 76min), Bridges.
Subs not used: Robinson, Hopkin, Mills, Duberry.
Bradford City: Clarke, Halle, Wetherall, O'Brien, Sharpe, Lawrence, Windass, McCall, Redfearn (Blake 64min), Beagrie (Myers 78min), Mills. Subs not used: Walsh, Westwood, Whalley.
Scorer: Windass.

■ **Nov 28 v Southampton (H) Won 1-0** (Bridges)
Att: 39,288 Ref: Rob Harris (Oxford) Position: 1st
Leeds United: Martyn, Kelly, Woodgate, Mills,
Harte, Bowyer, Batty (Bakke 31min), McPhail,
Kewell, Smith (Huckerby 62min) Bridges.
Subs not used: Robinson, Haaland, Hiden.
Southampton: Jones, Tessem, Lundekvam,
Richards, Colleter, Ripley, Soltvedt, Oakley,
Kachloul, Pahars (Dodd 89min), Hughes (Beattie
77min). Subs not used: Le Tissier, Moss, Boa
Morte.

■ **Dec 2 v Spartak Moscow (UEFA Cup 3rd rd, 1st
leg) (in Sofia) Lost 2-1** (Kewell).
Att: 6,000. Ref: Anders Frisk.
Spartak Moscow: Filimonov, Parfionov, Khlestov,
Boushmanov, Kovtun, Baranov, Bulatov, Titov,
Bezrodniy, Schirko, Robson. Subs not used:
Smetanin, Ananko, Ketchinov, Evseev, Melesehin,
Moi, Peniche. Scorers: Schirko, Robson.
Leeds United: Martyn, Kelly, Woodgate, Duberry,
Harte, Bakke, Haaland, Bowyer, McPhail, Kewell,
Bridges (Huckerby 55min). Subs not used:
Robinson, Smith, Mills, Jones, Hiden. Maybury.

■ **Dec 5 v Derby County (A) Won 1-0** (Harte pen).
Att: 29, 455 Ref: Paul Alcock Position: 1st
Derby County: Poom, Laursen (Prior 63min),
Carbonari, Elliott, Delap, Burley, Powell, Kinkladze
(Dorigo 75min), Johnson, Burton (Christie 80min),
Sturridge. Subs not used: Hoult, Nimni.
Leeds United: Martyn, Kelly, Woodgate, Radebe,
Harte, Bowyer, Bakke, McPhail (Jones 87min),
Kewell, Bridges, Huckerby (Smith 77min).
Subs not used: Robinson, Mills, Duberry.

■ **Dec 9 v Spartak Moscow (UEFA Cup 3rd rd, 2nd
leg) (H) Won 1-0** (Radebe)
Att: 39,732 Ref: Antonio Lopez Nieto (Spain)
Leeds United: Martyn, Kelly, Woodgate, Radebe,
Harte, Bakke, Bowyer, McPhail, Kewell, Bridges,
Smith (Huckerby 73min).
Subs not used: Robinson, Haaland, Mills, Jones,
Hiden, Duberry.
Spartak Moscow: Filimonov (Smetanin 38min),
Parfionov, Khlestov, Bouschmanov, Evseev,
Baranov, Bulatov, Titov, Tikhonov; Schirko, Robson.
Subs not used: Ananko, Ketchinov, Penishe,
Meleschin, Mor, Bezrodniy.

■ **Dec 12 v Port Vale (FA Cup 3rd rd) (H) Won 2-0**
(Bakke 2). Att: 11,912 Ref: Steve Dunn.
Leeds United: Martyn, Kelly, Woodgate, Radebe,
Harte, Bowyer (Bridges 75min), Bakke, McPhail,
Kewell, Smith (Jones 72min), Huckerby.
Subs not used: Robinson, Mills, Duberry.
Port Vale: Musselwhite, Burns, Snijders, Gardner,
Briscoe, Minton, Eyre, Widdrington, Tankard
(Naylor 67min), Foyle, Rougier. Subs not used:
Pilkington, Butler, Corden, Bogie.

■ **Dec 15 v Leicester City (Worthington Cup rd 4)
(A) 0-0 (Lost 4-2 on pens)** Att: Ref: Graham Barber.
Leicester City: Flowers, Taggart, Walsh, Elliott,
Impey, Oakes, Savage, Lennon (Zagorakis 15min),
Izzet, Cottee (Gunnlaugsson 91min) Heskey.
Subs not used: Gilchrist, Campbell, Arphexad.
Leeds United: Martyn, Kelly, Woodgate, Radebe,
Harte, Batty (Jones 20min), Bakke, Bowyer,
McPhail, Kewell, Bridges (Duberry 92min).
Subs not used: Robinson, Huckerby, Mills.

■ **Dec 19 v Chelsea (A) Won 2-0** (McPhail 2)
Att: 35,106. Ref: Jeff Winter Position: 1st
Chelsea: De Goey, Ferrer, Desailly (Hogh 46min,
Petrescu 64min), Lebouef, Harley, Wise, Di Matteo,
Deschamps, Poyet, Sutton, Flo (Zola 57min).
Subs not used: Morris, Cudicini.
Leeds United: Martyn, Kelly, Woodgate, Radebe,
Harte, Bowyer (Jones 85min), McPhail, Bakke,
Kewell, Huckerby, Bridges (Wilcox 48min).
Subs not used: Robinson, Mills, Duberry.

■ **Dec 26 v Leicester City (H) Won 2-1** (Bridges,
Bowyer) Att: 40,105. Ref: Mark Halsey
Position: 1st
Leeds United: Martyn, Kelly, Radebe, Woodgate,
Harte, Bowyer, Bakke, McPhail, Kewell; Huckerby
(Wilcox 77min), Bridges. Subs not used: Robinson,
Jones, Mills, Duberry.
Leicester City: Arphexad, Sinclair, Elliott, Taggart,
Gilchrist (Zagorakis 65min), Savage, Izzet, Oakes,
Eadie, Cottee, Heskey. Subs not used:
Gunnlaugsson, Campbell, Hodges, Thomas.
Scorer: Cottee.

■ **Dec 28 v Arsenal (A) Lost 2-0**
Att: 38,096. Ref: Graham Poll Position: 1st
Arsenal: Seaman, Grimandi, Adams, Luzhny,
Silvinho, Ljungberg, Vieira, Petit, Overmars, Henry,
Kanu. Subs not used: Dixon, Manninger, Barrett.
Scorers: Ljungberg, Henry
Leeds United: Martyn, Kelly, Woodgate, Radebe,
Harte, Bakke, Bowyer (Jones 80min), McPhail,
Kewell, Bridges, Smith (Wilcox 80min).
Subs not used: Robinson, Mills, Duberry.

■ **Jan 3 v Aston Villa (H) Lost 2-1** (Kewell).
Att: 40,027 Ref: Uriah Rennie Position: 1st
Leeds United: Martyn, Kelly, Duberry, Woodgate,
Harte, Haaland, Bakke, Jones (Wilcox 75min),
Kewell, Smith (Huckerby 75min) Bridges.
Subs not used: Robinson, Mills, Hiden.
Aston Villa: James, Watson, Southgate, Ehiogu,
Barry, Wright, Stone, Boateng, Merson, Joachim,
Carbone (Vassell 79min). Subs not used: Draper,
Cutler, Ghrayib, Calderwood. Scorer: Southgate 2.

■ **Jan 9 v Manchester City (FA Cup 4th rd) (A)**
Won 5-2 (Bakke, Smith, Kewell 2 Bowyer).
Att: 29,240 Ref: Dermot Gallagher
Manchester City: Weaver, Edghill, Wiekens, Jobson,
Granville (Peacock 65min), Horlock, Bishop, Grant
(J Whitley 54min), Kennedy, Dickov, Goater.
Subs not used: Crooks, Wright, Tiatto. Scorers:
Goater, Bishop.
Leeds United: Martyn, Kelly, Woodgate, Radebe,
Harte, McPhail, Bowyer, Bakke, Wilcox, Kewell,
Smith (Huckerby 86min). Subs not used:
Robinson, Mills, Jones, Duberry.

■ **Jan 23 v Sunderland (A) Won 2-1** (Wilcox,
Bridges) Att: 41,947. Ref: Peter Jones Position: 1st
Sunderland: Sorensen, Williams, Butler, Bould
(Craddock 77min), Gray (Holloway 46min), Roy
(Reddy 64min), Schwarz, Ray, Kilbane, McCann,
Phillips. Subs not used: Marriott, Oster.
Scorer: Phillips.
Leeds United: Martyn, Kelly, Woodgate, Duberry,
Harte, Bowyer, McPhail, Bakke, Wilcox, Kewell,
Bridges (Huckerby 75min).
Subs not used: Robinson, Haaland, Mills, Jones.

■ **Jan 30 v Aston Villa (FA Cup 5th rd) (A) Lost 3-2.**
(Harte, Bakke) Att: 30,026. Ref: Graham Barber.
Aston Villa: James, Ehiogu, Southgate, Barry,
Watson (Delaney 46min) Merson (Hendrie 73min),
Stone, Boateng, Wright, Carbone, Joachim.
Subs not used: Thompson, Cutler, Walker.
Scorer: Carbone 3.
Leeds United: Martyn, Kelly, Duberry (Mills 71min),
Woodgate, Harte, Bowyer, Bakke (Huckerby
84min), McPhail, Wilcox, Bridges (Smith 71min),
Kewell. Subs not used: Robinson, Jones.

■ **Feb 5 v Liverpool (A) Lost 3-1** (Bowyer).
Att: 44,793. Ref: Mike Reed Position: 2nd.
Liverpool: Westerveld, Carragher, Hyypia, Henchoz,
Matteo, Smicer, Gerrard, Hamann, Berger, Camara
(Murphy 72min), Meijer. Subs not used: Staunton,
Heggem, Nielsen, Newby. Scorers: Hamann,
Berger, Murphy.
Leeds United: Martyn, Kelly, Woodgate, Duberry,
Harte, Bowyer, Bakke, McPhail (Huckerby 75min),
Wilcox, Smith (Bridges 75min), Kewell.
Subs not used: Robinson, Mills, Jones.

■ **Feb 12 v Tottenham (H) Won 1-0** (Kewell).
Att: 40,127. Ref: Dermot Gallagher Position: 2nd
Leeds United: Martyn, Kelly, Duberry, Woodgate,
Harte, Bakke (Haaland 85min), Bowyer, Jones,
Wilcox, Smith, Kewell (Huckerby 68min).
Subs not used: Robinson, Mills, Maybury.
Tottenham: Walker, Carr, Campbell, Perry, Taricco,
Anderton, Sherwood, Clemence (Nielsen 74min),
Ginola (Dominguez 78min), Armstrong, Korsten.
Subs not used: Baardsen, Scales, Young.

■ **Feb 20 v Manchester United (H) Lost 1-0.**
Att: 40,160 Ref: Peter Jones Position: 2nd
Leeds United: Martyn, Kelly, Radebe, Woodgate,
Harte, Bakke, Bowyer, Jones, Wilcox, Smith,
Kewell. Subs not used: Robinson, Haaland,
Hopkin, Huckerby, Mills.
Manchester United: Bosnich, G. Neville, Stam,
Silvestre, Irwin, Giggs, Keane, Butt, Scholes, Cole,
Yorke (Sheringham 30min).
Subs not used: P. Neville, Cruyff, Van Der Gouw,
Berg. Scorer: Cole.

■ **Feb 26 v Middlesbrough (A) Draw 0-0.**
Att: 34,800. Ref: Uriah Rennie Position: 2nd
Middlesbrough: Schwarzer, Cooper, Festa,
Pallister, Fleming, Maddison (Cummins 73min),
Ziege, Summerbell, Juninho, Campbell (Armstrong
73min), Ricard (Vickers 86min).
Subs not used: Beresford, Stockdale.
Leeds United: Martyn, Mills, Radebe, Haaland,
Woodgate, Harte, Hopkin (Bridges 86min), Bowyer,
Wilcox, Smith (Huckerby 55min), Kewell.
Subs not used: Robinson, Duberry, Maybury.

■ **Mar 2 v AS Roma (UEFA Cup 4th rd 1st leg) (A)**
Draw 0-0. Att: 37,726. Ref: Gilles Veissiere (France)
AS Roma: Antonioli, Zago, Aldair, Mangone, Cafu,
Nakata, Tommasi, Candela, Totti, Montella,
Delvecchio. Subs not used: Lupatelli, Di Francesco,
Blasi, Tomic, Gurenko, Rinaldi, Fabio Junior.
Leeds United: Martyn, Kelly, Woodgate, Radebe,
Haaland, Harte, Jones, Bakke, Bowyer, Bridges
(Smith 71min), Kewell. Subs not used: Robinson,
Hopkin, Huckerby, Mills, Duberry, Maybury.

■ **Mar 5 v Coventry City (H) Won 3-0** (Kewell,
Bridges, Wilcox). Att: 38,710 Ref: Jeff Winter
Position: 2nd
Leeds United: Martyn, Kelly, Radebe, Woodgate
(Haaland 46min), Harte, Bakke, Bowyer (Jones
89min), McPhail, Wilcox, Bridges (Huckerby
80min), Kewell. Subs not used: Robinson, Smith.
Coventry City: Hedman, Quinn (Shaw 46min),
Breen, Hendry, Burrows, Eustace, Chippo,
McAllister, Whelan, Zuniga (Normann 60min),
Roussel. Subs not used: Konjic, Hyldgaard, Pead.

■ **Mar 9 v AS Roma (UEFA Cup 4th rd 2nd leg) (H)**
Won 1-0 (Kewell).
Att: 39,149 Ref: J M Garcia-Aranda Encinar (Spain)
Leeds United: Martyn, Kelly, Haaland, Radebe,
Harte, Bakke (Jones 84min), Bowyer, McPhail
(Huckerby 88min), Wilcox, Kewell, Bridges (Smith
81min). Subs not used: Robinson, Hopkin, Mills,
Duberry.
AS Roma: Antonioli, Zago, Aldair, Mangone,
Rinaldi, Nakata (Eusebio 77min), Tommasi,
Candela, Totti, Montella, Delvecchio. Subs not
used: Luatelli, Zanetti, Blasi, Tomic, Gurenko,
Lanzaro.

■ **Mar 12 v Bradford City (A) Won 2-1** (Bridges 2).
Att: 18,276. Ref: Paul Durkin Position: 2nd
Bradford City: Southall, Halle (Cadete 66min),
Wetherall, O'Brien, Jacobs, Lawrence, McCall,
Whalley (Blake 66min), Beagrie, Windass,
Saunders. Subs not used: Taylor, Sharpe, Dreyer.
Scorer: Beagrie
Leeds United: Martyn, Kelly, Haaland, Radebe,
Harte, Bowyer, Bakke, McPhail (Hopkin 73min),
Wilcox, Bridges (Huckerby 89min), Smith.
Subs not used: Robinson, Duberry, Maybury.

■ **Mar 16 v Slavia Prague (UEFA Cup QF 1st leg)**
(H) Won 3-0 (Wilcox, Kewell, Bowyer)
Att: 39,519 Ref: Markus Merk (Germany)
Leeds United: Martyn, Kelly, Haaland, Radebe,
Harte, Bowyer, Bakke, McPhail, Wilcox, Bridges,
Kewell. Subs not used: Robinson, Hopkin, Mills,
Jones, Duberry.
Slavia Prague: Cerny, Vicek (Vagner 55min), Rada,
Koller, L Dosek, Kuchar, Dostalek (Hysky 55min),
Horvath, Petrous, Ulich, T Dosek. Subs not used:
Lerch, Kozel, Skala, Vaclavik, Vozabal.

■ **Mar 19 v Wimbledon (H) Won 4-1** (Bakke 2,
Harte pen, Kewell)
Att: 39,256. Ref: Alan Wiley Position: 2nd
Leeds United: Martyn, Kelly, Radebe, Haaland,
Harte, Bakke (Jones 85min), Hopkin, McPhail,
Wilcox, Bridges (Smith 64min), Kewell (Huckerby
84min). Subs not used: Robinson, Duberry.
Wimbledon: Sullivan, Cunningham, Willmott,
Andersen, Kimble, Euell, Gayle, Earle, Ardley, Cort
(Badir 46min), Lund. Subs not used: Blackwell,
Heald, Hughes, Andresen. Scorer: Euell.

■ **Mar 23 v Slavia Prague (UEFA Cup QF 2nd leg)**
(A) Lost 2-1 (Kewell)
Att: 13,460. Ref: Orhan Erdemir
Slavia Prague: Cerny, L Dosek, Koller, Hysky, Kozel,
Ulich, Kuchar (Vozabal 85min), T Dosek (Vagner
54min), Dostalek (Lerch 54min), Skala, Zelenka.
Subs not used: Kristofik, Vaclavik.
Scorer: Ulich 2.
Leeds United: Martyn, Haaland, Woodgate,
Radebe, Kelly, Bakke, Jones, McPhail, Harte,
Kewell, Bridges (Smith 50min).
Subs not used: Robinson, Mills, Hopkin, Duberry,
Huckerby, Wilcox.

■ **Mar 26 v Leicester City (A) Lost 2-1** (Kewell)
Att: 21,095 Ref: Steve Lodge Position: 2nd
Leicester City: Flowers, Sinclair (Gilchrist 48min),
Taggart, Elliott, Guppy, Savage, Izzet, Lennon,
Oakes, Collymore, Eadie (Cottee 65min).
Subs not used: Marshall, Arphexad, Impey.
Scorers: Collymore, Guppy.
Leeds United: Martyn, Kelly, Radebe, Woodgate,
Harte, Bakke, Haaland, McPhail, Wilcox, Bridges
(Huckerby 71min), Kewell.
Subs not used: Robinson, Mills, Duberry, Maybury.

■ **Apr 1 v Chelsea (H) Lost 1-0.**
Att: 40,162. Ref: Jeff Winter Position: 2nd
Leeds United: Martyn, Kelly, Woodgate, Radebe,
Harte, Bowyer, Bakke, McPhail, Wilcox (Huckerby
74min), Kewell, Smith. Subs not used: Robinson,
Haaland, Mills, Jones.
Chelsea: De Goey, Ferrer, Thome, Lebouef,
Babayaro, Di Matteo, Morris, Wise, Harley
(Lambourde 88min), Sutton, Weah.
Subs not used: Hogh, Cudicini, Dalla Bona, Zola.
Scorer: Harley.

■ **Apr 6 v Galatasaray (UEFA Cup SF 1st lg) (A)**
Lost 2-0. Att: 18,00. Ref: Helmut Krug (Germany)
Galatasaray: Taffarel, Capone, Popescu, Bulent,
Hagi (Ahmet 88min), Okan (Hakan Unsal 62min),
Suat, Emre, Regun, Arif (Hasan 77min), Suker.
Subs not used: Bolukbasi, Akyel, Emrah, Dos
Santos. Scorers: Suker, Capone.
Leeds United: Martyn, Kelly, Woodgate, Radebe,
Harte, Bakke, Bowyer, Jones (Wilcox 65min),
McPhail, Kewell, Bridges (Huckerby 74min).
Subs not used: Robinson, Haaland, Smith, Mills,
Duberry.

■ **Apr 9 v Aston Villa (A) Lost 1-0**
Att: 33,889. Ref: Barry Knight Position: 3rd
Aston Villa: James, Watson, Ehiogu, Samuel, Barry,
Wright (Ghrayib 52min), Merson, Boateng, Hendrie
(Thompson 67min), Carbone (Dublin 59min),
Joachim. Subs not used: Delaney, Enckelman.
Scorer: Joachim.
Leeds United: Martyn, Kelly, Radebe, Woodgate,
Harte, Bakke, Bowyer, McPhail, Wilcox, Bridges
(Huckerby 59min), Kewell.
Subs not used: Robinson, Haaland, Mills, Jones.

■ **Apr 16 v Arsenal (H) Lost 4-0.**
Att: 39,307. Ref: Steve Dunn Position: 4th
Leeds United: Martyn, Kelly, Woodgate, Haaland,
Harte, Bowyer, Bakke, McPhail, Kewell, Bridges
(Wilcox 46min), Smith. Subs not used: Robinson,
Hopkin, Huckerby, Duberry.
Arsenal: Seaman, Dixon, Keown, Adams, Silvinho,
Parlour, Vieira, Petit, Winterburn (82min),
Ljungberg, Bergkamp (Kanu 66min), Henry
(Overmars 73min). Subs not used: Malz,
Manninger. Scorers: Henry, Keown, Kanu,
Overmars.

■ **Apr 20 v Galatasaray (UEFA Cup SF 2nd leg) (H)**
Draw 2-2 (Bakke 2)
Att: 38,406. Ref: Lubos Michel (Slovakia)
Leeds United: Martyn, Mills, Radebe, Woodgate,
Harte (Huckerby 46min), Bakke, Bowyer, McPhail,
Wilcox, Kewell, Bridges. Subs not used: Robinson,
Haaland, Hopkin, Smith, Jones, Duberry.
Galatasaray: Taffarel, Popescu, Korkmaz, Ergun,
Suat Kaya (Ahmet 80min), Belozoglu, Buruk
(Hasan Sas 87min), Capone, Hagi, Erdem (Hakan
Unsal 46min), Hakan Sukur. Subs not used: Akyel,
Davala, Inan, Marcio. Scorers: Hagi (pen), Suker.

■ **Apr 23 v Newcastle United (A) Draw 2-2**
(Bridges, Wilcox)
Att: 36,460 Ref: David Elleray Position: 5th
Newcastle United: Given, Barton, Hughes, Dabizas,
Helder (Mercelino 65min), Domi, Howey, Gavilan
(Antunes 86min), Lee, Dyer (Maric 80min), Shearer.
Subs not used: Harper, McClen. Scorer: Shearer 2.
Leeds United: Martyn, Mills, Radebe, Duberry,
Harte (Bowyer 76min), Bakke, Haaland, McPhail,
Wilcox, Bridges (Huckerby 78min), Kewell.
Subs not used: Robinson, Hopkin, Smith.

■ **Apr 30 v Sheffield Wed (A) Won 3-0** (Hopkin,
Bridges, Kewell)
Att: 23,416.Ref: Rob Harris Position: 4th
Sheffield Wednesday: Pressman, Nolan,
Hinchcliffe, Walker, Atherton, Horne (Sibon 63min),
Alexandersson (Briscoe 76min), Jonk, Quinn,
De Bilde (Sonner 76min), Booth.
Subs not used: Haslam, Srnicek.
Leeds United: Martyn, Kelly, Radebe, Duberry,
Mills, Hopkin, Bakke (Haaland 69min), Jones,
Wilcox, Kewell, Bridges (Huckerby 84min).
Subs not used: Robinson, Woodgate, Smith.

■ **May 3 v Watford (H) Won 3-1** (Bridges, Duberry, Huckerby).
Att: 36,324 Ref: Paul Alcock Position: 3rd
Leeds United: Martyn, Kelly, Duberry, Radebe (Woodgate 46min), Mills, Bakke, Bowyer, McPhail, Kewell, Bridges, Huckerby (Smith 80min). Subs not used: Robinson, Hopkin, Wilcox.
Watford: Day, Cox, Page, Ward, Robinson, Hyde, Palmer, Perpetuini, Helguson (Wooter 66min), Smith, Foley (Mooney 66min). Subs not used: Gibbs, Bonnot, Chamberlain. Scorer: Foley.

■ **May 8 v Everton (H) Draw 1-1** (Bridges)
Att: 37,713. Ref: Andy D'Urso Position: 3rd
Leeds United: Martyn, Kelly, Woodgate, Duberry, Mills, Bakke, Bowyer, McPhail, Wilcox (Haaland 56min), Kewell, Bridges (Huckerby 81min). Subs not used: Hopkin, Jones, Robinson.
Everton: Gerrard, Weir, Dunne, Unsworth, Ball, Barmby, S Hughes, Collins, Pembridge (Ward 79min), M Hughes (Cadamarteri 73min), Hutchison. Subs not used: Jevons, Clarke, Simonsen. Scorer: Barmby.

■ **May 14 v West Ham (A) Draw 0-0.**
Att: 26,044 Ref: Graham Barber Position: 3rd
West Ham United: Bywater, Margas, Ferdinand, Stimac, Potts, Sinclair, Foe, Moncur, Di Canio, Wanchope, Kanoute. Subs not used: Newton, McCann, Alexander, Forbes, Feuer.
Leeds United: Martyn, Kelly, Radebe, Woodgate, Mills, Jones, Bakke (Bowyer 78min), McPhail, Wilcox (Huckerby 88min), Bridges (Smith 29min), Kewell. Subs not used: Duberry, Robinson.

PREMIERSHIP FINAL TABLE 1999-2000

		HOME					AWAY					TOTAL					
	P	W	D	L	F	A	W	D	L	F	A	W	D	L	F	A	GD	Pts
Manchester Utd	38	15	4	0	59	16	13	3	3	38	29	28	7	3	97	45	+52	91
Arsenal	38	14	3	2	42	17	8	4	7	31	26	22	7	9	73	43	+30	73
LEEDS UNITED	38	12	2	5	29	18	9	4	6	29	25	21	6	11	58	43	+15	69
Liverpool	38	11	4	4	28	13	8	6	5	23	17	19	10	9	51	30	+21	67
Chelsea	38	12	5	2	35	12	6	6	7	18	22	18	11	9	53	34	+19	65
Aston Villa	38	8	8	3	23	12	7	5	7	23	23	15	13	10	46	35	+11	58
Sunderland	38	10	6	3	28	17	6	4	9	29	39	16	10	12	57	56	+1	58
Leicester City	38	10	3	6	31	24	6	4	9	24	31	16	7	15	55	55	+0	55
West Ham Utd	38	11	5	3	32	23	4	5	10	20	30	15	10	13	52	53	-1	55
Tottenham H	38	10	3	6	40	26	5	5	9	17	23	15	8	15	57	49	+8	53
Newcastle Utd	38	10	5	4	42	20	4	5	10	21	34	14	10	14	63	54	+9	52
Middlesbrough	38	8	5	6	23	26	6	5	8	23	26	14	10	14	46	52	-6	52
Everton	38	7	9	3	36	21	5	5	9	23	28	12	14	12	59	49	+10	50
Coventry City	38	12	1	6	38	22	0	7	12	9	32	12	8	18	47	54	-7	44
Southampton	38	8	4	7	26	22	4	4	11	19	40	12	8	18	45	62	-17	44
Derby County	38	6	3	10	22	25	3	8	8	22	32	9	11	18	44	57	-13	38
Bradford City	38	6	8	5	26	29	3	1	15	12	39	9	9	20	38	68	-30	36
Wimbledon	38	6	7	6	30	28	1	5	13	16	46	7	12	19	46	74	-28	33
Sheffield Wed	38	6	3	10	21	23	2	4	13	17	47	8	7	23	38	70	-32	31
Watford	38	5	4	10	24	31	1	2	16	11	46	6	6	26	35	77	-42	24

CARLING OPTA STATISTICS

■ Total Shots Attempted

Harry Kewell	107
Michael Bridges	78
Lee Bowyer	72

■ Total Shots On Target

Harry Kewell	43
Michael Bridges	42
Lee Bowyer	30

■ Total Shots Off Target

Harry Kewell	64
Lee Bowyer	42
Michael Bridges	36

■ Total Passes

Ian Harte	1517
Harry Kewell	1240
Gary Kelly	1102

■ Total Successful Passes

Ian Harte	995
Harry Kewell	814
Stephen McPhail	811

■ Tackles Attempted

Woodgate	116
Lucas Radebe	106
Lee Bowyer	105

■ Dribbles and Runs Attempted

Harry Kewell	336
Darren Huckerby	119
Michael Bridges	114

■ Total Crosses Attempted

Ian Harte	181
Jason Wilcox	119
Harry Kewell	94

■ Offsides

Michael Bridges	56
Harry Kewell	33
Darren Huckerby	28

■ Total Fouls Conceded

Michael Bridges	65
Harry Kewell	65
Alan Smith	57

■ Total Fouls Won

Harry Kewell	80
Lee Bowyer	57
Michael Bridges	49

■ Harry Kewell - here, there and everywhere judging by Opta's stats!

APPENDIX TWO

THE PLAYERS

■ **GOALKEEPER Nigel Martyn**

The Cornishman became England's first £1million player when he was transferred from Bristol City to Crystal Palace in 1989 and when he joined Leeds United seven year's later his value had more than doubled - Leeds beating off fierce competition from Everton to sign him for £2.25m.

His form has continued to improve, to such an extent that many people believe he should be England's first choice goalkeeper ahead of Arsenal's David Seaman. At least he must now be considered on the same level as the Arsenal keeper.

A consistent performer, Martyn managed to stay clear of injury last season and was the only Leeds player to appear in all 55 of the club's league and cup games.

Date of Birth:	August 11th, 1966
Birthplace:	St Austell, Cornwall
Height:	6ft 1in
Signed for Leeds:	July 24th, 1996
Signed from:	Crystal Palace
Transfer fee:	£2.25million
Leeds goals:	-
Debut for Leeds:	August 17th, 1996 v Derby County (a) D 3-3
International Honours:	England full, Under 21

■ **RIGHT-BACK Gary Kelly**

Although still only 26, Kelly is the longest serving player with Leeds and has made more first team appearances than any other of the club's present players. He has bounced back in style after having missed the whole of the 1998-99 season with shin splint problems.

The Republic of Ireland international provided the perfect answer to those who felt he might have difficulty in battling his way back into the side following the signing of Danny Mills from Charlton Athletic.

Though he was not in the side at the start of the 1999-2000 season, once he got back his form was such that he stayed there and finished the season having made 47 appearances.

Date of Birth:	July 9, 1974
Birthplace:	Drogheda, Ireland
Height:	5ft 8in
Signed for Leeds:	July 9, 1991
Signed from:	Home Farm, Ireland
Transfer fee:	Nil
Leeds goals:	2
Debut for Leeds:	October 8th, 1991 Rumbelows Cup 2nd rd 2nd lg v Scunthorpe (h)
International honours:	Republic of Ireland Full and Under 21

■ **LEFT-BACK Ian Harte**

After an indecisive period under previous Leeds manager George Graham, when although playing regularly for the Republic of Ireland he found himself relegated to the Leeds reserve side, Harte is now established as first choice left back.

He had to shed some weight to do it but there is no doubting the skills of the Irishman who, although a left-footed player, possesses as much power in his right foot - as a few goalkeepers have found out to their cost in the last couple of seasons.

In fact he probably has the hardest shot of all

the players at the club - a talent he uses to good effect at free kicks and from the penalty spot.

Date of Birth:	August 31, 1977
Birthplace:	Drogheda, Ireland
Height:	5ft 9in
Signed for Leeds:	December 11, 1995
Signed from:	Trainee
Transfer fee:	Nil
Leeds goals:	17
Debut for Leeds:	January 10th, 1996
	Coca-Cola Cup rd 5
	v Reading
International honours:	Republic of Ireland
	Full, Under 21, Under 18

■ CENTRE-BACK Lucas Radebe

Widely regarded among Leeds fans as one of the best and most cultured central defenders to have appeared in a Leeds side dating back to the golden era of the late 1960s and early 1970s.

Not the quickest of defenders, but one of great vision and determination. His timing of a tackle is second to none. Made captain of the team when George Graham was manager and he held on to the honour after David O'Leary took over.

■ Lucas Radebe

Highly respected in the game, Radebe, captain of South Africa, has been an excellent ambassador as his country made a successful bid to be recognised on football's world stage. Led his country to their African Nations Cup final triumph in 1996 and in their first ever World Cup finals in 1998.

Date of Birth:	April 12th, 1969
Birthplace:	Johannesburg,
	South Africa
Height:	6ft 1in
Signed for Leeds:	August 5th. 1994
Signed from:	Kaiser Chiefs, South Africa
Transfer fee:	£250,000
Leeds goals:	3
Debut for Leeds:	September 21, 1994
	Coca-Cola Cup 2nd rd
	1st lg v Mansfield Town
International honours:	South Africa Full

■ CENTRE-BACK Jonathan Woodgate

Enjoyed a rapid rise to the top when given his first team chance in October 1998, shortly after David O'Leary had become manager. He began that season playing in Leeds' youth team but ended it with 25 first team appearances - and a call up by Kevin Keegan to the full England squad.

A player with a down to earth approach, the teenager seemed completely unfazed by his elevation to senior team soccer and formed a sound partnership with Lucas Radebe.

Off the field problems interrupted his international career but he continued to be a regular choice for the first team. Although his form dipped midway through the second half of the 1999-2000 season he worked hard in extra training sessions with his manager to put his career back on track.

Date of Birth:	January 22nd, 1980
Birthplace:	Middlesbrough
Height:	6ft 2in
Signed for Leeds:	January 22nd, 1997
Signed from:	Trainee
Transfer fee:	Nil
Leeds goals:	3
Debut for Leeds:	October 17th, 1998 v
	Nottingham Forest (a)
International honours:	England Full and Under 18

■ **CENTRE-BACK Michael Duberry**

Leeds paid £4.5million to bring Duberry from Chelsea where after making an impact he had found himself shut out by the West London club's overseas signings, notably those of Frank Leboeuf and Marcel Dessailly.

Although he got into the Leeds side in the early part of last season a thigh injury interrupted his progress.

It took him the best part of two months to recover from the injury and when he did he found it difficult to force his way back into the senior side. He did however come back towards the end of the season top make a handful of first team outings.

Date of Birth:	October 14th, 1975
Birthplace:	Enfield
Height:	6ft 1in
Signed for Leeds:	July 12th, 1999
Signed from:	Chelsea
Transfer fee:	£4.5million
Leeds goals:	1
Debut for Leeds:	August 11th, 1999 v Southampton (h)
International honours:	England Under-21

■ **MIDFIELD Olivier Dacourt**

The French midfielder became Leeds United's record signing when he became manager David O'Leary's first signing of the summer in a £7.2million transfer from RC Lens.

The transfer enabled the 25-year-old tough tackling midfield man to return to the English Premier League after just one season back in French football having been with Everton before that. He previously played for Strasbourg

Dacourt was at the top of O'Leary's wanted list following the club's qualification for the Champions' League and he is seen as being able to add some much needed steel as well as more quality to the Leeds midfield.

Date of Birth:	25th September 1974
Birthplace:	Montreuil, France
Height:	5ft 9in
Date signed:	15th May 2000
Signed from:	RC Lens
Transfer fee:	£7.2m
Previous clubs:	Strasbourg, Everton, RC Lens.

■ **MIDFIELD Eirik Bakke**

When Leeds United paid Norwegian club Sogndal £1.75m for Bakke, manager David O'Leary said the player had been bought with the intention that he would first gain further experience in reserve team football.

But injuries forced the manager to bring Bakke into the senior side and the budding young Norwegian international made such an impression that he quickly became a regular. A measure of how well he played came when Leeds supporters voted him the club's Young Player-of-the-Season.

Bakke was captain of Norway's Under-21 side when he joined Leeds and his progress in the English Premiership was duly noted by Norway who selected him in their Euro 2000 squad.

Date of Birth:	September 13th, 1977
Birthplace:	Sogndal, Norway
Height:	5ft 11in
Signed for Leeds:	May 25th 1999
Signed from:	Sogndal
Transfer fee:	£1.75million
Leeds goals:	8
Debut for Leeds:	August 11th, 1999 v Southampton (a)
International honours:	Norway Full and Under-21

■ Eirik Bakke

■ **MIDFIELD Lee Bowyer**

The player Leeds' coaching staff have christened 'Mr Perpetual Motion' because of his amazing ability to keep up on running from penalty area to penalty area throughout the full 90 minutes of a match.

When Bowyer signed for Leeds in the summer of 1996, he cost £2.6million and that made him Britain's most costly teenage footballer. Leeds felt he was a player with huge potential and that it would be money well spent.

So far the aggressive midfield man with an eye for goals has shown that is likely to be money very well spent. He was the club's Player-of-the-Year in 1998-99 and was in great form for the first half of last season, until off the field problems appeared to affect him.

Date of Birth:	January 3rd, 1977
Birthplace:	West Ham
Height:	5ft 9in
Signed for Leeds:	July 3rd, 1996
Signed from:	Charlton Athletic
Transfer fee:	£2.6m
Leeds goals:	30
Debut for Leeds:	August 17th, 1996 v Derby County (a)
International honours:	England Under-21

■ **MIDFIELD Stephen McPhail**

Another of the Leeds youngsters to rise rapidly through the ranks, McPhail has surprised no one on the Elland Road coaching staff who predict a very bright future for the lad from Ireland after watching him develop in the lower ranks.

Injuries hampered his career at the start of last season but once he got over them he was quickly back in the first team displaying his creative skills in the Leeds midfield. Another of the club's left-footed players, McPhail has the ability to split open defences with quality passes and also to unleash inch perfect passes substantial distances.

Well through off, too, by the Republic of Ireland who have played him at Under-21 level and, last summer gave him his full international debut. His play making ability is admired my many.

■ Lee Bowyer celebrating one of 30 goals for Leeds.

Date of Birth:	December 9th, 1979
Birthplace:	London
Height:	5ft 8in
Signed for Leeds:	December 9th, 1996
Signed from:	Trainee
Transfer fee:	Nil
Leeds goals:	2
Debut for Leeds:	February 7th, 1998 v Leicester City (a)
International honours:	Republic of Ireland Full, Under-21, Under-18.

■ **MIDFIELD Jason Wilcox**

At 29 years of age, Wilcox is one of the most experienced players in the Leeds side. Brought in from Blackburn Rovers midway through last season when David O'Leary strengthened his squad - at the cost of £3m.

The transfer caused surprise among Leeds fans and the suddenness of it all also surprised Wilcox, who had spent his career with Blackburn and had not been seeking a move. But once he knew of Leeds' interest he quickly agreed to the transfer.

O'Leary made his move for Wilcox to play on the left side of midfield so that he could move Australian international Harry Kewell to a front running role and Wilcox played his part in the final stages of Leeds' successful bid for Champions' League qualification.

Date of Birth:	July 15, 1971
Birthplace:	Bolton
Height:	6ft
Signed for Leeds:	December 17th, 1999.
Signed from:	Blackburn Rovers
Transfer fee:	£3million
Leeds goals:	4
Debut for Leeds:	December 19th, 1999 v Chelsea (a)
International honours:	England Full.

■ Matthew Jones

■ **MIDFIELD David Batty**

Batty's return to his home city club in December 1998 delighted supporters and the experienced England international was playing some of the best football of his career when struck by injuries.

An Achilles tendon injury suffered three and half months into last season ruled him out for the rest of the season and as time dragged on cast doubts over his future in the game. But medication he was taking to recover from a previous injury that caused a heart problem was slowing his recovery.

After an operation on the Achilles problem last summer Batty is expected to be back in action in the New Year.

Date of Birth:	December 2nd, 1968
Birthplace:	Leeds
Height:	5ft 8in
Signed for Leeds:	July 1985
Signed from:	Trainee
Debut for Leeds:	November 21st, 1987 v Swindon Town (h)
Transferred to Blackburn:	October 1993.
Re-Signed for Leeds:	December 8th, 1998
Signed from:	Newcastle United
Transfer fee:	£4.4million
Leeds goals:	4
International honours:	England Full and 'B'

■ **MIDFIELD Matthew Jones**

Coaches predict a bright future for the talented young midfielder from Llanelli in South Wales. Although he can not yet claim to be a regular first team player with Leeds it was a measure of the faith manager David O'Leary has in him that he played him in most of the club's biggest games of last season.

Although he played in most positions, other than left-back or in goal at reserve and youth level, playing in the centre of midfield is the position he would eventually like to settle into.

An elegant player, Jones is tough in the tackle and never shirks his responsibilities. Captained Wales Under-21 side when still only 18 years of age. Has played at every level for his country.

Date of Birth:	September 1st, 1980
Birthplace:	Swansea
Height:	5ft 11in
Signed for Leeds:	September 1st, 1997

Signed from:	Trainee.
Transfer fee:	Nil
Leeds goals:	-
Debut for Leeds:	January 23rd, 1999 FA Cup
	5th rd v Portsmouth (a)
International honours:	Wales, Full, 'B,' Under-18,
	Under-16, Under -15

■ STRIKER Michael Bridges

Not a great deal was known about Michael Bridges when David O'Leary targeted him the summer before last as the player he needed to pep up his side's attack and agreed to pay a then club record fee of £5m for him.

As a player who had not been an automatic choice for Sunderland as they earned promotion to the Premier League, some thought the fee excessive. But the young player for m the North East quickly settled in and established himself with a brilliant hat-trick in his second game for Leeds at Southampton.

■ Michael Bridges

His goalscoring ability and his skills in attack made him a firm favourite with Leeds fans. An England Under-21 international, he spearheaded Leeds' attack in productive fashion and finished the 1999-2000 campaign as the club's top marksman with 21 goals.

Date of Birth:	August 5th, 1978
Birthplace:	North Shields
Height:	6ft 1in
Signed for Leeds:	July 23rd, 1999
Signed from:	Sunderland
Transfer fee:	£5million
Leeds goals:	21
Debut for Leeds:	August 7th, 1999 v Derby
	County.
International honours:	England Under-21

■ STRIKER Harry Kewell

Regard as the jewel in Leeds United's crown, the young Australian international, possesses just about everything a top class player needs. Already established as one of the best players in world football, Kewell finished the season as 17 goal second highest scorer.

His efforts earned him the club's Player-of-the-Year award and he was further honoured by being voted Young-Player-of-the-Season by the Professional Footballers' Association and third best player in the country, behind Manchester United's Roy Keane and Kevin Phillips of Sunderland.

His skills with the ball, his ability to go past defenders almost at will and with pace and his shooting ability makes the player who joined Leeds from the New South Wales soccer Academy, a prized asset.

Date of Birth:	September 22nd, 1978
Birthplace:	Sydney, Australia
Height:	5ft 11in
Signed for Leeds:	July 1st, 1995
Signed from:	New South Wales Soccer
	Academy
Transfer fee:	Nil.
Leeds goals:	34
Debut for Leeds:	March 30th, 1996
	v Middlesbrough (h)
International honours:	Australia Full

■ **STRIKER Mark Viduka**

Australian international Mark Viduka signed a five-year contract with Leeds United at the start of the season when left Scottish League side Glasgow Celtic in a £6million transfer.

Powerfully built 6ft 2in 13st 9lb, Viduka will add power and height in the penalty area which was something Leeds had lacked following the departure of Jimmy Floyd Hasselbaink to Atletico Madrid.

Player of the year in Scotland last season after scoring 27 goals for Celtic, Viduka's move to Leeds will enable him to form a front strike partnership with fellow Australian Harry Kewell. The 24-year-old played his football with Croatia Zagreb until he moved to Celtic two years ago but was keen to put his skills to the test in the English Premiership.

Date of Birth:	9th October 1975
Birthplace:	Melbourne, Australia
Height:	6ft 2in
Date signed:	3rd July 2000
Signed from:	Glasgow Celtic
Transfer fee:	£6m
International honours:	Full international
Previous clubs:	Melbourne Knights, Croatia Zagreb, Glasgow Celtic

■ **STRIKER Alan Smith**

Made a terrific impact when brought into the first team midway through the 1998-99 season and scored on his debut in a 3-1 victory against Liverpool at Anfield. A niggling ankle injury hampered his progress last season.

Underwent an operation on the ankle during the summer in the hope of being fully fit to press his claim for first team football against increased competition following the signing of Viduka.

Although still young, Smith has shown the aggression, tenacity and strength to deal with the meanest and most experienced of defenders. In addition to having an eye for goal he possesses the ability to shield the ball well.

Date of Birth:	October 28th, 1980
Birthplace:	Leeds
Height:	5ft 10in
Signed for Leeds:	February 1st, 1998
Signed from:	Trainee
Transfer fee:	Nil
Leeds goals:	15
Debut for Leeds:	November 14th, 1998 v Liverpool (a)
International honours:	England Under-21, Under-18

■ Alan Smith shoots versus Spurs

■ STRIKER Darren Huckerby

Speed merchant Huckerby joined Leeds in a £4m deal just over a year ago as Leeds manager David O'Leary looked to boost his squad following the departure of Jimmy Floyd Hasselbaink.

However, the England Under 21 international had to be content for the large part of last season with making substitute appearances as later signing Michael Bridges made an impressive start to his career at Leeds.

Huckerby is seen as a valuable member of United's first team squad and his pace - he's the fastest player in the Leeds camp - makes him the ideal player to come on late in a game and run at defenders who by that stage might not be too fresh.

Date of Birth:	April 23rd, 1976
Birthplace:	Nottingham
Height:	5ft 11in
Signed for Leeds:	August 11th, 1999
Signed from:	Coventry City
Transfer fee:	£4million
Leeds goals:	3
Debut for Leeds:	August 8th, 1999
	v Manchester United (a)
International honours:	England Under-21.

■ Darren Huckerby

■ DEFENDER Danny Mills

A £4m signing from Charlton Athletic before the start of last season, Mills began the 1999-2000 campaign at right-back for Leeds. He made an encouraging start and scored the winning goal against Sunderland and, in the Worthington Cup against Blackburn.

But once Gary Kelly, recovered from shin problems, was given a first team opportunity, Mills lost his first team place

After that Norwich born Mills had to be content for the most part with a place on the substitutes bench but he did return to play in United's last six games of the season and he was a regular choice for the England Under 21 squad.

Date of Birth:	May 18th 1977
Birthplace:	Norwich
Height:	5ft 10in
Signed for Leeds:	June 15th, 1999
Signed from:	Charlton Athletic
Transfer fee:	£4million
Leeds goals:	2
Debut for Leeds:	August 7th, 1999
	v Derby County (h)
International honours:	England Under-21

■ GOALKEEPER Paul Robinson

Robinson has shown himself to be a more than capable deputy for first choice goalkeeper Nigel Martyn. But because of Martyn's great ability, fitness and freedom from injury he never got a chance to show his skills at first team level last season.

Leeds, however, showed how highly they value the England Under-21 keeper by handing him a new improved four-year contract 18 months ago.

Date of Birth:	October 15th, 1979
Birthplace:	Beverley, Yorkshire
Height:	6ft 4in
Signed for Leeds:	May 8th, 1997
Signed from:	Trainee
Transfer fee:	Nil
Leeds goals:	-
Debut for Leeds:	October 25th, 1998
	v Chelsea (h)
International honours:	England Under 21,
	Under-18

■ **CENTRE-BACK Robert Molenaar**

No Leeds player worked harder last season than Molenaar - but sadly for him his activity was not on the pitch. It was off it as he staged a determined battle to recover from a serious knee injury.

The muscular defender, who joined Leeds from Dutch club FC Volendam in January 1997 in a £1million deal, suffered a cruciate ligament injury mid-way through the 1998-99 season and has been striving to recover ever since.

His ability to overcome the problems has impressed backroom staff at Leeds and Molenaar is now hoping for better fortune in the 2000-2001 season.

Date of Birth:	February 27th, 1969
Birthplace:	Zaadam, Holland
Height:	6ft 2in
Signed for Leeds:	January 9th, 1997
Signed from:	FC Volendam
Transfer fee:	£900,000
Leeds goals:	6
Debut for Leeds:	January 11th, 1997
	v Leicester City (h)

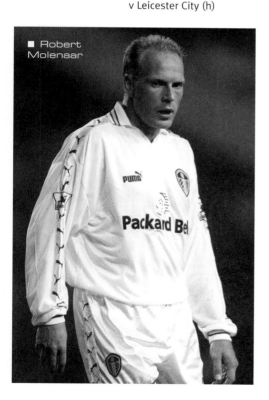

■ Robert Molenaar

■ **CENTRE-BACK Danny Hay**

Hay arrived at Leeds at the start of last season when David O'Leary made a surprise move for the New Zealand international from Australian club Perth Glory.

Standing 6ft 3in tall, Hay came to Leeds's attention when O'Leary made a trip to Australia. Impressed by Hay's display he arranged for the player to have a short trial at Elland Road after which he was duly signed for £200,000.

Date of Birth:	15th May 1975
Birthplace:	Auckland, New Zealand
Height:	6ft 3in
Date signed:	19th August 1999
Signed from:	Perth Glory, Australia
Transfer fee:	£200,000
International honours:	New Zealand Full
Previous clubs:	Central United (NZ),
	Perth Glory (Aus)

■ **RIGHT-BACK Alan Maybury**

Injuries have hampered the development of Alan's career with United. After missing half of the 1998-99 season with shin problems similar top those that kept Gary Kelly out for the entire campaign, he recovered but was unable to fight his way back into the first team.

He suffered further misfortune towards the end of the 1999-2000 season when, playing for the second team, he broke a leg in a reserve game against Manchester United. With Kelly and Danny Mills ahead of him in the pecking order for the right-back role, he faces a tough task to win back a first team place at Leeds.

Date of Birth:	August 8th, 1978
Birthplace:	Dublin
Height:	5ft 11in
Date signed:	August 17th, 1995
Signed from:	St Kevins BC
Transfer fee:	Nil
International honours:	Republic of Ireland B
	and Under 21
Previous clubs:	St Kevins BC

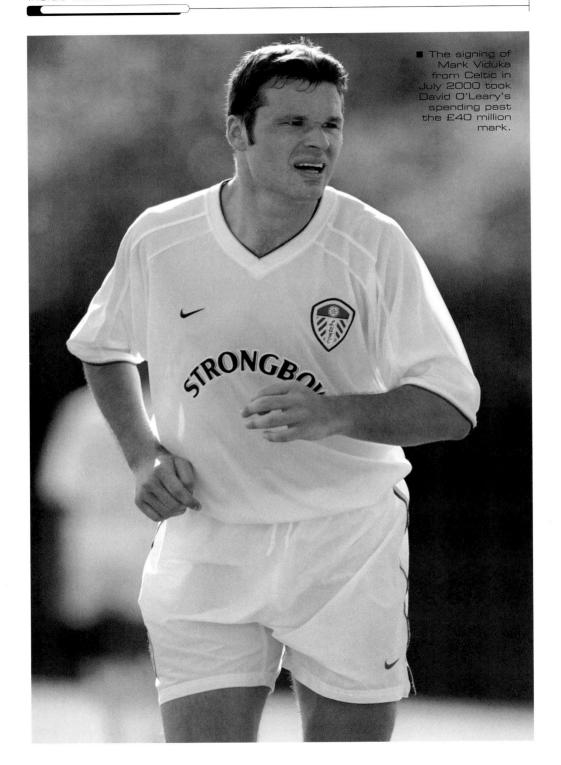

■ The signing of
Mark Viduka
from Celtic in
July 2000 took
David O'Leary's
spending past
the £40 million
mark.

APPENDIX THREE

TRANSFER MARKET ACTIVITY

THE quest to equip Leeds United for a challenge to Manchester United's Premier League supremacy has gone on unabated since David O'Leary took over the managerial reins at Elland Road from George Graham.

As well as giving his talented youngsters a chance to show their capabilities he has been very active in the transfer market in an effort to increase the size of his first team squad by bringing in high-class players.

If United are to compete with the best of Europe's football teams it is essential they have the kind of quality squad capable of dealing with the large number of matches successful sides have to play. Whether players like it or not, football in the higher echelons is now very much a squad game.

David O'Leary has not been found wanting in adding to the quality of his squad - and neither has United's chairman Peter Ridsdale and his board who have backed their manager financially.

The summer signings of Olivier Dacourt and Mark Viduka at a total cost of £13.2million left United with a deficit of just over £19million on transfer market dealings - a comparatively small amount in building a top team in these days of sky high transfer fees.

Coincidentally, David Hopkin's move to neighbouring Bradford City left Dutch defender Robert Molenaar as the only survivor from those players brought to the club in George Graham's occupancy of the manager's chair at Elland Road.

A full list of United's transfer market dealings - both 'in' and 'out' - since O'Leary became United team boss makes for interesting reading. It is as follows: -

DAVID O'LEARY'S BUYS

December 8th, 1998	David Batty from Newcastle United	£4,400,000
May 25th, 1999	Eirik Bakke from Sogndal	£1,750,000
June 16th, 1999	Danny Mills from Charlton	£4,000,000
July 12th, 1999	Michael Duberry from Chelsea	£4,500,000
July 24th, 1999	Michael Bridges from Sunderland	£5,000,000
August 19th, 1999	Danny Hay from Perth Glory	£200,000
September 11th,1999	Darren Huckerby from Coventry City	£5,500,000
December 17th, 1999	Jason Wilcox from Blackburn Rovers	£3,000,000
January 15th, 2000	Danny Milosevic from Perth Glory	£ 100,000
March 4th, 2000	Shaun Allaway from Reading	£200,000
May 15th, 2000	Olivier Dacourt from RC Lens	£7,200,000
July 3rd, 2000	Mark Viduka from Celtic	£6,000,000
	Total outlay	**£41,850,000**

DAVID O'LEARY'S SALES

June 10th, 1999	Gunnar Halle to Bradford City	£250,000
June 15th 1999	Lee Sharpe to Bradford City	£200,000
June 30th, 1999	David Wetherall to Bradford City	£1,400,000
July 16th, 1999	Clyde Wijnhard to Huddersfield Town	£750,000
August 4th, 1999	J-F Hasselbaink to Atletico Madrid	£12,000,000
August 5th, 1999	Derek Lilley to Oxford United	£50,000
October 19th, 1999	Danny Granville to Manchester City	£1,000,000
October 22nd, 1999	Bruno Ribeiro to Sheffield United	£500,000
May 25th, 2000	Martin Hiden to SV Salzburg	£500,000
June 13th, 2000	Alfie Haaland to Manchester City	£2,800,000
July 7th, 2000	David Hopkin to Bradford City	£2,500,000
	Total income	**£21,950,000**
	Deficit on Transfer market dealings	**£19,900,000**

GEORGE GRAHAM'S BUYS

December 13, 1996	Gunnar Halle from Oldham	£475,000
January 9, 1997	Robert Molenaar from FC Volendam	£900,000
March 26, 1997	Pierre Laurent from Bastia	£275,000
March 27, 1997	Derek Lilley from Greenock Morton	£500,000
May 13, 1997	David Robertson from Rangers	£500,000
June 12, 1997	Alfie Haaland from Nottm Forest	£1,600,000
June 17, 1997	Bruno Ribeiro from Vitoria Setubal	£500,000
June 19, 1998	Danny Granville from Chelsea	£1,600,000
July 1, 1997	J-F Hasselbaink from Boavista	£2,000,000
July 21,1997	David Hopkin from Crystal Palace	£3,250,000
February 25, 1998	Martin Hiden from Rapid Vienna	£1,500,000
May 15,1998	Clyde Wijnhard from Willem II	£1,500,000
	Total outlay	**£14,600,000**

GEORGE GRAHAM'S SALES

February 7, 1997	Paul Beesley to Manchester City	£500,000
March 25, 1997	Mark Tinkler to York City	£75,000
July 15, 1997	Andy Couzens to Carlisle United	£100,000
July 16, 1997	Mark Ford to Burnley	£275,000
July 25 1997	Brian Deane to Sheffield United	£1,500,000
September 23, 1997	Carlton Palmer to Southampton	£1,000,000
January 5,1998	Pierre Laurent to Bastia	£500,000
	Total income	**£3,950,000**
	Deficit on transfer market dealings	**£10,650,000**